T0329945

American Indian Business

AMERICAN INDIAN BUSINESS

Principles and Practices

EDITED BY

DEANNA M. KENNEDY

CHARLES F. HARRINGTON

AMY KLEMM VERBOS

DANIEL STEWART

JOSEPH SCOTT GLADSTONE

GAVIN CLARKSON

UNIVERSITY OF WASHINGTON PRESS

Seattle and London

American Indian Business was supported by a generous grant from the Tulalip Tribes Charitable Fund, which provides the opportunity for a sustainable and healthy community for all.

www.tulalipcares.org

Additional support was provided by generous gifts from Sidney Anderson, Charles Atkinson, David Cannon, Rosanna Garcia, Marina Grosso, Mistyne Hall, June Birdrattler Humphrey, Felix McGowan, Natalie Cotton Nessler, Miguel Olivas-Lujan, Tara Perino, Cara Peters, Terence Pitre, Alex Rodriguez, Jose Rosa, Shalei Simms, Brent Smith, and Ron and Gail Tilden, and from Martha Atelia Clarkson in honor of her late husband, Cdr. Charlie J. Clarkson (USN), the first American Indian to fly a jet.

UNIVERSITY OF WASHINGTON PRESS
www.washington.edu/uwpress

Library of Congress Cataloging-in-Publication Data
Names: Kennedy, Deanna M., editor of compilation.
Title: American Indian business : principles and practices / edited by Deanna Kennedy . . . [and five others].
Description: 1st edition. | Seattle : University of Washington Press, [2017] | Includes bibliographical references and index.
Identifiers: LCCN 2016056653 | ISBN 9780295742083 (hardcover : alk. paper) | ISBN 9780295742090 (pbk. : alk. paper)
Subjects: LCSH: Indian business enterprises—United States. | Indians of North America—Economic conditions. | Indians of North America—Legal status, laws, etc. | Business. | Tribal government—United States.
Classification: LCC E98.B87 A56 2017 | DDC 338.7089/97—dc23
LC record available at https://lccn.loc.gov/2016056653

Cover photo by Marc Studer. Eighth Generation is a Native-owned and operated company in Seattle, Washington, founded by Louie Gong. More information at http://eighthgeneration.com.

We collectively thank the forces and tricksters that brought us together at this time in American Indian history so that we could work together and contribute to improving the quality of life for tribal people on and off reservation.

We also thank the support of all of our family, colleagues, friends, and each other for the support and encouragement that you provided.

We dedicate this book to our mentors, our students, and others who diligently work to improve the well-being of Native people.

CONTENTS

FOREWORD

AMERICAN INDIAN BUSINESS: PRINCIPLES AND PRACTICES IS A necessary document appearing at an opportune time for American Indian (and other indigenous) communities. Most modern Native communities have high levels of individual and social problems that need attention but too few community resources or services to address them. Economic development in Indian Country is weak, while economic resources are needed to address Indian community problems. Chapter 3, on American Indians and entrepreneurship, provides a good overview of the challenges that Indian communities face. In general, both Indian health and Indian community health systems are comparatively poor. Indian communities lack adequate infrastructure. Indian educational success is low, and consequently practical and technical skill levels are low in Indian communities. Creative economic development that fits with the norms and values of American Indian communities is needed. This edited volume provides examples for generating such economic development and is therefore an important tool toward American Indian self-determination.

Since contact, the struggle for Indian communities has been, and remains, to hold on to culture, land, and natural resources in the face of human and technological encroachment. Recently, a new struggle has developed: to hold onto the *people*. Indian and indigenous communities worldwide are bleeding young people into surrounding societies. The 2010 US Census illustrates this. In that census more American Indian/Alaska Native (AI/AN) people lived *away* from tribal lands than *on* them; the majority of AI/AN people live in urban areas (Norris, Vines, and Hoeffel 2012). Reservation and village Natives are increasingly relocating to cities, largely motivated by a search for economic opportunity. Where once relocation was forced at gunpoint or through cultural coercion, today it is often voluntary (or as "voluntary" as a choice among limited life options can be). Urban Indian migration is substantially driven by young people's efforts to escape poverty and find jobs. According to a recent report from the Canadian Centre for Policy Alternatives

(Macdonald and Wilson 2016), 60 percent of on-reserve and 41 percent of off-reserve First Nations households were in poverty. Even in the cities, indigenous people experience high levels of unemployment, low incomes, and the many outcomes that tend to accompany poverty (e.g., poor nutrition and lower life expectancy).

Viewed differently, though, the "problems" in Indian Country are actually opportunities for developing the resources needed to address the goals of Indian people. As Coyote learns in chapter 11, health is economics (health provides jobs and needs systematic [i.e., organized] attention if it is to be good) and economics is health (a certain amount of green is good for red). Schools and colleges employ many people—too few of them Indian; and a well-educated populace generates more economic resources than does a poorly educated one. Building roads and bridges, or patching runways, or stabilizing riverbanks, or laying optical fibers, and other forms of infrastructure creation all pay well. Economic development in Indian Country could therefore form a virtuous circle with the educational, health, and infrastructure goals and needs of Indian communities. *American Indian Business* provides exemplars for Indian communities and individuals who seek to create such a virtuous circle.

The book touches on many key topics of American Indian business, which is commonly defined as an economic enterprise operated by one or more American Indians. That seems tautological. The current volume extends the definition by focusing on Indian businesses operating within one or more Indian communities. An Indian business, then, is one that serves an Indian community and/or employs Indian community members. The best-known version of the latter is tribal casinos. They are attended to in this book from a legal perspective in chapter 8 and from a community- and corporate-development perspective in chapter 10 and elsewhere. Those chapters provide important insights and interesting introductions to a number of issues. Chapter 8 is entirely focused on the opportunities and challenges inherent in creating tribal gaming compacts and tribal casinos. It provides a good background for both applied tribal gaming operations and for researchers interested in studying gaming and its impacts. Some casinos have proven to be engines of economic and community development. Chapters 12, 13, and 14 include, respectively, outlines of community successes developed out of the Pechanga, the Muckleshoot, and the Seminole casinos. Other tribes, such as the Lummee and the Menominee, have also successfully used tribal casinos as starting points for wide-reaching community development.

However, most of the 570 federally recognized tribes in the United States have either no casino or one that yields little economic impact on the community. While certain casinos do provide the cornerstone of full-fledged community capacity building, a few have generally produced negative community impacts (e.g., internecine battles over revenues). The casino-jaded but particularly practice-minded reader will find satisfaction in the chapters on Indian business law (chapters 5, 6, and 8), finance (chapters 7 and 8), business structures (chapter 6), human resources (chapters 12 and 13), and marketing (chapter 14). Potential Indian business owners will learn basic lessons from the information in these chapters as well as from the one on business strategy (chapter 4). As this listing of topics shows, the chapters in this work tend to follow standard business textbook and degree-program contents. By presenting an Indian (indigenous) perspective on these topics, though, this book should be of practical use to Indian business people and it potentially could spark new research directions.

In addition to reviewing major knowledge and functions that prospective business owners need to attend to, this volume makes the case that each major process or functional aspect of a business can be (successfully) operated on the basis of American Indian cultural values and norms. We can support, these contributions tell us, ecological and community health (business ethics) and worker well-being (leadership; human resource and service management) in unique and positive ways by looking to the traditional values, norms, and tactics of Indian cultures. I have written things along the same lines (e.g., James 2006) but do wonder whether such ideas reflect stereotypes as much as cultural reality. Indian cultures and communities are variable, both comparatively across them and internally within them (see, especially, chapter 14 in this book). James et al. (2008), for instance, presents a case of a (group of) Navajo communities and tribal members who were divided in their views of a mining enterprise, at least in part because of differences in dominant cultural values.

The ideas in this volume stimulate critical discussion and even debate. How strong is the evidence for some of the arguments made? Are there circumstances or environmental conditions that may interact with (moderate) values or norms to influence Indian business approaches, the success of such approaches, or Indian perceptions of business? What new evidence might help shed light on those and other issues raised throughout this book? Of additional value is that this work can help stimulate new scholarship on the nature and effectiveness of Indian business practices, the nature of Indian views of business, and the mechanisms that shape all that both involve.

Along the same lines, while outsiders sometimes impose stereotypes on Indian people, Indians sometimes impose the stereotypes on themselves. This is consistent with the arguments in chapters 2, 3, and 4 that Indians (and outsiders) frequently see "Indian-ness" and "business" as antithetical to one another, while a look at Indian prehistory and history shows this to be untrue.

Before contact with Europeans (or, from the indigenous perspective, before invasion from Europe), American Indians had robust production and trade economies, even if they did not meet the definition of modern capitalism. In chapter 1, for instance, Charles F. Harrington outlines two eras (pre-1491 and twentieth- and early twenty-first-century tribal economics) and finds much of value in both. Similarly, Joseph Scott Gladstone (in chapter 2) recounts precontact and historical trade patterns among a variety of Indian groups. He looks at trends in more recent postcontact history that have tended to undermine Indian trade and business. Postcontact economic activity in indigenous communities has historically been largely top-down, driven by (mainstream and/or indigenous) government policies and officials. This is illustrated in Daniel Stewart's chapter 4, where "American Indian firms" in the chapter title largely translates to "tribal (government) business" in the text. As Stewart notes, tribal government control over community laws and codes, land and natural resources, and certain distinctive financial opportunities gives tribal governments the potential for strategic advantage. Tribal businesses have produced some notable successes, some of which are described in chapters 7 and 12. As Charles F. Harrington, Carolyn Birmingham, and Daniel Stewart note in chapter 3, however, tribal governments (along with non-Indian governments at all levels) have also been a major source of difficulties for, and barriers to, Indian economic development.

The Navajo Nation (which spans parts of Arizona, New Mexico, and Utah) provides examples of what tribal governments could do, but have often failed to, and of barriers to Indian economic development that non-Indian governments often create. The Navajo Nation recently created code that allows, for the first time, the creation of limited liability corporations (LLCs) by tribal members. Chapter 6, by Amy Klemm Verbos, surveys major organizational-structure approaches for Indian businesses, including LLCs. Legal provision for LLC formation and operation circumvents potential problems such as risk to the nonbusiness resources of the business owners and frequent turnover of tribal governments that creates the peril of post-hoc changes to demands on companies. By setting up the legal basis for

LLCs, the Navajo Nation has provided a potentially valuable tool to tribal businesses and businesses run by tribal members. However, a recent effort by the Navajo Nation to develop a large-scale solar energy production business on tribal lands was stymied by a (non-Indian) county government that refused to approve the needed tie-in of the planned tribal solar array to the electrical grid.

Given the poverty, unemployment, and relocation patterns that occur among Indian peoples, direct tribal-government-directed business and economic development have clearly not met the need. Recent decades have seen increases in nation-state and non-Indian corporate efforts at economic development in indigenous territories (UN Global Compact 2013). Many of those projects, though, have been characterized by poor economic outcomes for indigenous communities, along with expropriation of lands and other abuses (Blaser et al. 2010; Gow 2008; James et al. 2008; UN Global Compact 2013). Indian peoples and Indian communities therefore need other approaches to business creation. In line with that, this edited volume extends the idea of American Indian business to the possibility that many such are defined by their being *informed by the contents of one or more indigenous culture*. For instance, one difference between historical mainstream entrepreneurship and American Indian entrepreneurship is that the former is likely to be more individualistic—driven by charismatic, risk-taking individuals—while the latter tends toward collectivistic (family, clan, cohort, tribe) approaches. In recent years, mainstream entrepreneurship scholarship has "discovered" collaborative business creation (e.g., Tiessen 1997). A collectivistic approach to entrepreneurship should, based on studies of Indian culture, work best for establishing successful Indian businesses. More direct research on this theory is needed, however. Research is also needed on conditions that may lead collective entrepreneurship to have mainly beneficial, versus mainly harmful, effects on overall community goals (see, e.g., Wated and Sanchez 2012).

Chapters 3, 4, and 14 especially make the case for business products and business models centered around distinctive, core Indian cultural content ("culture of origin"). Chapter 14, by Stephanie Lawson Brooks and Cara Peters, describes the potential for Indian businesses to market on the basis of tribal culture and Indian iconography as well as the paradoxes of attempting to do so. That same chapter examines the problem of cultural appropriation by non-Native individuals, groups, and companies. Cultural appropriation is part of the larger problem of expropriation and exploitation of Indian and indigenous "intellectual property" by non-Natives that has been occurring for centuries, continues through today, and may be an area that tribes (and their lawyers) will increasingly turn their attention to in the future (Keoke and Porterfield 2005; UN Global Compact 2013; Weatherford 1988).

As Lawson Brooks and Peters point out in their chapter on marketing paradoxes for Indian businesses, the various tribal groups need to collaborate to assert control over Indian cultural contents (aka "intellectual property"). The authors point out, however, some of the challenges (e.g., resource competition among tribes) that can make such collaborations difficult to achieve. Nevertheless, tribes should be able to collaborate on some things while competing on others. For instance, development of mechanisms for certifying Indian businesses, products, and services seems feasible even as individual businesses and tribes compete for specific resources. Certifications could extend beyond simple Indian ownership to aspects of "culture of origin" that would benefit business marketing. The Menominee tribe, for example, is renowned for its sustainable forestry practices. The large non-Indian timber companies have worked together to undermine the general certification of "sustainably grown" lumber such that many of their tree-farm products qualify equally for that designation with the Menominee's much more ecologically (and community) healthy lumber. A tribally controlled certification of "sustainably and American Indian produced" could therefore potentially be of value—and not just for lumber but for other products.

American Indian entrepreneurship is a major element of creative economic development that is often focused on cultural content. American Indian (and indigenous) entrepreneurship is business creation or business expansion/innovation based on the principles and targeted toward the needs of one or more indigenous communities. Indigenous entrepreneurship also deals with Indian businesses that are bottom-up, by and for grassroots community members, rather than top-down. Many Indian people are entrepreneurs—artists, writers, food makers, and many other fields—even if the label "entrepreneur" is one that they sometimes do not recognize or acknowledge. We know that there are numerous barriers to Indian/indigenous entrepreneurship, such as lack of availability of financing as well as knowledge and skill deficits. Gavin Clarkson's chapter 7, on tribal finance and economic development, addresses financial barriers and some approaches to overcoming them. Similarly, many contributions in this book are intended to aid the development of the knowledge and skills that prospective Indian business owners need. Therefore, this volume should help reduce barriers to

American Indian entrepreneurship and, by doing so, help address the economic goals and needs of Indian individuals and communities.

This book also serves a global need. There are about a half billion indigenous people worldwide (World Bank 2015). Those who reside outside the northern two-thirds of North America—barring a few exceptions, such as the Maori—lack even the limited legal recognition and community control seen (in varying degrees) in Canada and the United States. Other indigenous groups experience similar or even greater unemployment and poverty than their North American siblings. For them, these challenges are compounded by lack of self-determination and territorial control (see UN Global Compact 2013). This book is thus likely to also be of value to non–North American indigenous groups.

This initial effort at addressing the scope and potential of American Indian business should spark further scholarship. For instance, additional areas of research may include the effects of economic globalization or how Indian communities might deal with them. Some of those impacts create challenges, such as low-cost foreign labor or foreign appropriation of cultural content. Others create opportunities, such as the appetite for American Indian goods and products in foreign markets like Germany and Japan. Indian businesses should be better able to directly tap those markets today, because of economic globalism, than they would have been thirty, twenty, ten, or even five years ago. International indigenous collaboration on such things as certifications or cooperative marketing could be particularly useful in today's globalized economic regime. The International Co-operative Alliance (ICA) defines a *co-op* as "an autonomous association of persons united voluntarily to meet their common economic, social, and cultural needs and aspirations through a jointly owned and democratically controlled enterprise." Co-ops seem to be increasing in number and economic impact in both the "developed" and the "developing" worlds. The need to exert control of "culture of origin" as a business resource and the benefits of scale (e.g., reduced costs per unit) make it likely that there would be benefits to developing new Indian/indigenous co-ops to market and distribute the products of indigenous businesses.

Another topic to explore is the importance of technology for Indian businesses. This volume largely addresses reservation/village Indian communities, but there is opportunity in the growing population of urban Indians. Most urban Indians go back and forth to tribal lands, so urban economic development by Indians could potentially feed into and off of reservation economic development. Similarly, market distance—long seen as a major barrier to Indian economic development—may matter less today because of technological changes such as the advent of the Internet. But technology and automation have also eliminated many jobs (my father was a skilled machinist; today, computer-controlled machines largely perform the type of skilled labor that he once provided) and look likely to eliminate even more in the future (imagine what self-driving cars will mean to taxi services and taxi-substitutes such as Uber drivers). Technology and technological change are important issues for Indian businesses and deserve further attention.

A final example of important research that could grow out of this collection involves the so-called gig (or, at the high end, "portfolio") economy, which is fueled by globalization and technology. More and more people are piecing together several different sources of economic input to replace the type of long-term, full-time, decently paying jobs that old-school businesses once provided to many. More and more people are becoming solo-preneurs, running a one-person multifocused business. The gig economy is not really new to Indian people. In order to meet personal and family needs, many Indian people have long cobbled together several economic efforts—say, craftwork plus humping a food truck from powwow to powwow, added to some "shade-tree" auto repair, combined with subsistence hunting and gathering.

American Indian Business: Principles and Practices is a valuable contribution and addresses many important issues involved in doing business in Indian Country. In fact, perhaps the importance of the topic, combined with this book's kindling of ideas for future research, calls for a second volume soon.

KEITH JAMES
TUCSON, ARIZONA
JULY 7, 2016

References

Blaser, M., R. de Costa, D. McGregor, and W. D. Coleman, eds. 2010. *Indigenous Peoples and Autonomy: Insights for a Global Age.* Vancouver: UBC Press.

Gow, D. D. 2008. *Countering Development: Indigenous Modernity and the Moral Imagination.* Durham: Duke University Press.

James, K. 2006. "Identity, Values, and American Indian Beliefs about Science and Technology: A First Wave of Data." *American Indian Culture and Research Journal* 30: 45–58.

James, K., M. Hiza, D. Hall, and R. Doppelt R. 2008. "Organizational Environmental Justice and Community Sustainability with a Navajo (Diné) Case Example." In S. Gilliland, D. Steiner, and D. Skarlicki, eds., *Research in Social Issues in Management*. Vol. 6, *Justice, Morality, and Social Responsibility*. Pp. 263–90. Greenwich, CT: Information Age Publishing.

Keoke, E. D., and K. A. Porterfield. 2005. *American Indian Contributions to the World*. New York: Checkmark Books.

Macdonald, D., and D. Wilson. 2016. *Shameful Neglect: Indigenous Child Poverty in Canada*. Online at www.policyalternatives.ca/publications/reports/shameful-neglect. Accessed on June 18, 2016.

Norris, T., P. L. Vines, and E. M. Hoeffel. 2012. *The American Indian and Alaska Native Population: 2010 Census Briefs*. Washington, DC: US Department of Commerce, Economics, and Statistics Administration, US Census Bureau.

Tiessen, J. H. 1997. "Individualism, Collectivism, and Entrepreneurship: A Framework for International Comparative Research." *Journal of Business Venturing* 12: 367–84.

United Nations (UN) Global Compact. 2013. *A Business Reference Guide: United Nations Declaration on the Rights of Indigenous Peoples*. New York: UN Global Compact.

Wated, G., and J. I. Sanchez. 2012. "The Cultural Boundary of Managing Nepotism." In R. G. Jones, ed., *Nepotism in Organizations*. Pp. 199–218. New York: Routledge/Taylor and Francis Group.

Weatherford, J. 1988. *Indian Givers: How the Indians of the Americas Transformed the World*. New York: Fawcett.

World Bank. 2015. *Indigenous Peoples Overview 2015*. Online at www.worldbank.org/en/topic/indigenouspeoples/overview. Accessed on June 18, 2016.

PREFACE

THIS BOOK IS MEANT FOR BUSINESS PRACTITIONERS, STUDENTS, and educators as an accessible introduction to business topics and business applications for American Indian businesspeople. It is equally useful for tribal program administrators, tribal leaders, and business professionals seeking to conduct business with tribal communities. Most contributors to this edited volume are American Indians who are business school professors or business PhD students. Our other contributors are non-Native business scholars who value and appreciate the contributions that Native peoples and their philosophies have to offer to the business community in general.

We, the editors of this volume, are enrolled tribal members and business scholars specializing in management, finance, or business law. Deanna M. Kennedy, PhD, is enrolled in the Cherokee Nation of Oklahoma; Amy Klemm Verbos, JD, PhD, is enrolled in the Pokagon Band of Potawatomi; Daniel Stewart, PhD, is enrolled in the Spokane Tribe; Joseph Scott Gladstone, PhD, is enrolled in the Blackfeet and is a Nez Perce descendant; and Gavin Clarkson, JD, DBA, is enrolled in the Choctaw Nation of Oklahoma. All of us met through our association with The PhD Project either as business doctoral students or faculty alumna.[1] We are motivated by our shared interest in identifying the means by which Native American tribes and business owners could contribute to developing vibrant and successful tribal economies defined by unique tribal values, including attracting and mentoring future Native American business PhD students and assistant professors. Both together and separately we have for more than a decade researched and taught in the areas of Native American business, management education, finance, and policy.

The genesis of this book came about from a series of long and fruitless searches to locate material relative to the history, philosophy, and practice of American Indian business. Without question, there is a void in the research literature on the contributions of American Indians to business, management and organization, leadership, applied economic development, and entrepreneurship. Furthermore, to our knowledge there is currently not one textbook that addresses the nuances of American Indian business. Quite frankly, we have been exceedingly hard pressed to locate any textbooks on business topics viewed from a Native American perspective. Even before the discussions about a business reader began, we realized a growing emphasis and interest within the business community in seeing the world through an indigenous lens, including that of Native Americans (also called American Indians).[2]

Today, more than 1.7 million Americans are enrolled in the 567 federally recognized tribes by the US Bureau of Indian Affairs (BIA). Indeed, the size of the American Indian population poses a large potential market that remains untapped to many local and national businesses. Yet the business practices in American Indian communities may be different than what is applied in mainstream business; recognizing this, it is important to reflect on business from an indigenous perspective. Indeed, the United Nations General Assembly adopted its Declaration of the Rights of Indigenous Peoples in 2007 that calls for more attention to the way business activities involve Native peoples and benefit from the involvement. To increase this conversation in the mainstream business community, we need a broad shift in management philosophy. Therefore, another aim of this book is to motivate the conversation in institutions of higher education by introducing and integrating a Native American perspective of business concepts.

To organize the different management areas discussed, we begin with historical perspectives of American Indian business, then we progressively work our way through business decisions needed for starting, structuring, and creating strategy for your business, understanding the legal environment of business in Indian Country. Next we focus on issues related to leading and managing businesses and finally implementing various business functions. The chapter contributions come from a number of scholars and practitioners with knowledge about how business concepts (e.g., strategy, finance, management, business law, and marketing) are demonstrated in Native American businesses, casinos, and service organizations. Starting with chapter 1, Charles F. Harrington, a professor of management, provides a brief overview of the history of American Indian business. As he suggests, the concept of Native business is not new, yet it has evolved across the generations since European contact. In chapter 2, Joseph Scott Gladstone, a management professor in public health sciences, discusses the development of business practices through sovereign trade and how these practices have existed for a long time.

Chapter 3, by Harrington, Carolyn Birmingham, and Daniel Stewart, presents an introduction to American Indian entrepreneurship, offering extensive detail about entrepreneurship as practiced by Native people, its challenges, and its decision-making processes. In chapter 4, Stewart, a professor of entrepreneurship, examines different business strategies for competitive advantage. Business strategy helps managers identify a unique position of the firm in the marketplace that can set it apart from competitors. Chapter 5, by Gavin Clarkson, professor of finance, provides insights about the way business and law intersect. In chapter 6, Amy Klemm Verbos, professor of business law, introduces the different types and forms that business can take under state, federal, and tribal law. In chapter 7, Clarkson discusses tribal finance and economic development. He introduces concepts to develop a toolkit of knowledge that applies to these areas. In chapter 8, Clarkson and James K. Sebenius discuss high-stakes gaming and the management of gaming enterprises.

Chapter 9, by Stephanie Lee Black and Carolyn Birmingham, discusses the role of leaders in American Indian business, including important clarifications about the way that cultural values influence American Indian leadership practices. In chapter 10, Carma M. Claw, a doctoral student of indigenous business management, Verbos, and management professor Grace Ann Rosile focus on business ethics and values that Native American business leaders bring to an organization. In chapter 11, Gladstone uses a Native storytelling approach to demonstrate how management thought is applied to managing a tribal health program. Chapter 12, by Matthew S. Rodgers, professor of management, and Shad Morris, professor of organizational leadership and strategy, discuss a values-infused approach to human resources. Their chapter covers the Native American influence on corporate recruiting, selection, assessment, development, retention, and compensation/benefits practices. In chapter 13, Deanna M. Kennedy, a professor of operations management, in collaboration with Denise Bill, of the Muckleshoot Tribal College, and university tribal liaisons Rachael Meares and Ross Braine, discusses insights for service management and the need for better access and cultural salience. In chapter 14, Stephanie Lawson Brooks and Cara Peters, professors of marketing, discuss the use of Native American images in marketing. The chapter explores the cultural misappropriation of images and the ensuing social movement by Native Americans to remove negative stereotypes from the media.

Our goal for this book is to contribute to learning about unique aspects of American Indian business. We've accomplished this in three ways. First, this book increases exposure to Native American perspectives in business and management, potentially increasing interest in developing alternative organizational practices to uniquely identify and position Native American business within Native culture. Indeed, rather than deferring Native American cultural practices for dominant cultural practices, this book provides a different cultural perspective that could lead to richer conversations about business approaches. Second, reading and discussing business principles from a Native perspective may be used by business instructors as a pedagogical approach that may help them improve their own teaching skills.

Students may discover business philosophies that challenge conventional business practices and inspire a broader approach to defining what constitutes success. Such readings may help management educators facilitate critical thinking in students and provide more well-rounded coverage of alternative business concepts and content. Because we wish for a future that includes Native commerce with indigenous businesses built by and for the needs of Native tribes and peoples, our third goal for this book contributes to helping our Native people become well versed in business without blindly assimilating into dominant business cultural practices that have and continue to wreak devastation on the Earth, our Mother, in the name of short-term profits. It is only by becoming strengthened in who we are today and by acknowledging our ways of being from past generations that we can conduct commerce in a sustainable way for the benefit of future generations.

DEANNA M. KENNEDY
CHARLES F. HARRINGTON
AMY KLEMM VERBOS
DANIEL STEWART
JOSEPH SCOTT GLADSTONE
GAVIN CLARKSON

Notes

1   The PhD Project is an alliance of foundations, corporations, universities, and professional and academic organizations dedicated to increasing minority representation in the business world. The project helps African Americans, Hispanic Americans, and Native Americans attain their business PhDs and become business school professors and serve as role models to attract the next generation of minority business

leaders. All royalties from book sales go to support The PhD Project. For more information about The PhD Project, visit www.phdproject.org.

2   Both we and the contributing authors use the terms *American Indian* and *Native American* interchangeably throughout this work. *American Indian* is the socially constructed racial category used in the United States and the term attributed to Columbus when he thought he had reached the Indies. Yet since both terms are used broadly as identifiers of the indigenous peoples of the United States, both terms are used throughout this edited volume.

American Indian Business

1 A BRIEF HISTORY OF AMERICAN INDIAN BUSINESS

Charles F. Harrington, *University of South Carolina–Upstate*

ABSTRACT

American Indians have a long and proud history of productive trade, commerce, and entrepreneurship. Existing long before European colonialism, Native people created and sustained numerous and complex trade and barter alliances that provided for their various needs. Despite horrendous injustices inflicted upon American Indians at the hands of white settlers and colonial and federal governments, Native business and entrepreneurship have thrived.

KEYWORDS: business and management, history, American Indians

INTRODUCTION

AMERICAN INDIANS HAVE A LONG AND PROUD HISTORY OF PRO-ductive trade, commerce, and entrepreneurship. Existing long before European colonialism, Native people created and sustained numerous and complex trade and barter alliances that provided for their various needs. Because Native economies are intimately linked with tribal governments and tribal cultures, business development in Indian Country in the United States has often been dependent on the creation of new tribal government institutions, ranging from regulatory commissions to tribal economic development corporations. American Indian and Alaska Native business development, up until the past three decades, can be reduced to a generic scenario: the overriding focus was on what the federal government could do to "help" Native nations, most of whom were in poverty.

As is necessary for survival and social order, early Native Americans (individually and collectively) were required to provide daily for the needs of their families and their tribes. This responsibility manifest itself in constant effort in areas of agriculture, tool production, assemblage of clothing, creation of appropriate shelter, and other domestic activities. Native people also routinely engaged in trade with other individuals and groups, from both near and far, in order to survive and to make life more comfortable (Weinberg 2002). Most, if not all, of this trade activity was undertaken in free-market situations where individuals came together voluntarily to buy, sell, and trade items that they had manufactured for such purpose.

Anthropological evidence suggests that Native people inhabited and civilized the Western Hemisphere long before the arrival of European "settlers" and perhaps could be considered the first to traverse and inhabit North America. The welfare and survival of early Native Americans depended entirely on their own resourcefulness, ingenuity, and persistence. They created and sustained their own culture and societies, technologies and means of production, habitats, and both land- and water-based transportation routes. R. J. Miller (2001) reports that Indian cultures have always fostered, encouraged, and supported their tribal people in private economic endeavors, argued for and protected their property rights, and allowed individuals to pursue their own ways.

From their first contact, Europeans experienced significant difficulties in productive interaction with the indigenous population. Europeans began with the racist assumption that Native people were "savage" and "uncivilized," yet these early settlers found themselves with little option but to attempt to engage these indigenous people. Short on supplies and grossly outnumbered, the Pilgrims opted to embrace the opportunity to establish beneficial and productive contact and eventually were able to gain substantially from trading and bartering with the Native Americans (Driver 1961). New trade goods represented another big change that European explorers and colonists brought to American Indians (Weinberg 2002). Soon after meeting their European visitors, Indians became very interested in things that the colonists could provide. In a short time the Indians began using these new materials and products in their everyday lives. Native hunters were eager to trade prepared deer hides and other pelts for lengths of colored cloth. Metal tools (such as axes, hoes, and knives) became valuable new resources. The desire to get European goods changed ancient trading patterns. The tradition of simple hunting for food began to become less important than getting animal hides to trade. According to Weinberg (2002), it appeared that American Indians depended on European items for daily needs.

Weinberg's (2002) view, however, is an oversimplification. Consider the Nez Perce, who for many years after contact could more than hold their own against the US Cavalry with their own traditional technologies, their special bows, and their much faster horses—not to mention their alternative military strategies. It was not really until after tribes had their economic base and cultural integrity weakened that dependency on Western trade arose.

THE HISTORY OF TRADE

American Indian trade has historically been characterized as the web of economic relationships between Europeans and their successors (Euro-Americans and Euro-Canadians) with Native people. The purposes of such activities included exchange of goods with material and cultural significance between American Indians and whites as part of diplomatic and economic interactions in order to secure goods, to establish and maintain political treaties, and to ensure mutual and peaceful cohabitation of lands. By this same convention, Indian trade has been portrayed as a Euro-American or Euro-Canadian male engaged in supplying Native Americans (male and female) with goods and services in exchange for Indian-made or Indian-processed commodities such as furs, pelts, hides, and foodstuffs; geographic information; and, at times, political and social alliances (Sturtevant 1988).

A more accurate view of American Indian trade, however, would be to describe an existing and well-established trade practice that was firmly in place long before European contact and colonization. Connecting tribes and regions, precolonial Indian trade involved individual traders as well as trader cultures that served as conduits between tribes separated by considerable distances. Indian traders—female as well as male—met at trading centers located strategically along major river systems and at locales where several tribes seasonally passed en route to hunting, gathering, or fishing grounds. Examples include Cahokia in present-day Illinois, the Mandan-Hidatsa-Arikara villages (often called Middle Missouri Indian towns) in the present-day states of North Dakota and South Dakota, Zuni Pueblo in contemporary New Mexico, and confluences intersecting important waterways such as Sault Sainte Marie and Niagara Falls in the Great Lakes region and the Dalles on the Columbia River. In addition to foodstuffs, fiberware and clayware, hides, and exotics ranging from obsidian and flint to seashells and pearls to precious gems and minerals passed hands in Indian lodges and at Native trade fairs before CE 1500 (Chittenden 1902).

EARLY EUROPEAN-INDIAN TRADE

After 1600 these same trails, watercourses, and meeting grounds became routes of European traffic and footprints for forts, factories, and towns placed at such strategic points as Albany, Augusta, Chicago, Detroit, Kodiak, Michilimackinac, Mobile, Natchitoches, Portland (Oregon), Saint Louis, and San Antonio. Colonists introduced European mercantile ideas of inventories and profits based on dynamics of supply and demand, often compromising Native systems, which operated on principles of barter exchange, gift-giving, and reciprocity. Whites who adhered to norms of Native trade did better than those who ignored or bypassed Indian protocol. The French succeeded best in the Indian trade business, becoming social as well as economic partners across North America. Up to the fall of New France in 1760 and beyond, French-Indian relations along the Saint Lawrence and Mississippi Rivers and in the Great Lakes region remained cordial, tied by kinship as well as economic partnerships (Sturtevant 1988).

Spanish, Dutch, English, Russian, and Swedish traders were less successful because of their more rigid expectations: they insisted that Indians conform to European trading standards. All colonists sought furs and hides, including deerskins, for a lucrative European and Cantonese fur market, making the occupation of the white or mixed-blood (Métis or French-Indian and mestizo or Spanish-Indian) trader a common occupational type on all national and ethnic frontiers in North America. Each had government-licensed trading companies with wide powers to expand the respective nation's interests in addition to authority to trade, trap, hunt, and settle. Also, each country had independents, known in French parlance as *coureur de bois* ("runners of the woods"). From the Saint Lawrence to the Rio Grande and on to the Pacific Ocean, these "free" trappers and traders trekked and traded, earning reputations for adventure and exploration, and often compromising national interests for personal gain.

Many major cities benefitted from this burgeoning Indian trade, including Albany and New York City (Dutch); Detroit, Mobile, Natchez, and Montreal (French); Charleston, Philadelphia, and Savannah (English); Pensacola, Santa Fe, and Saint Louis (Spanish); Wilmington, Delaware (Swedish); and Kodiak, Alaska, and Fort Ross, California (Russian). Native economic dependency did not rest solely upon trade of guns, blankets, kettles, knives, and other utilitarian items with whites. Nearly all Native tribes engaged in European-based trade to a certain degree with some tribes prospering and others suffering hardship and economic loss. Throughout the eighteenth century, most tribes of eastern and southeastern North America were locked into the Indian trade as a way of life and expected French, British, and Spanish traders to protect their respective trade spheres from outside aggressors and internal rebellion (Ewers 1997).

TRADE AFTER THE AMERICAN REVOLUTION

In the aftermath of the American Revolution, the Indian trade continued under different flags and more restrictive rules. Congress regulated Indian trade under a series of Trade and Intercourse Acts beginning in 1790, establishing government "factories" in the heart of Indian territories in 1796 with the intent of keeping settlers and alcohol out of Indian Country. This segregationist approach was abandoned in 1822, allowing large and small companies to compete for Indian furs and favors in the Western territories. In both Canada and the United States, independent traders and smaller firms were historically leveraged out of business by oligarchies such as the Montreal-based North West Company; the Philadelphia firm of Baynton, Wharton, and Morgan; and Spanish, Indian, and English traders working for the British firm Panton, Leslie, and Company, based in Florida (Washburn 1988).

As smaller, fur-bearing habitats were trapped out or settled, a new economic Indian trade prevailed from 1840 to 1890 on the Western plains and prairies. This buffalo-hide trade supplied water- and steam-powered factories' demand for leather belts as well as military overcoats, rugs, and blankets. Once the buffalo were gone, economic dependency on reservations in Canada and the United States gripped Indian communities, now reliant on annuities and the need to become herders and farmers. Still, the Indian trade and the Indian trader, part of an international fur industry, continued in Alaska and in Canada's remote Yukon and Northwest Territories, where it remains important, as well as in the eastern Arctic. Across North America, Indians themselves have continued to function as Indian traders, many dealing in arts and crafts, others in horse breeding and trading; others in restoring buffalo, trading calves for other livestock and goods from one reserve to another; and still others in mitigating violations of treaties by swapping further litigation for restoration of tribal lands or monetary compensation (Hanner 1981).

Deprived of their historic homelands, sacred places, and hunting and fishing grounds, American Indians also lost control of their traditional livelihood. Agriculture, hunting, and gathering all required the places to which Native peoples had a deep and spiritual connection. They could continue to fashion various productive implements such as spades for digging, but these could not be employed without access to land. The same held true for animal traps and other technology. Thus, if they were to remain in their traditional areas of the country, their only alternative was to work for the new owners of the land.

After the Revolutionary War the new national government developed its own Indian policy. Chief Justice John Marshall set the stage for present Indian policy by asserting that tribes were sovereign nations. In 1831 he wrote in his famous *Cherokee Nation v. Georgia* opinion that Indian tribes were "nations within a nation," but he went on to call them "domestic dependent nations," implying that they had alienated their power to negotiate with foreign nations by virtue of treaties with the federal government (Anderson and Parker 2004). While implying that the tribes had retained their internal powers to govern themselves, Marshall described the relationship between tribes and the United States as "that of a ward to his guardian." Under this interpretation the federal government attempted to monopolize treaty negotiations with tribes in order to reduce conflicts over land and forced the tribes into a subservient position by declaring them "wards" (M. Miller 1988).

The federal government eventually took control of tribal assets by holding them in trust, a relationship fraught with mismanagement and depletion of resources over time. Tribal sovereignty might have allowed Indians to devise their own property rights and governance structures had the federal government not established the trust relationship with American Indians and had it truthfully been willing to grant broad autonomy to Indians over providence and control of their property. The Dawes Act enacted in 1887 implied the potential to release Indians from trusteeship by allotting reservation lands to individual Indians in fee simple ownership (Carlson 1992). However, the act's true intent was to assimilate American Indians into mainstream society. The act offered 160 acre tracts of reservation land to individual Indians and families that they could use to settle and become farmers. US citizenship was also offered to allotment holders. A condition of accepting the allotment and citizenship was surrendering tribal ties. As part of the allotment plan, "surplus" reservation lands were opened up for settlement by non-Indians. Of course, designated "surplus" lands were good-quality farmlands coveted by non-Indians who supported Dawes's efforts to help Native people through assimilation into the Western world (Otis 1973).

According to the Indian Land Tenure Foundation: "As a result of the General Allotment Act of 1887 (also called the Dawes Act), 90 million acres of Indian land—nearly two-thirds of the total Indian land base—were taken out of Indian ownership and control. From 1887 to 1934, 60 million acres of 'surplus' Indian lands were sold or transferred to non-Indians and another 30 million acres were lost due to the 1906 Burke Act, forced sales and other takings. All of these alienated Indian lands remained within reservation boundaries but were no longer under Indian ownership and control" (Indian

Land Tenure Foundation 2016). In 1934 the fee simple ownership allotments ended with the passage of the Indian Reorganization Act. Since then, the US Department of Interior has struggled to programmatically fulfill its trust responsibility and eliminate corruption. Not only does the trust authority raise the cost of managing Indian lands, timber, minerals, and wildlife, it provides opportunities for corruption in the use of those resources and the funds generated therefrom. Because the federal government controls tribal assets, it is not surprising that corruption prevails (McChesney 1992).

MODERN AMERICAN INDIAN BUSINESS

The history of American Indian and Alaska Native business development, up until the past three decades, can be reduced to this scenario: the overriding focus was on what the federal government could do to "help" Native nations, most of whom were in poverty. This approach tended toward grant-making for projects and programs designed by non-Natives and a development agenda that was driven almost wholly by the federal government. Tribal nations were often caught up in what was essentially a transfer economy, where tribes were left to manage federal monies, if they were able to secure these grants at all. This "projects and grants" mentality, where tribal ventures were often dictated by the federal government's funding priorities rather than the talents and opportunities of the tribes themselves, failed to create or support business development in any meaningful way because it did not address the overriding characteristic of Indian Country: its vast heterogeneity. In addition, this federal grant-making approach sparked grant-seeking behavior in many tribes, ultimately undermining many of the Native nations' own plans because precious tribal resources had to be invested in applying for federal grants in the first place.

A shift in federal policies toward tribal self-determination means that business development in Indian Country today is less dependent on federal government prerogatives. However, business development in Indian Country continues to rely on numerous important factors ranging from a tribe's access to (or lack of) markets, their development strategy, and having reformed government institutions in place to support their strategy (Jorgensen 2007). This chapter provides a brief overview of the opportunities and challenges of business development in Indian Country today, with an emphasis on the ways that tribal governments (and individual tribal members) can—and do—leverage their competitive advantages and core competencies both on and off the reservation.

At the most basic level an economy is the way a society is organized to meet the needs of its people. There are local, regional, national, and international economies. Because Native economies are intimately linked with tribal governments and tribal cultures, business development in Indian Country in the United States often depends on the creation of new tribal government institutions, ranging from regulatory commissions to tribal economic development corporations. The structure and effectiveness of these institutions depends on a range of factors, including cultural appropriateness and political stability.

One of the most common and effective strategies employed by tribal governments in the United States has been the creation of tribal development corporations to manage the business research and development arm of the tribal government, to strengthen management, and to streamline business decision-making. For some tribes, creating a triangular approach works to most efficiently generate, protect, and invest tribal capital and assets. Research out of Harvard University into nation building supports the general premise that separation of powers can increase accountability and support more efficient governmental functions. However, it is critical that these institutions are also culturally appropriate and tribally generated so they best reflect the goals of the tribe (Jorgensen 2007). While it is difficult to generalize about business development in Indian Country, there is an identifiable pattern of business development among many tribes in the United States. For example, in order to exploit core competencies in hospitality and gaming, many tribal governments have begun business development in such gaming-related ventures as hotels, restaurants, spas, RV parks, convention centers, and gas stations. These amenities directly enhance the gaming experience while creating additional (and often significant) employment opportunities and revenue streams for the tribal government.

Another business development trend in Indian Country is tourism development more generally, with many tribal governments building and managing golf courses, museums, outlet malls, water parks, convention centers, and other businesses that attract visitors to the reservation for gaming and nongaming purposes. As has been thoroughly documented, Native nations and peoples have supported, engaged in, and enriched themselves with entrepreneurial private and family-oriented economic activities throughout history (R. J. Miller 2001). American Indian cultures and traditions have historically demonstrated the principles of entrepreneurship and do not oppose them as some believe. Indian history and culture encourages and supports entrepreneurship. This history underscores the potential benefits and successes that modern American Indian entrepreneurs can and have achieved.

The majority of revenue-generating enterprises in Native American communities are tribally owned. However, recently, small individually owned enterprises have also become an increasingly important economic base for these communities. Reports from the Community Development Financial Institutions (CDFI) Fund of the US Department of Treasury characterize Native American communities as America's "domestic emerging market." The CDFI Fund cites the sales growth rates of Native American–owned business as double the US average and business creation rates as seven times the US average (Johnson Strategy Group 2002). Data from the 2012 census shows that since 1997, the number of Native American– and Alaska Native–owned businesses has risen to 272,919 and that their gross incomes have increased to $38.8 billion (Minority Business Development Agency 2016). The "Native American Entrepreneurship Report," written by First Nations Development Institute Native Asset Research Group (FNDI 2002), estimates that 170,083 of these businesses are microenterprises—that is, businesses that are owned and operated by one person or family, have fewer than five employees, and are usually financed with loans of less than $50,000 (NAIHC 2010).

Tribal governments with a limited land base or a remote location are pursuing business development that does not rely on the local market or attracting tourists to the reservation. In many cases these businesses include development of the tribe's natural resources for export to national or international markets. Examples of these businesses include water-bottling plants, farms, orchards, ranches, or energy development. In addition, many tribal governments have purchased or created banks, developed restaurants or hotels, and pursued franchising off the reservation, building on their hospitality experience and taking advantage of larger national and international markets. Finally, a significant number of agencies, organizations, and entities whose primary existence is to support Native entrepreneurs now exists. These organizations include, but are not limited to, the National Center for American Indian Enterprise Development, American Indian Business Leaders, the American Indian Chamber of Commerce, the Harvard Project on American Indian Economic Development, the US Department of Commerce Minority Business Development Agency, and the National Congress of American Indians.

CURRENT STATE OF AMERICAN INDIAN-/ALASKAN NATIVE-OWNED BUSINESS IN THE UNITED STATES

The Survey of Business Owners: American Indian– and Alaska Native–Owned Businesses defines these businesses as firms in which American Indians and Alaska Natives own 51 percent or more of the equity, interest, or stock of the business. Additional reports from the survey highlighting other minority- and veteran-owned businesses were issued in 2017. Subsequently, separate publications should be issued soon highlighting additional characteristics of all businesses and their owners. According to data from the US Census Bureau, there were 272,919 American Indian– and Alaska Native–owned businesses in 2012, an increase of 13.3 percent from 2007. The total number of US businesses increased by just 2 percent. American Indian– and Alaska Native–owned businesses generated $38.8 billion in receipts in 2012, an increase from $34.4 billion in 2002. These data come from the 2007 and 2012 editions of *The Survey of Business Owners: American Indian– and Alaska Native–Owned Businesses*. The survey provides detailed information every five years for American Indian– and Alaska Native–owned businesses.

Data are presented by geographic area (nation, state, including the number of firms, sales and receipts, number of paid employees and annual payroll, county, city, and metro area), industry, and size of business. Preliminary national and state data were released in December 2015 from the 2012 survey and in 2010 from the 2007 survey. Among states, in 2012, California had the largest number of American Indian– and Alaska Native–owned businesses with 41,254, down from 45,629 in 2007. California was followed by Oklahoma, with 27,450, up from 21,194 in 2007. While American Indian– and Alaska Native–owned firms accounted for 1.0 percent of all US firms, they made up 2.7 percent of those in the agriculture, forestry, and fishing and hunting sector. By comparison, American Indians and Alaska Natives accounted for 1.8 percent of the eighteen and older population in 2012.

Among counties, Los Angeles, California, had the largest number of American Indian– and Alaska Native–owned businesses with 11,081, down from 14,195 in 2007. In 2012, American Indian– and Alaska Native–owned firms comprised 11.0 percent of all firms in the state, the highest percentage in any state. Other highlights from the 2007 survey include:

- Of the 236,967 American Indian– and Alaska Native–owned businesses in 2007, 23,704 had paid employees, a decrease of 3.2 percent from

2002. These businesses employed 184,416 people, a decrease of 3.6 percent from 2002. Their payrolls totaled $5.9 billion, an increase of 15.4 percent. Receipts from these employer businesses totaled $27.5 billion, an increase of 25.1 percent.

- In 2007, 213,263 American Indian– and Alaska Native–owned businesses had no paid employees, an increase of 20.6 percent from 2002. These nonemployee businesses generated $6.9 billion in receipts, an increase of 40.7 percent from 2002.

- The number of American Indian– and Alaska Native–owned businesses with receipts of $1 million or more increased 26.7 percent from 3,631 in 2002 to 4,599 in 2007.

- The number of American Indian– and Alaska Native–owned businesses with 100 employees or more decreased by 9.0 percent from 178 to 162.

- In 2007, 30.5 percent of American Indian– and Alaska Native–owned businesses operated in construction and repair, maintenance, personal, and laundry services.

- In 2007 construction, retail trade, and wholesale trade accounted for 52.9 percent of American Indian– and Alaska Native–owned business receipts.

CONCLUSION

American Indians have a long and proud history of productive trade, commerce, and entrepreneurship. Existing long before European colonialism, Native people created and sustained numerous and complex trade and barter alliances that provided for their various needs. Despite horrendous injustices inflicted upon American Indians at the hands of white settlers and colonial and federal governments, Native business and entrepreneurship have thrived. American Indian businesses have the potential to contribute significantly to the welfare of tribes, to strengthen tribal sovereignty and self-determination, and to contribute to the national economy.

DISCUSSION

1. How did preexisting trade practices help tribes engage in trade with early European traders?
2. Describe examples of cooperative economic relationships that developed between Native Americans and early European traders.

3. Characterize the impact of US federal government policy on Indian trade following the Revolutionary War.

4. What has been the impact of tribal sovereignty on American Indian business?

References

Anderson, T., and D. Parker. 2004. "The Wealth of Indian Nations: Economic Performance and Institutions on Reservations." Paper presented at the 2004 Annual Meeting of the Western Economic Association. Vancouver, BC.

Carlson, L. 1992. "Learning to Farm: Indian Land Tenure and Farming before the Dawes Act." In T. L. Anderson, ed., *Property Rights and Indian Economies*. Pp. 64–84. Lanham, MD: Rowman and Littlefield.

Chittenden, H. 1902. *The American Fur Trade of the Far West*. New York: Francis P. Harper.

Driver, H. 1961. *Indians of North America*. Chicago: University of Chicago Press.

Ewers, J. 1997. *Plains Indian History and Culture*. Norman: University of Oklahoma Press.

First Nations Development Institute, Native Assets Research Group (FNDI). 2002. *The Native American Entrepreneurship Report*. March. Fredericksburg, VA: FNDI.

Hanner, J. 1981. "Government Response to the Buffalo Hide Trade, 1871–1882." *Journal of Law and Economics* 24, no. 2 (October): 239–71.

Indian Land Tenure Foundation. 2016. "Land Loss." Online at https://www.iltf.org/land -issues/land-loss. Accessed on April 17, 2016.

Johnson Strategy Group, Inc. 2002. *CDFI Fund Native American Lending Study Equity Investment Roundtable and Research Report*. Washington, DC: US Department of the Treasury.

Jorgensen, M., ed. 2007. *Rebuilding Native Nations: Strategies for Governance and Development*. Tucson: University of Arizona Press.

McChesney, F. 1992. "Government as Definer of Property Rights: Indian Lands, Ethnic Externalities, and Bureaucratic Budgets." In T. L. Anderson, ed., *Property Rights and Indian Economies*. Pp. 109–46. Lanham, MD: Rowman and Littlefield Publishers.

Miller, M. 1988. "Tribal Responses to Federal Land Consolidation Policy." Harvard Project on American Indian Economic Development. Online at www.ksg.harvard.edu/hpaied /pubs/pub_129.htm. Accessed on August 1, 2015.

Miller, R. J. 2001. "Economic Development in Indian Country: Will Capitalism or Socialism Succeed." *Oregon Law Review*, 80: 757.

Minority Business Development Agency. 2016. *Fact Sheet U.S. Minority-Owned Firms*. Washington, DC.: US Department of Commerce. Online at www.mbda.gov/sites /default/files/FactSheet-Minority-OwnedFirms.pdf. Accessed on April 17, 2016.

National American Indian Housing Council (NAIHC). 2010. "Native Americans Often Victims of Predatory Lending." Press Release. Washington, DC: NAIHC

Otis, D. S. 1973. *The Dawes Act and the Allotment of Indian Lands*. Edited by F. P. Prucha. Norman: University of Oklahoma Press.

Sturtevant, W., ed. 1988. *Handbook of North American Indians*. Vol. 4, *Indian-White Relations*. Edited by W. Washburn. Washington, DC: Smithsonian Institution Press.

US Department of Commerce. 2012. *Survey of Business Owners—American Indian– and Alaska Native–Owned Firms: 2012*. US Census Bureau. Washington, DC: US Department of Commerce.

———. 2007. *Survey of Business Owners—American Indian– and Alaska Native–Owned Firms: 2007*. US Census Bureau. Washington, DC: US Department of Commerce.

Washburn, W., ed. 1988. *Handbook of North Americans*. Vol. 4, *History of Indian-White Relations*. Washington, DC: Smithsonian Institution Press.

Weinberg, M. 2002. "Indian America." In *A Short History of American Capitalism*. Pp. 13–30. Chicago, IL. New History Press.

2 EMBRACING CULTURAL TRADITION

Historic Business Activity by Native People in the Western United States

Joseph Scott Gladstone, *New Mexico State University*

ABSTRACT

Research exploring challenges faced by some American Indian entrepreneurs include findings that reveal apprehensions that as they practice business as private individuals or families, these entrepreneurs risk stepping outside American Indian cultural norms for collectivism. This chapter addresses and counters these apprehensions by providing some historical examples through archaeological evidence and reports by Western traders showing that private business activity at the family level has traditionally existed within American Indian tribes. I reveal this history with the hope that it relieves any anxiety that current and future private American Indian entrepreneurs might have as they contemplate entering into private profit-oriented business activity. This chapter also briefly suggests a possible source for the perception that tribal governments are solely responsible for creating and managing business activity on reservations. The examples provided in this chapter specifically address Western US tribes, thus demonstrating the need for advanced scholarship that explores this history.

KEYWORDS: entrepreneurship, culture, history

INTRODUCTION

CURRENT RESEARCH EXPLORING ENTREPRENEURIAL ACTIVITY BY individual Native American people reveals that these entrepreneurs are anxious that their for-profit business activities conflict with collective tribal norms (Frantz 1999; Gallagher and Selman 2015; Garsombke and Garsombke 2000; Miller 2012; Stewart and Schwartz 2007) and that for-profit business activity by private individuals can seriously harm tribal culture (Miller

2008). This chapter presents a few historical examples about Native trade that should help relieve some anxiety that readers might have as they contemplate entering in or continuing to perform in private for-profit business practice. Some may be especially concerned that owning a for-profit business might conflict with tribal values for collectivism. My intent in this chapter is not to present and discuss a comprehensive historical examination of American Indian trade in North America. Readers seeking to learn more about tribal trading history are encouraged to read chapter 1 in this edited volume, by Charles F. Harrington, as well as Miller 2012 and especially Swaggerty 1988, who discusses this historic record in detail.

The trading histories presented in this chapter are meant to reveal that tribal people have for a very long time practiced business as private individuals—that is, they practiced their trade independent from large collective tribal influences. Knowing the history about Western Native American trading activity improves one's understanding that entrepreneurial activity practiced by modern-day Native individuals and families does not conflict with perceived tribal community ideas about collectivism. It is important to point out that the examples provided here refer only to the tribes in the Western United States. Readers curious about tribal trading history in other regions are encouraged to expand their inquiry into these places. Research into Native American and other indigenous people from a business-school perspective is a burgeoning field of study.

The brief examples presented here open with an archeological history in what is today called the US Southwest as well as an anthropological history in the US Pacific Northwest, notably the Celilo Falls region on the Columbia River, which bisects today's Washington-Oregon state line. These two examples are followed with historical reports describing trading activity between white fur traders and individual tribal people and families. These reports include those by the French trader La Vérendrye and journal entries written by Hudson's Bay Company men who actively traded with individuals and families. Following this illustration of the distant past, the chapter suggests a possible source for modern-day community perceptions within some tribes that businesses must be collectively owned and operated at the tribal level: the Indian Reorganization Act. The chapter concludes with an affirmation that owning and running one's own business today is okay. A Native business owner is doing what tribal people have done for millennia: identifying unfulfilled needs and wants in the community and taking the initiative on to fulfill them.

HISTORICAL INDIAN BUSINESS ACTIVITY IN THE WEST:
AN ARCHEOLOGICAL AND ANTHROPOLOGICAL LOOK

Tribal people in today's "Americas" have conducted trade for several millennia. But who was responsible for initiating, organizing, and controlling (i.e., managing) these trading activities? Did tribal leaders historically hold sole responsibility for trading activity? Was business activity controlled so as to discourage personal accumulation of wealth? Some tribal people today believe that this second question is the case (Frantz 1999). This section suggests answers to these questions by presenting archeological and anthropologic historical examples that reveal trading (i.e., business) activity in two distinct parts of the US West. The intent in this first examination is to show that business activity done by individual Native Americans and families has a very long history. These examples come from archeological records in the Mesa Verde region in the high desert Southwest as well as from anthropological descriptions about Celilo Falls along what is today called the Columbia River. I admit that these two examples are brief, and readers are encouraged to refer to the resources cited throughout the chapter for additional information.

THE DESERT SOUTHWEST

Long before Spanish incursions in the area, Pueblo tribes participated in economic activity among themselves. Evidence revealing a robust production and trading culture remains today in archeological sites such as Chaco Canyon and Mesa Verde near the Four Corners area in New Mexico and Colorado. Trade goods came from as far south as central Mexico and Mesoamerica (Carter 1993; Ericson and Baugh 1993). The nature of these goods implies that acquiring personal wealth was acceptable among these people (Carter 1993; Ericson and Baugh 1993). Evidence exists revealing a way that trade might have been conducted during this historical era. Let's briefly look at the Mesa Verde community near the Four Corners region.

MESA VERDE

Mesa Verde today is a collection of small community sites built onto cliff ledges. One theory explaining this architectural choice is safety from marauders since the ladders serving as the sole access to these sites could be raised whenever threats appear. A popular site that remains protected today is Mesa Verde National Park in southeastern Colorado. Mesa Verde is relatively young when included in the region's history of trade. It is estimated that the cliff dwellings were built during the end of the twelfth century and inhabited for only about a hundred years (National Park Service 2016).

Visitors to Mesa Verde today will find several cliff dwellings scattered throughout the park. These vary in size from the large Cliff Palace to the small Balcony House. Populations in the largest of these complexes were perhaps about a hundred people. There are two ways to travel from dwelling site to dwelling site: either by traveling up and over the mesas that they are built into or traversing through the canyons in between the mesas, which seems the logical option if one was carrying trade goods. Such intra-mesa routes existed, and they extended beyond the Mesa Verde metro area. When visiting an individual dwelling site such as Cliff Palace within the complex, one can see how life was possibly organized. These structures were essentially large apartment complexes that archeologists assume served to house family groups and, this being a text about business, to divide labor.

The Mesa Verde region held diverse communities that included other cliff dwellings and surface-based farming sites (Rohn 1985). Trade roads connected each of these small community sites (National Park Service 2016). Visiting just this one large area called Mesa Verde National Park makes one realize that this collection of communities is a small part within the greater Mesa Verde region that greatly outsizes the park site. It's quite overwhelming to sense that the scattered cliff sites within the national park are just one place within a much broader region on the Colorado Plateau, spreading from southeastern Colorado and extending west to the Colorado River in southern Utah, especially since intercommunity travel by motor vehicle today still requires hours to complete.

When visiting Mesa Verde National Park and directly observing these historical structures, questions arise about how productive activity was coordinated. One must take into account the size, layout, and relationship to nearby dwelling sites, and connect these observations with knowledge about the region, especially the national park's tie with the greater Chaco Canyon metropolis a hundred miles south. I take the liberty for inference here. These individual sites exchanged among themselves. Surplus production moved out of the area while scarce resources moved in. But did this activity occur via a command economy? A *command economy* is one in which a central government bureaucracy determines and sets specific guidelines for producing and distributing goods within a society. A command economy seems unlikely within the Mesa Verde region. Given the obvious relative isolation for each community, and the communication network limited to foot and visual signals, directing a command economy would be a logistics nightmare.

Further inference about the nature of the producers within this region is grounded in knowledge about tribal societies in the Plains and Pacific Northwest. Drawing on this knowledge about family structures in the northern part of the country, it is possible to assume that like these northern tribes, communities in Mesa Verde were essentially large family groups. It is then possible to legitimately assume that these family-based communities operated and managed their own production activities (i.e., businesses) independent from a central government oversight and control. I admit for now that this is conjecture. But it does raise food for thought regarding the role that larger government has on individuals within historical tribal communities when it comes to producing and distributing goods. Let's now work our way up the US map and move from the southwest corner of the United States to its northwest corner.

CELILO FALLS AND THE DALLES

Celilo was a historical tribal community along a set of massive river rapids given the Western name, The Dalles. The Dalles region was described as "one of the most important trade centers in Aboriginal America" (French and French 1998, 374). The Dalles was a key part of a continental trade network connecting the plains to the coast and both to what is now called Alaska and present-day California (Barber 2005). This vast marketplace network "[created] a hybrid space, one in which coastal and plateau trades thrived" (Barber 2005, 22–23). This area is now inundated by the floodwaters of The Dalles Dam straddling the Washington-Oregon state line along the Columbia River. Before its flooding in the late 1950s, Celilo was the longest inhabited community in the region, estimated to be at least fifteen thousand years old (Dietrich 1995; Robbins 2001).

Celilo was more than a fishing village; it was a trading hub like Chaco Canyon and Mesa Verde in the US Southwest. It connected the coast to the plains, placing tribes in a position to establish trade relationships that served the needs and wants of both coastal and plains tribes. People living along the damp Pacific coast appreciated the warmth provided by buffalo robes that came from the plains, while inland tribes enjoyed the salmon pemmican (a Native North American food made primarily from dried meat) produced on the coast (Stern 1993). Celilo was one of the more significant communities serving as a gateway for trading these goods.

Barber (2001, 50) has described The Dalles as "a confluence of cultures," adding that the area was a traditional marketplace with trade goods extending beyond material things. It included "languages, social systems, technologies,

and mythologies" plus "cultural intermixing" (Barber 2001, 50) that characterized the region. Celilo was very active during large fish migration that
occurred in the spring and fall. With the fish came Natives from all over the
Northwest who "came to trade, socialize, and fish with local residents" (Barber 2001, 51). Barber illustrates life on The Dalles as such:

> Both men women and men traded goods and strengthen[ed] the relation-
> ship with neighboring tribes through marriages and renewed friendships.
> According to trapper and explorer Alexander Ross's estimation, 3,000
> Indians gathered at the river to trade, gamble, and socialize each year in the
> early 1800s. In his often-repeated words, The Dalles was "the great Empo-
> rium or Mart of the Columbia." By the 1950s, the Indian fishery at Celilo
> supported five thousand Indians who traveled from as far away as Montana
> and California to harvest salmon at nearly 480 different fishing station[s]
> spread out along the banks of the roaring River." (Barber 2001, 50–51)

While Barber described The Dalles as a network of cooperative villages
that included Celilo Falls, Stern (1993) added a caveat that these communities dominated passage along the river. Despite community control along the
river, the people conducting trade were individual entrepreneurs, middlemen who conducted trade "to their own advantage, serving as carriers, rather
than primary producers" (Stern 1993, 20). Exchanges were deeply embedded social relationships (Stern 1993). Barber supports Stern's description
about tribal entrepreneurs. These people were savvy and wealthy middlemen
conversant in many languages; being multilingual was essential for trade
(Barber 2005).

These two regions in the Western United States shed some light on the
effects that independent tribal businesspeople had within their communities. Reports by European traders, seen through extensive logs and intra-
organization letters describing their experiences with the tribes within their
business territories, reveal more about the nature of ancestral Native businesspeople. Let's move inland from Celilo and explore the encounters that
the English Hudson's Bay Company experienced with tribal people with
whom they traded.

THE FUR TRADER OBSERVATIONS

Founded in 1670 by British royal charter, the Hudson's Bay Company was
granted a monopoly over fur trade in the Hudson's Bay drainage (Rich 1958).

The Hudson's Bay Company region extended from Hudson's Bay southwesterly toward and reaching what is now the US Pacific Northwest. The Hudson's Bay Company first established forts along the western shores of Hudson's Bay, placing themselves well north of the forts established by the French-Canadian trader Pierre Gaultier de Varennes Sieur de La Vérendrye, on Lake Winnipeg (Rich 1958). These competitors offered two options for local tribes to conduct trade for their goods. They provide insight about business activity that was regulated by tribal leaders in addition to revealing that individuals worked independently from tribal control.

Both the Hudson's Bay Company and La Vérendrye found that tribes, such as the Mandan, sometimes negotiated business only through a tribal headman (Cowie 1993; La Vérendrye 1730; Stern 1993). These headmen, however, were not the political leaders of the tribe; rather, they were headmen during the trading process and often required additional gifts above and beyond the bartered goods (Cowie 1993; Stern 1993). James Isham, a fort manager with Hudson's Bay Company, shared in his journals examples of trade conducted directly with families (1739). It is important to note here that not only does Isham report trade at the family level; he also points out that these family traders were assertive in demanding good value in the items they received from Hudson's Bay in exchange for the furs that they used for barter. Isham reported a list of returned goods and the reasons why they were returned: kettles that were too small to be useful, low-quality knives, low-quality gunpowder, fabric cloth that was thin and weak, yarn clubs that were "noways pleasing nor serviceable to Indians" and oatmeal that was "course, foul, and very bitter" (Isham 1739, 279, 281). The Hudson's Bay Company also reported that women were active in facilitating trade, serving as translators and helping prepare furs (Brown 1980).

Through Western trader reports such as these we discover three significant facts: (1) some tribes did control trade at a government label; (2) individual families worked outside government control; and (3) family-level traders understood a value for trade goods and asserted this understanding through demand for useful quality products.

EMBRACING HISTORIC TRADING TRADITIONS

This chapter presented a very brief history of trade in the Western United States. Readers seeking more comprehensive descriptions about tribal economic history are encouraged to read Robert Miller's 2012 book *Reservation "Capitalism"* as well as work produced by the Harvard Project for American

Indian Development (hpaied.org) and the Native Nations Institute (nni
.arizona.edu). Alexandra Harmon provides an extensive examination of
tribal values toward wealth in her 2010 book *Rich Indians: Native People
and the Problem of Wealth in American History*. The examples described
here illustrate the intent of this chapter's lesson: business activity within
American Indian tribes in the Western United States had been practiced at
the individual and family level for a very long time. Individual American
Indians and their families who venture into entrepreneurial activity today
are not shunning their cultures; rather, they continue to embrace traditions
that predate Western contact. Despite evidence revealing that owning and
running a business as a private individual is a tribal norm, where did some
Native people today get the idea that owning and operating a for-profit business conflicts with tribal values?

A THEORY EXPLAINING THE PERCEPTUAL SHIFT AWAY
FROM PRIVATE ENTERPRISE

Tribes began losing their inherent sovereignty after Spain and the United
States claimed tribal lands for themselves. These governments did not see
tribes as equal partners in trade, but rather, in the case of Spain, as subjects
to be exploited, and, in the case of the United States, as primitive people
dependent on federal paternalism. Amid this loss were tribal identities as
savvy traders, a loss that became more prominent after Western US tribes
were placed on reservations and, through the Indian Reorganization Act of
1934 (IRA), were prescribed government systems with sole responsibility
for economic development. The IRA was a law meant to return tribal sovereignty by allowing tribes to govern themselves. It created tribal councils that
served as the conduit for economic development. The IRA, however, placed
this responsibility for tribal economic development into the hands of tribal
business councils who had little knowledge or skill in profitably managing
such enterprises. Many IRA government systems persist today, and although
some flourish, many do not.

History shows that while tribes practiced trade at both a collective and
individual level, the IRA shifted the paradigm by placing all of the responsibility and power for economic activity (trade) onto tribal governments. After
nearly eighty years under such a system, this may be seen among tribal communities as the normal expectation about who is responsible and permitted
to conduct business on reservations (Gladstone 2012). Perhaps this is why
community animosity perceived by tribal entrepreneurs exists for many

living on reservations. The IRA system is the only economic system that they are familiar with. What influence the IRA has on the ancient history of a strong Native trading spirit remains an unanswered question today (Gladstone 2012).

CONCLUSION

American Indians have always conducted trade, and throughout this history many practiced trade specifically for profit. Even while seeking profit, these long-ago entrepreneurs, such as those out of Celilo, were aware of their social roles in the community. The custom for relying on tribal governments to initiate and manage business is a modern concept less than a decade old compared to the thousands of years that tribal people traditionally conducted trade. Exposing community members today to their rich trading history will help them understand that they are members of a culture that has always permitted individuals and families to practice their trades.

DISCUSSION

1. Given the history of sovereign American Indian trade before the reservation era, it is interesting to hear about cultural barriers experienced by modern-day Native American entrepreneurs. How did these cultural barriers come about?
2. This chapter asserts that tribal people have practiced business in one form or another for centuries and that modern perceptions saying otherwise are inaccurate. Do you agree or disagree with these modern perceptions? Why or why not?
3. What value do entrepreneurs bring to their reservation communities today? How do these contributions compare to tribally managed enterprises?

References

Barber, K. 2005. *Death of Celilo Falls*. Seattle: University of Washington Press.
———. 2001. "Narrative Fractures and Fractured Narratives: Celilo Falls in the Columbia Gorge Discovery Center and the Yakama Nation Cultural Heritage Center." In W. G. Robbins, ed., *The Great Northwest: The Search for Regional Identity*. Pp. 47–65. Corvallis: Oregon State University Press.
Brown, J. S. H. 1980. *Strangers in Blood: Fur Trade Company Families in Indian Country*. Vancouver, BC: University of British Columbia Press.

Carter, W. B. 2009. *Indian Alliances and the Spanish in the Southwest, 750–1750*. Norman: University of Oklahoma Press.

Cowie, I. 1993. *The Company of Adventurers: A Narrative of Seven Years in the Service of the Hudson's Bay Company during 1867–1874 on the Great Buffalo Plains*. Lincoln: University of Nebraska Press.

Dietrich, W. 1995. *Northwest Passage: The Great Columbia River*. New York: Simon & Schuster.

Ericson, J. E., and T. G. Baugh. 1993. *The American Southwest and Mesoamerica: Systems of Prehistoric Exchange*. New York: Plenum Press.

Frantz, K. 1999. *Indian Reservations in the United States*. Chicago: University of Chicago Press.

French, D. H., and K. S. French. 1998. *Wasco, Wishram, and the Cascades*. In D. Walker Jr., ed., *Handbook of North American Indians: Plateau*. Vol. 12. Pp. 360–77. Washington, DC: Smithsonian Institution.

Gallagher, B., and M. Selman. 2015. "Warrior Entrepreneur." *American Indian Quarterly* 39, no. 1: 73–94.

Garsombke, D. J., and T. W. Garsombke. 2000. "Non-traditional vs. Traditional Entrepreneurs: Emergence of a Native American Comparative Profile of Characteristics and Barriers." *Academy of Entrepreneurship Journal* 6, no. 1: 93–100.

Gladstone, J. S. 2012. "Old Man and Coyote Barter: An Inquiry Into the Spirit of a Native American Philosophy of Business." Thesis (PhD)–Business Administration (Order No. 3537767, New Mexico State University). ProQuest Dissertations and Theses, 284 pages.

Harmon, A. 2010. *Rich Indians: Native People and the Problem of Wealth in American History*. Chapel Hill: University of North Carolina Press.

Indian Reorganization Act. 1934. 25 U.S.C. 478 (1934).

Isham, J. 1739. "Letter to Hudson's Bay Headquarters." In E. E. Rich, ed., *The History of the Hudson's Bay Company, 1670–1870. Volume 1, 1670–1763*. London: Hudson's Bay Company Record Society, 1958.

La Vérendrye, P. G. 1730. "Continuation of the Report of the Sieur de la Vérendrye Touching upon the Discovery of the Western Sea." In L. J. Burpee, ed., *Journals and Letters of Pierre Gaultier de Varennes de La Vérendrye and His Sons*. Pp. 43–513. Toronto: Champlain Society, 1927.

Miller, R. J. 2012. *Reservation "Capitalism": Economic Development in Indian Country*. Westport, CT: Praeger Publishing.

———. 2008. "American Indian Entrepreneurs: Unique Challenges, Unlimited Potential." *Arizona State Law Journal* 40: 1297.

National Park Service. 2016. "Mesa Verde National Park." Online at https://www.nps.gov /meve/index.htm. Accessed on August 1, 2016.

Rich, E. E., ed. 1958. *The History of the Hudson's Bay Company, 1670–1870. Volume 1, 1670–1763*. London: Hudson's Bay Company Record Society.

Robbins, W. G. 2001. *The Great Northwest: The Search for Regional Identity*. Corvallis: Oregon State University Press.

Rohn, A. H. 1985. "Prehistoric Developments in the Mesa Verde Region." *Exploration: Annual Bulletin of the School of American Research*. Pp. 3–10.

Stern, T. 1993. *Chiefs and Chief Traders: Indian Relations at Fort Nez Percés, 1818–1855.* Corvallis: Oregon State University Press.

Stewart, D., and R. G. Schwartz. 2007. "Native American Business Strategy: A Survey of Northwest US Firms." *International Journal of Business Performance Management* 9, no. 3: 259–77.

Swaggerty, W. R. 1988. "Indian Trade in the Trans-Mississippi West to 1870." In D. Walker Jr., ed., *Handbook of North American Indians: History of Indian-White Relations.* Vol. 4. Pp. 351–74. Washington, DC: Smithsonian Institution Press.

3 AMERICAN INDIAN ENTREPRENEURSHIP

Charles F. Harrington, *University of South Carolina–Upstate*
Carolyn Birmingham, *Florida Institute of Technology*
Daniel Stewart, *Gonzaga University*

ABSTRACT

Entrepreneurship and entrepreneurial endeavors have proven to be effective avenues for the pursuit of tribal economic development, sustained economic independence, and sovereignty of Native American people. Despite significant gains in entrepreneurship, there remain significant challenges facing Native American entrepreneurs. These include lack of access to capital, insufficient business development support, and bureaucratic entanglements within tribal, state, and federal government agencies. Often, the lack of supportive infrastructure hampers new business development. A mixed strategy of traditional economy, individual market enterprise, and tribal government–managed corporations can coexist and provide multiple strategies and tools for moving toward sustained economic sovereignty in ways that are informed by indigenous values, culture, and interests. Native American entrepreneurs have specific and unique characteristics that impact business decision-making, strategy, and enterprise growth. American Indian entrepreneurs can leverage knowledge of their distinct history, institutions, indigenous culture, and local economic resources to add value to their entrepreneurial ventures.

KEYWORDS: entrepreneurship, Native American entrepreneurs, economic sovereignty

INTRODUCTION

AMERICAN INDIAN NATIONS AND PEOPLES HAVE SUPPORTED, engaged in, and enriched themselves with entrepreneurial private and family-oriented economic activities throughout history. They have always fostered, encouraged, and supported tribal people in their private economic endeavors, protected their private property rights, and allowed individual

American Indians to pursue their own ways (Miller 2008, 2001).[1] As in all societies, Indians and their governing bodies had to provide for the daily needs of their families and their tribes. Hence Indians were continuously involved in the production of food, tools, clothing, shelter, and all sorts of objects for personal use. Indians regularly traded goods with other peoples from near and far, both for survival and to make life as comfortable as possible. The majority, if not all, of this trade was conducted in free-market situations where private individuals voluntarily came together to buy and sell items they had manufactured for sale, which they exchanged by barter and sometimes even sold for money. The only way in which Indian principles of economics and private property differed from the European/American concepts was in the conflicting views these societies had on the private ownership of land (Guzman 2000).

As discussed in chapter 1, many indigenous nations in what is now the United States recognized and protected private property rights in all conceivable items of property, such as river-fishing rocks, wooden fishing platforms, ocean fishing and sealing sites, beaches, housing and housing plots, fruit and nut trees, berry patches, and beached whales. Many of these real and personal property rights were inheritable. Commanding large quantities of financial resources is not always a secure path to economic development, since contemporary success in the market also requires large co-investments in education and skilled workforces that allow organizations and communities to effectively deploy their resources. Most tribal communities do not have access to investments necessary to assure competitiveness with national or international economies to develop sustaining economies. Many, if not most, American Indian communities are located on reservations where there are limited resources and often limited market opportunities because of their isolation from urban business districts (Pascal and Stewart 2008).

American economic policy for American Indians has largely focused on providing education to American Indians so they can join the American workforce. This solution assumes Indian labor will move to where there is work, and the migration from reservations to cities of Indian labor supports that view. Research, however, indicates that if there were sufficient jobs on their home reservation, most Indians would prefer to stay in their communities (Verbos et al. 2015). If Indian communities are to uphold and extend tribal political and cultural sovereignty, they will need capabilities to maintain sustained economic independence. The reservation system of dependence on federal funds has helped support tribal communities, but it does not provide communities and individuals with resources that will ensure the continuity of community, culture, and political government (Indian Country Today 2010).

While prevailing economic development strategists suggest that developing communities can be successful using the current market economy, in many places in the world this has not been the case. The results are often highly mixed, a situation that also characterizes present-day American Indian economies. Instead of imposing economic development models that work in highly developed market systems, development strategists look to work cooperatively with local communities and use their knowledge of their history, institutions, culture, and local economic resources. This approach uses indigenous knowledge and should be part of the philosophy of economic development in American Indian communities.

Tribally managed businesses, such as tribal casinos and other enterprises, already exemplify the indigenous-knowledge approach when they use profits for improving tribal economic well-being and supporting tribal government, cultural, and sovereignty projects. To survive in the current world, indigenous communities can use traditional economic knowledge and apply it in a modern context. A mixed strategy of traditional economy, individual market enterprise, and tribal government–managed corporations can coexist and provide multiple strategies and tools for moving toward sustained economic self-sufficiency in ways that are informed by indigenous values, culture, and interests (Indian Country Today 2009). Economic development need not present a forced choice between dependent poverty or middle-class assimilation. Contemporary tribal economies need to provide enough well-being to sustain healthy, culturally creative, socially interrelated, and politically capable communities.

TRIBAL ECONOMIC DEVELOPMENT

Tribal economic development in rural/reservation communities tends to be more complicated than in larger population centers because tribes continue to struggle with the historical legacies of centuries of genocidal, paternalistic, and assimilationist federal policies that have obstructed their efforts to become self-determined, self-governing nations. Tribes have historically focused their economic-development efforts on creating new jobs and generating increased revenues by recruiting new industries, promoting entrepreneurship, training/retraining their workforces, and developing essential infrastructure (e.g., roads, shopping centers, and telecommunications systems). Increasingly, these efforts have taken into consideration tribal cultural values, environmental impacts, and long-term economic sustainability. Owing to this history, tribes are striving to reacquire and reclaim their lands and rivers (often contaminated or otherwise deteriorated by decades of poor mining, logging, and other resource-extraction practices); to develop basic physical infrastructure (e.g., roads, water/sewer/solid waste management systems, power and telecommunications systems); to provide basic community services (e.g., health, education housing, safety/security, and child/ family services); and to develop their internal capacity to govern their tribal nations and manage complex tribal organizations.

Until the advent of tribally operated casinos in the 1980s, these kinds of tribal community development efforts generally preceded tribal efforts to attract new industries, support local entrepreneurship, and develop tribally owned enterprises (other than natural resource extraction). Between 1990 and 2000 the per capita incomes of tribal communities grew at two to three times the rate of the nation as a whole (US Census Bureau 2002a) yet remained at less than half the national average. This is true for both gaming and nongaming tribes. According to the Harvard Project on American Indian Development, the key to successful tribal economic development has not been solely the cash flowing from casinos or natural resource endowments (many successful tribes have neither), but rather a strong belief in self-determination and a "focus on developing the legal, regulatory, and physical infrastructure that rewards productivity, holds decision makers accountable, and holds down the risks of political instability for individuals and businesses" (Cornell and Kalt 2007, 113).

Tribes that create favorable conditions for economic investment—and fully utilize their human capital—can be as successful as those with far greater natural resource bases. "On many reservations, comprehensive and multifaceted development approaches are supplanting single-strategy interventions that are project-driven or focused on a specific sector such as resource extraction, manufacturing, or tourism" (Cornell and Kalt 2007, 114). While some gaming tribes have realized significant economic gains in recent years, remote rural/reservation communities have not benefited significantly from gaming. Yet the Harvard Project points out:

> The gaming revolution in Indian Country is but one manifestation of
> Indian nations' assertions of self-determination and the development payoff
> to those assertions . . . perhaps the most encouraging aspect of the

economic growth that is taking hold in Indian Country is the thickening of the economic fabric of many Native nations. These nations are beginning to develop sustained economies, often generating export-oriented enterprises that seek to build upon tribal comparative advantages based on natural resources, labor costs, regulatory flexibility, human capital, and/or geographic position. They have also sought to diversify their local economic bases by fostering small business creation that supplants off-reservation retail sectors. (Cornell and Kalt 2007, 117)

NATIVE ENTREPRENEURSHIP

The national report *Native Entrepreneurship: Challenges and Opportunities for Rural Communities* (Malkin and Aseron 2006) defined *entrepreneurship* as the process by which an individual creates and grows an enterprise. Building on this broad definition of entrepreneurship, the report defined *Native entrepreneurship* to include an emphasis on the role of cooperation; value of group goals; and the importance of placing material success after emotional, family, or community relationships. The report *Native Entrepreneurship in South Dakota: A Deeper Look* (Malkin and Aseron 2010) reinforced this idea of a culturally relevant definition for Native entrepreneurship. A common sentiment was that people who owned their own businesses were not solely seeking personal financial gain, but that they showed initiative and had utilized their strengths and abilities.

As the authors conducted interviews for the report, the very terminology *entrepreneurship* evoked discussion, confusion, and at times resistance over a sense of what *entrepreneurship* represented to tribal community members. In many instances, when asked, "What is Native entrepreneurship," respondents expressed uncertainty in either defining or identifying themselves as entrepreneurs. For many respondents the move from abject poverty and the survival mode to entrepreneurial vision and success was daunting. Very few respondents claimed outright to be Native entrepreneurs. Despite this perception, the majority of those interviewed also noted that entrepreneurship plays an important role in their tribal past, present, and future and that entrepreneurship activities and engagement are increasing.

The national report *Native Entrepreneurship: Challenges and Opportunities for Rural Communities* (Malkin and Aseron 2006) explored perceptions about Native culture as it relates to entrepreneurship development strategies. Those interviewed for the national report, mostly Native and non-Native leaders of national nonprofit organizations, offered the following distinctions with regard to Native culture and entrepreneurship:

- The issues of control and use of Native assets are critical to any Native entrepreneurship development strategy or discussion.
- While the traditional Native model of business development may differ from mainstream models, Native communities have had a long history of trade and commerce (entrepreneurship).
- For many Native Americans, entrepreneurship is about utilizing individual initiative to benefit the whole community. Part of this community interest includes sustainable utilization of natural resources.
- While a lack of experience in business development and entrepreneur role models are not unique to Native communities, it is particularly prevalent on many reservations today.
- Native entrepreneurship development includes holistic support strategies that deal with both personal and economic empowerment.

CHALLENGES TO NATIVE ENTREPRENEURSHIP

Creating economic development and activity in Indian Country is an absolutely crucial issue today. In fact, it is probably the most important modern-day political, social, and financial concern that Indian nations and Indian people face. Tribal governments and Indians need to create jobs and economic activity on their reservations and also for tribal citizens who live off reservations. One obvious problem that plagues the development of economic activity in Indian Country is the total lack of functioning economies on the vast majority of reservations (Miller 2008). This is caused by an absence of small businesses on reservations and the fact that Indian people own private businesses at the lowest rate per capita for any ethnic or racial group in the United States. Certainly, if tribes can increase the entrepreneurial activities of tribal citizens and the number of privately operated businesses in Indian Country that would greatly benefit reservation communities. Notwithstanding the phenomenal results from tribal gaming, American Indians remain as a group the poorest within the United States. Indians suffer under the highest unemployment and substandard housing rates of any ethnic or racial group (US Commission on Civil Rights 2003).

American Indian entrepreneurs face important cultural and social issues when determining whether to start a business and whether to locate it in Indian Country. Cultural and social traditions impact business development in Indian Country and elsewhere. The history of federal Indian policies, economic development, and activities on reservations has left many tribal communities leery of the "businessman" and the "get-rich" development scheme that is going to "save" the reservation. A long history of having their lands, sacred sites, and assets exploited by the majority society has understandably made many tribes and Indians cautious about business. In fact, the very word *capitalism* causes a visceral reaction for many Indians. Given this, Indian entrepreneurs stand out, and they ignore cultural and social concerns at their peril.

Miller (2008, 7) has stated that for "many Indian development is the road to cultural ruin . . . a further walk down that non-Indian road to assimilation and 'civilization.' " He adds that many Indians have "a profound ambivalence about the ethos of economic development that values only production and acquisition." It is an exercise of economic sovereignty when tribal governments and communities decide what types of businesses to allow in Indian Country and what business endeavors a reservation community will support. It is also the individual right of tribal entrepreneurs to pursue their own goals and economic self-sufficiency. What can be problematic is that at times successful Indian business owners stand out on many reservations and sometimes encounter resistance for seeming to have pushed ahead of others (Frantz 1999). This phenomenon has been called "social jealousy" and is a well-known idea in many cultures, especially in poorer areas that are beginning to develop economically. This principle is often referred to by Indians with the "crickets in the bucket" analogy, where any cricket that tries to climb out of the bucket is pulled back in by the others.[2] This is a serious issue that Indian entrepreneurs have to understand, deal with, and factor into their business analysis and decision. Will reservation residents support your business, seek employment with your company, and support you in the community, legal, and bureaucratic issues you as an entrepreneur will face? Some entrepreneurs have addressed these questions and made the conscious decision to locate their businesses off reservation for these very reasons.

Social and cultural issues can seriously affect the success of a business in Indian Country if reservation residents will not patronize a particular business. Some Indian entrepreneurs have stated that this concern and others have led them to locate their business off reservation because of questions about profitability. They mention specifically being expected to extend credit, employment, and assistance to relatives and tribal citizens who would not be granted such under usual economic standards. When these types of social and cultural issues are present on a reservation, one change is necessary before entrepreneurs will be able to operate there successfully. It is for those tribal communities and governments to decide whether they want the specific type of economic development proposed and whether they will support businesses operated by their fellow citizens and relatives instead of only patronizing off-reservation businesses. As a result, many Indian entrepreneurs face unique cultural challenges in starting, locating, and operating a business.

ACCESS TO CAPITAL

Access to capital, both financial and human, is needed for any successful entrepreneurial endeavor. Resource acquisition (in terms of money, time, and people) is a constant challenge to entrepreneurship in Indian Country. Despite these daunting challenges, American Indian entrepreneurs often acquire the resources necessary to launch their businesses in one of three ways: accumulated family wealth, bank loans backed by home mortgages, and regular bank loans (Miller 2008). The majority of prospective entrepreneurs simply do not have access to these regular opportunities for new business funding. First, because of a history of impoverishment and lack of meaningful economic opportunities, few Indian people have accumulated family wealth that can be utilized for new business development. Second, most homes owned by Indians in Indian Country are located on "trust land"—that is, land in which the legal estate is owned by the United States and the Indian family is the beneficial owner and is therefore unable to grant a mortgage on the real property. Thus home equity, even where that exists in Indian Country, cannot be used for bank loans in the majority of cases. Finally, Indian people have difficulties getting regular uncollaterized bank loans, or signature loans. In addition to the historical fact that most banks did not even consider loaning in Indian Country, tribal entrepreneurs face unique challenges in getting bank loans. Due to the poverty and the near absence of economic activity in Indian Country, many tribal people do not have the permanent employment histories and near-perfect credit scores needed to acquire bank loans (Miller 2008).

EDUCATION AND VOCATIONAL PREPARATION

Indian people have among the lowest educational attainment rates of any ethnic or racial group in the United States. Reservation and urban Indian unemployment rates are far above the general American rate. As a result, there is a lack of work experience and general business education among many Indians—a challenge for entrepreneurs. Presently, there are almost no instructors at mainstream universities who have the technical or cultural knowledge of reservation social and economic systems that would allow them to provide effective entrepreneurship training for American Indian students (Miller 2012). One solution would be to use the extensive network of tribal colleges to provide instruction at the undergraduate level. However, many tribal colleges lack strong access to a pool of academically qualified MBA or PhD instructors who would be eligible to teach these courses (Stewart and Pepper 2011).

There are also challenges related to formal business education. Fortunately, there has been some progress initiated on this front. For example, unique programs such as the MBA in American Indian Entrepreneurship at Gonzaga University aspire to provide tribal members with graduate-level business training that will allow them to teach at tribal colleges. The PhD Project, sponsored by the accounting firm KPMG, connects qualified business professionals with doctoral programs in business, with the hopes that the number of American Indian business professors at research universities will increase. Because of the paucity of Indians who are private business owners, there are too few mentors to train others or to pass on such information. Many Indians lack significant work experience because of a dearth of employment opportunities on reservations. As a result, dealing with banks; legal, business, and accounting issues; federal, tribal, and state bureaucracies; and so on can be more difficult for an inexperienced entrepreneur. The frequent lack of business role models, mentors, and job training for youth and adults to gain experience creates additional obstacles for entrepreneurs.[3] These endemic issues pose major challenges for Indian entrepreneurs and their potential employees.

HEALTH AND WELLNESS

Health and wellness issues further compound the challenges and difficulties confronting Indian entrepreneurs. American Indians suffer from low life expectancy, major health issues, and a number of health-related challenges that plague their communities. Health care is at an abysmal level in Indian Country and has been for over a century. The United States has woefully underfunded its treaty and trust responsibilities in this arena. The US Indian Health Service budget increases for decades have not even kept pace with inflation, and that assumes the budgets started at a reasonable level to being with, which they did not. The United States spends, for example, far less on health care for American Indians, for whom it owes health care trust and treaty responsibilities, than it does for other Americans in general and for incarcerated federal prisoners (Miller 2008, 2012).

TRIBAL GOVERNMENTS AND RESERVATION INFRASTRUCTURE

Establishing a successful business in Indian Country has other challenges that must be addressed, specifically the challenges inherent in tribal governments. Many tribal governments and reservations are not considered "business friendly" places. This is not enacted the policies, laws, and regulatory frameworks for business, which is necessary in attracting new businesses and business development (Miller 2008). Many tribes, for example, do not have incorporation, business standards, or uniform commercial codes. There is also an absence of precedent in written tribal case law for the incorporation, existence, and operation of businesses as well as enforcement of contracts and various related rights and responsibilities.

In addition, most tribal constitutions do not contain a prohibition on ex post facto laws or on the impairment of the obligation of contracts. This ironic situation can be blamed initially on the United States because most tribal constitutions were originally suggested and nearly imposed on tribes by the federal government in the 1930s. These boilerplate constitutions did not contain these important provisions. Entrepreneurs are rightly concerned about the powers of the government they are thinking of operating under, and the absence of legal protections in Indian Country against ex post facto laws and impairment of contracts raises serious questions for all private businesses (Miller 2012).

Tribal governments can also impose problematic bureaucratic "hurdles" that consume valuable resources spent dealing with governments and business regulations that could have been used to develop and run a business. Like all governments, tribes have good and bad bureaucracies. Entrepreneurs will encounter varying levels of bureaucratic knowledge, experience, and helpfulness on different reservations. But one bureaucracy that is present on almost all reservations is the Tribal Employee Rights Office (TERO). TERO ordinances, for example, usually require on-reservation businesses to register, file paperwork and reports, give hiring preferences to tribal citizens and Indians (something non-Indian entrepreneurs may struggle with as they are used to hiring whomever they want), and perhaps pay certain fees. Entrepreneurs have to understand and comply with these laws, which can be an obstacle for some business startups and ongoing operations (Miller 2008).

Entrepreneurs considering locating on reservations face other unique challenges pertaining to infrastructure. A principle and confounding issue is the same faced by all rural economic concerns: the distance from markets, cities, clients, employees, resources, and so on. Reservations were often purposely located by the United States far from valuable resources and population centers, and many remain very isolated today. A primary deterrent to success on reservations is the lack of access to supporting industries (Pascal and Stewart 2008). Urban areas have a higher concentration of business activity, which creates a better environment for successful partnerships with potential suppliers and buyers. "Economic clusters" are concentrated numbers of firms in related industries that support one another. For example, a technology company needs access to parts distributors for inputs, trained labor that can develop new products, manufacturing plants to build its equipment, and retail or wholesale stores to sell its goods. The likelihood of finding these types of supporting activities is much higher near urban areas. American Indian entrepreneurs located near economic clusters have higher revenue than those located in rural areas (Pascal and Stewart 2008).

Indian entrepreneurs have many unique challenges to overcome in starting, locating, and operating their businesses. Many of the issues discussed here impact Indian entrepreneurs no matter where they locate their business. It is no wonder that Indians are underrepresented per capita in private business ownership. This fact is not due to a cultural prohibition on economic activity and private initiative; instead, it is rooted in commonly understood obstacles to business formation and entrepreneurship.

FEDERAL AND STATE GOVERNMENTS

Federal and state governments impose challenges for businesses in Indian Country that are quite different than challenges faced by off-reservation entrepreneurs. As with all governments, these entities are eager to apply broadly their taxation, regulatory, and jurisdictional authority, even into reservations. That is nothing unique for entrepreneurs, but Indians are faced with conflicting and perhaps unsettled federal claims of regulatory authority and state claims of taxation and jurisdiction that overlap with tribal claims to the same authority. Businesses can get caught in the middle of these disputes, and the uncertainty alone is often sufficient to convince Indian and non-Indian entrepreneurs to avoid reservations as business locations.

In addition, the federal government plays a major role in the day-to-day economic activities on non-self-determining reservations in Indian Country. The United States assumed this role due to (a) the US Constitution, (b) hundreds of treaties the United States signed with Indian Nations, (c) the fiduciary responsibilities it owes tribes and individual Indians in many circumstances, and (d) its ownership as the trustee of much of tribal land and assets in addition to about eleven million acres of individual Indian-owned trust land. Since the United States holds the legal ownership of many of the assets of tribes and individual Indians, federal law requires that anyone seeking to buy or lease tribal or individual Indian trust assets has to secure the approval of the United States. Moreover, tribes and individuals cannot pledge these assets as collateral for loans, or even develop or sometimes even use the assets themselves, without time-consuming federal bureaucratic approvals. Needless to say, this situation slows down and increases the cost of economic activities regarding these assets and interjects enormous uncertainty, sometimes completely hampering certain types of economic activity in Indian Country.

A few examples will suffice to demonstrate some of the problems federal control and bureaucratic red tape can cause Indian entrepreneurs. The US General Accounting Office reported that as of 2003, the Bureau of Indian Affairs had a multiyear staff backlog for title search requests. These searches are needed for many reasons, including the acquisition of private mortgages and site leases. A person can get a title search off reservation in a few days, but some Indians have waited up to six years to get a BIA title search. No business and no entrepreneur can operate under that kind of regulatory climate. In addition, federal employees are often required to review tribal and individual economic plans for reservation and trust land developments and pass judgment on whether federal approval should be granted. These federal employees often have no expertise in the business subjects they are reviewing and approving. That is a significant obstacle for Indian entrepreneurs.

State governments wreak their own special brand of business and investment uncertainty on reservations. They are often interested in what they can get from Indian Country, either tax dollars or jurisdictional control. States have often attempted to tax individual Indian and tribal enterprises on reservations and to control economic activities. State governments and courts have also intervened in the on-reservation activities of Indian entrepreneurs. Congress contributed to this situation and uncertainty in 1953 when it granted certain states criminal and civil jurisdiction on certain reservations. Clearly, in light of the foregoing discussion, federal and state governments impose numerous obstacles, obligations, and uncertainties on Indian entrepreneurs.

ENTREPRENEURIAL DECISION-MAKING PROCESSES

Researchers have tried to gain a better understanding of what factors contribute to the existence of entrepreneurial opportunities (Sarasvathy 2008; Venkataraman 1997). The decision to invest or to become involved in a specific type of venture within an industry determines the nature of resources required to achieve economic sustainability (Chandler et al. 2011). There has been little research into entrepreneurial motivation of Indian entrepreneurs other than many Indians want to stay on the reservation with their families and start businesses that are needed locally and help the community/tribe. A better awareness of the actions and behaviors of entrepreneurs is crucial to gaining a better understanding of the entrepreneurial economy (Chandler et al. 2011).

Decision-making processes influence choices that are made and the effectiveness of the venture (Dean and Sharfman 1996). Sarasvathy (2008) advances our understanding of the entrepreneurial decision process by elucidating two approaches: causation and effectuation. "Causation processes take a particular effect as given and focus on selecting between means to create that effect. Effectuation processes take a set of means as given and focus on selecting between possible effects that can be created with that set of means" (Sarasvathy 2008, 245). A causation approach to entrepreneurial decisions looks at opportunity recognition as a planned process where opportunities are recognized after a purposeful, rational, and systematic search process. This school is based on causation logic (Sarasvathy 2001) and is derived from the rational decision-making perspective of neoclassical microeconomics (Chandler et al. 2011). Consistent with this approach, competitive advantage for emerging firms is conceptualized to be largely determined by competencies related to discovering and exploiting opportunities and utilizing current firm resources (e.g., Chandler and Jansen 1992; Cooper, Gimeno-Gascon, and Woo 1994). In a causation process an economic development entity (EDE) for a tribe may decide to enter into entrepreneurial ventures that will meet a need for the tribe, such as a grocery store on a relatively remote reservation. In new venture creation entrepreneurs following a causation process clearly define the objectives they want to accomplish up front and systematically search (Herron and Sapienza 1992) for entrepreneurial opportunities within developed industries that meet those objectives.

In the second approach, effectuation, opportunities are unknown until discovered (Ardichvili, Cardozo, and Ray 2003; Kirzner 1997). Entrepreneurs using an effectuation approach intend to create a new venture but are not driven toward one specific goal and are more flexible in the decision-making process before settling on a business model. The entrepreneur develops the opportunity by experimenting, changing directions, and using emergent (e.g., Crick and Spence 2005; Mintzberg and Waters 1985) or nonpredictive strategies (Wiltbank et al. 2009). Under effectuation theory, entrepreneurs utilize existing skills and prior knowledge, which influences the opportunity recognition process. Goals emerge by developing potential courses of action that are based on the available means of who a person is, what they know, and whom they know. The entrepreneur starts from a given set of capabilities and know-how. Entrepreneurs using an effectuation approach work with means within their control and make adjustments as necessary (Dew et al. 2009).

Effectuation helps to explain how "in the absence of current markets for future goods and services, these goods and services manage to come into existence" (Venkataraman 1997, 120). This appears to better describe the actual thoughts and behaviors that some entrepreneurs experience when starting a venture. In an effectuation process, the economic development entity may consider its status as minority-owned in order to enter into any number of businesses that may be enhanced through that status.

BUSINESS STRATEGY OF TRIBAL ENTERPRISES

Much of the mainstream literature in strategic management builds on Porter (1985) and Barney (1991), which focus on internal capabilities. Porter develops the idea of competing with the "value chain," a series of organizational activities (i.e., research and development, marketing, production), which the firm could utilize to create value for the buyer. Barney argues that either capabilities or resources could be a source of competitive advantage, so long as those resources and capabilities are valuable, rare, costly to imitate, and exploitable by the organization. One resource that is particularly valuable to American Indian entrepreneurs is their unique knowledge of their own culture. Understanding of a particular culture is referred to as cultural capital, since that knowledge is valuable to those have it. Many American Indian entrepreneurs use their cultural capital to market and sell their goods. This is called the culture-of-origin strategy (Stewart et al. 2014). In the American Indian community, entrepreneurs who market their goods as "Made in Native America" are following a culture-of-origin strategy.

The culture-of-origin strategy is viable for American Indian entrepreneurs because it cannot be imitated easily by non–American Indian firms. For example, an American Indian entrepreneur specializing in American Indian art or music can claim cultural authenticity, whereas a competing non–American Indian firm cannot. For the culture-of-origin strategy to work, the particular good or service must be made more valuable by its cultural content or association with American Indian culture. As such, cultural authenticity can easily add value to art, music, or even medicine, but it is a more difficult strategy to use with more generic goods or services such as modern building construction or plastics manufacturing. In these types of industries, there is usually no value added by being associated with the Native American culture. Tribally owned enterprises operate on a for-profit basis for the benefit of the tribe and as such are often hybrid (profit combined with mission) organizations. For-profit entities may follow mission-driven strategies (Russo 2010) that incorporate and couple economic, social, and ecological logics. These logics are perhaps more balanced in tribal enterprises than in mainstream enterprises.

SUSTAINABILITY AND SOCIAL RESPONSIBILITY

Native American philosophy and culture differ from that of the dominant US culture. Native Americans have a deep respect for and relationship with Mother Earth (Cajete 2000; Gladstone 2015). There is also a future orientation that is often absent in the dominant culture. Native Americans traditionally consider the effects of their actions seven generations into the future (LaDuke 1999). This reflects a relational ethic (Verbos and Humphries 2014) that is important to the social and ecological logics of American Indian culture. Sustainability is embedded in Native American culture (Cajete 2000; Wildcat 2009), and because of its importance, it is likely that socially responsible and ecologically sustainable practices are present, legitimized, and institutionalized in Native American businesses.

In mainstream corporate businesses there is increasing pressure to pay attention to the "triple bottom line" of economic, social, and environmental returns. For instance, carbon offsets are becoming increasingly important for large corporations to implement, since publicly traded firms can experience tremendous scrutiny for their attention (or lack thereof) to global pollution policies and trends. This is one area in which Native American companies can set the example and potentially utilize a culture-of-origin strategy. Because American Indian communities are well-known for their sensitivity toward the natural environment, American Indian entrepreneurs are perhaps in a position to take leadership in the provision of services in this area.

Businesses in the dominant culture generally focus first on economic outcomes and second on other social or environmental goals. The limited research on Native American businesses indicates that the tribe and its needs come first, and economic considerations are second (cf. Hindle et al. 2005; Hindle and Lansdowne 2005; Hindle and Moroz 2007). This does not mean these companies are, in effect, nonprofits; instead, they are hybrid in nature. Tribal enterprises are explicitly profit-driven because the profits support reservation economies through job creation, paying for tribal government, social services, education, tribal culture, and tribal community activities. They are nonprofit with respect to the strong social mission and claim the tribe has on a significant portion of their profits. It is harder therefore for some of the reservation-owned companies to reinvest enough money back into the business because of the claim the tribe has on profits. The social logic of tribal enterprises should thus be paramount.

CONCLUSION

Indian nations and peoples have supported, engaged in, and enriched themselves with entrepreneurial private and family-oriented economic activities throughout history. They have always fostered, encouraged, and supported tribal people in their private economic endeavors, protected their private property rights, and allowed individual Indians to pursue their own ways. Entrepreneurship and entrepreneurial endeavors have proven to be effective avenues for the pursuit of tribal economic development, sustained economic independence, and sovereignty of Native people. These activities leverage development strategies, leverage local resources, and utilize their knowledge of their history, institutions, culture, and local economic resources. This approach uses indigenous knowledge and is part of the philosophy of economic development in American Indian communities.

A mixed strategy of traditional economy, individual market enterprise, and tribal government–managed corporations can coexist and provide multiple strategies and tools for moving toward sustained economic self-sufficiency in ways that are informed by indigenous values, culture, and interests. Native entrepreneurs have specific and unique characteristics that impact business decision-making, strategy, and enterprise growth. Despite significant gains in entrepreneurship, there remain significant challenges facing Native entrepreneurs, including lack of access to capital, insufficient business development support, and bureaucratic entanglements within tribal, state, and federal government agencies. Often, the lack of supportive infrastructure hampers new business development.

DISCUSSION

1. In what ways has US federal economic policy affected American Indian entrepreneurship?

2. How does entrepreneurship contribute to tribal economic development?

3. What are some of the challenges facing American Indian entrepreneurs?

4. Describe the role that tribal governments can take to stimulate tribal entrepreneurial activity.

5. In what ways does the concept of social responsibility impact American Indian entrepreneurship?

Notes

1   In this chapter we use the terms *American Indian*, *Indian*, and *Native American* interchangeably.

2   In some coastal regions this analogy is known as the "crab pot problem."

3   This is especially true for private business owners. Stewart and Schwartz (2007) polled Native American businesses in the Pacific Northwest and found that managers of tribally owned businesses felt that they had sufficient role models in their environment. However, entrepreneurs from privately owned companies did not claim to know many successful businesspeople of American Indian descent.

References

Ardichvili, A., R. Cardozo, and S. Ray. 2003. "A Theory of Entrepreneurial Opportunity Identification and Development." *Journal of Business Venturing* 18, no. 1: 105–23.

Barney, J. 1991. "Firm Resources and Sustained Competitive Advantage." *Journal of Management* 17, no. 1: 99–120.

Cajete, G. 2000. *Native Science: Natural Laws of Interdependence*. Santa Fe, NM: Clear Light Publishers.

Chandler, G., D. DeTienne, A. McKelvie, and T. Mumford. 2011. "Causation and Effectuation Processes: A Validation Study." *Journal of Business Venturing* 26: 375–90.

Chandler, G., and E. Jensen. 1992. "The Founder's Self-Assessed Competence and Venture Performance." *Journal of Business Venturing* 7: 223–36.

Cooper, A., F. Gimeno-Gascon, and C. Woo. 1994. "Initial Human and Financial Capital as Predictors of New Venture Performance." *Journal of Business Venturing* 9, no. 5: 371–95.

Cornell, S., and M. Jorgensen. 2007. "The Nature and Components of Economic Development in Indian Country." Research Brief, 2007. National Congress of American Indians Policy Research Center. Washington, DC.

Cornell, S., and J. P. Kalt. 2007. "One Works, the Other Doesn't: Two Approaches to Economic Development on American Indian Reservations: Strategies for Governance and Development." In M. Jorgensen, ed., *Rebuilding Native Nations: Strategies for Governance and Development*. Tucson: University of Arizona Press.

———. 2000. "Where Is the Glue? Institutional and Cultural Foundations of American Indian Economic Development." *Journal of Socio-Economics* 29: 443–70.

Crick, D., and M. Spence. 2005. "The Internationalization of High Performing, High Tech, SME's: A Study of Planned and Unplanned Strategies." *International Business Review* 14, no. 2: 167–85.

Dean, J., and M. Sharfman. 1996. "Does Decision Process Matter? A Study of Strategic Decision-Making Effectiveness." *Academy of Management Journal* 39, no. 2: 368–96.

Dew N., S. Read, S. D. Sarasvathy, and R. Wiltbank. 2009. "Effectual versus Predictive Logics in Entrepreneurial Decision-making: Differences Between Experts and Novices." *Journal of Business Venturing* 24, no. 4: 287–309.

Frantz, K. 1999. "Indian Reservations in the United States: Territory, Sovereignty, and Socioeconomic Change." Geography Research Papers. University of Chicago, 1999.

Gladstone, J. S. 2015. "Native American Transplaner Wisdom." In C. Spiller and R. Wolfgramm, eds., *Indigenous Spiritualties at Work: Transforming the Spirit of Business Enterprise*. Pp. 21–32. Charlotte, NC: Information Age Publishing.

Guzman, K. 2000. "Give or Take an Acre: Property Norms and the Indian Land Consolidation Act." *Iowa University Law Review* (January): 597–632.

Herron, L., and H. J. Sapienza. 1992. "The Entrepreneur and the Initiation of New Venture Launch Activities." *Entrepreneurship Theory and Practice* 17, no. 1: 49–55.

Hindle, K., R. Anderson, R. Giberson, and B. Kayseas. 2005. "Relating Practice to Theory in Indigenous Entrepreneurship: A Pilot Investigation of the Kitsaki Partnership Portfolio." *American Indian Quarterly* 29 (1-2 Winter–Spring): 1–23.

Hindle, K., and M. Lansdowne. 2005. "Brave Spirits on New Paths: Toward a Globally Relevant Paradigm of Indigenous Entrepreneurship Research." *Journal of Small Business and Entrepreneurship* 18, no. 2: 131–41.

Hindle, K., and P. Moroz. 2010. "Indigenous Entrepreneurship As a Research Field: Developing a Definitional Framework from the Emerging Canon." *International Entrepreneurship and Management Journal* 6, no. 4: 357–85.

Indian Country Today. 2010. "Tribal Economies Informed By Culture Are Key." Editorial. October 22.

———. 2009. "Indigenous Knowledge for Economic Stability." Editorial. August 21.

Kirzner, I. 1997. "Entrepreneurial Discovery and the Competitive Market Process: An Austrian Approach." *Journal of Economic Literature* 35: 60–85.

LaDuke, W. 1999. *All Our Relations: Native Struggles for Land and Life*. Boston: South End Press.

Malkin, J., and J. Aseron. 2010. *Native Entrepreneurship in South Dakota: A Deeper Look*. Saint Paul, MN: Northwest Area Foundation.

———. 2006. *Native Entrepreneurship Nationwide and in South Dakota: A Summary Report to the Northwest Area Foundation*. Saint Paul, MN: Northwest Area Foundation.

Miller, R. 2012. *Reservation Capitalism*. Westport, CT: Praeger Publishing.

———. 2008. "American Indian Entrepreneurs: Unique Challenges, Unlimited Potential." *Arizona State Law Journal* (Winter 2008): 1297–1341, 1297–1300.

———. 2001. "Economic Development in Indian Country: Will Capitalism or Socialism Succeed?" *Oregon Law Review* 80, no. 3 (Fall): 757–860.

Mintzberg, H., and J. Waters. 1985. "Of Strategies, Deliberate and Emergent." *Strategic Management Journal* 6, no. 3: 257–72.

Pascal, V., and D. Stewart. 2008. "The Effects of Geographic Location and Economic Cluster Development on Native American Entrepreneurship." *International Journal of Entrepreneurship and Innovation* 9, no. 2: 121–31.

Porter, M. E. 1985. *The Competitive Advantage: Creating and Sustaining Superior Performance*. New York: Free Press.

Russo 2010. *Companies on a Mission: Entreprenurial Strategies for Growing Sustainability, Responsibility, and Profitability*. Redwood City, CA: Stanford University Press.

Sarasvathy, S. 2008. "What Makes Entrepreneurs Entrepreneurial?" *Social Science Research Network* 1: 1–9.

Stewart, D., J. Gladstone, A. Verbos, and M. Katragadda. 2014. "Native American Cultural Capital and Business Strategy: The Culture-of-Origin Effect." *American Indian Culture and Research Journal* 38, no. 4: 127–38.

Stewart, D., and M. B. Pepper. 2011. "Close Encounters: Lessons from an Indigenous MBA Program." *Journal of Management Education* 35: 66–83.

Stewart, D., and R. G. Schwartz. 2007. "Native American Business Strategy: A Survey of Northwest US Firms." *International Journal of Business Performance Management* 9, no. 3: 259–77.

US Census Bureau. 2002a. *Economic Census: Survey of Business Owners Characteristics of Businesses and Characteristics of Business Owners*. (2006).

———. 2002b. *A Half-Century of Learning: Historical Statistics on Educational Attainment in the United States, 1940 to 2000*. Internet release April.

US Commission on Civil Rights. 2003. *A Quiet Crisis: Federal Funding and Unmet Needs in Indian Country*. July. Washington, DC.

US Department of Commerce, Economics, and Statistics Administration and the Minority Business Development Agency. 2002. *Keys to Minority Entrepreneurial Success: Capital, Education, and Technology*. P. Buckley. Washington, DC.

Venkataraman, S. 1997. "The Distinctive Domain of Entrepreneurship Research." *Advances in Entrepreneurship, Firm Emergence, and Growth* 3: 119–38.

Verbos, A., and M. Humphries. 2014. "A Native American Relational Ethic: An Indigenous Perspective on Teaching Human Responsibility." *Journal of Business Ethics* 123, no. 1: 1–9.

Verbos, A. K., D. Kennedy, J. Gladstone, and C. Birmingham. 2015. "Native American Cultural Influences on Career Self-Schemas and MBA Aspirations." *Equality, Diversity, and Inclusion: An International Journal* 34, no. 3: 201–13.

Wildcat, D. R. 2009. *Red Alert!: Saving the Planet with Indigenous Knowledge*. Golden, CO: Fulcrum.

Wiltbank, R., S. Read, N. Dew, and S. Sarasvathy. 2009. "Marketing under Uncertainty: The Logic of an Effectual Approach." *Journal of Marketing* 73, no. 3: 1–18.

4 BUSINESS STRATEGY

Building Competitive Advantage in American Indian Firms

Daniel Stewart, *Gonzaga University*

ABSTRACT

Businesses compete by positioning themselves strategically relative to competitors. This chapter covers the processes by which a firm creates a unique position in its industry or market. By using resources and capabilities, a firm develops a distinct competence, which becomes the basis of its strategy. The typical strategy involves either having a low-cost structure or having a highly differentiated product. Implications for American Indian organizations are discussed.

KEYWORDS: business strategy, distinct competence, resources, capabilities, cost leadership, differentiation, diversification, value creation

INTRODUCTION

BUSINESS STRATEGY REFERS TO THE PROCESSES AND TACTICS AN organization uses to effectively achieve its goals. Usually this goal is profitability, but other goals are important as well. For example, many tribal organizations are considered to be "not-for-profit," since their main objective is not profitability but the delivery of a valued service. For instance, a tribal health clinic or employment office delivers a valuable service, but the success of the clinic or employment office is probably measured by some other metric (patient counts or job placements) instead of profits. Regardless of the end goal, all organizations need a strategy to communicate to important stakeholders the direction the organization is headed and the means by which it will get there. Proper execution of a good strategy helps organizations sell their products or acquire the funding they need to deliver their services.

VALUE CREATION

To sell a product or receive funding to deliver a service, all organizations must deliver something that buyers value. By *buyers* we mean either customers who purchase a product directly or funding agencies that provide resources to others to deliver a service. For example, the BIA offers funds to tribes for tribes to offer social services on their reservations. In essence, this makes the BIA a buyer of services. It buys/funds social services on behalf of tribal members, using tribal government as a middleman who delivers the service. To ensure it is making products or services that buyers value, an organization should focus on meeting the needs of the potential customer. By focusing on addressing a particular need, the organization is creating value (Ghemawat 1991). Therefore, *value creation* can be thought of as the process of need satisfaction. One way to pinpoint the value of a firm's product is to answer the questions, "Who? What? How?" *Who* is your customer, *what* is their need, and *how* is my company meeting that need? If you cannot answer these questions, it is not clear that you have a market for your product or service.

Who refers not to specific buyers, but to different groups of buyers with distinct needs. Those needs are the *what*. The buyer groups are referred to as *customer segments*. Many companies will sell to only a narrow range of customer segments. For example, a construction firm might target residential consumers who want homes instead of government buyers who want office spaces. An apparel company might target athletes who need workout gear instead of office workers who need suits. The general idea is that not all buyers are the same, so a company should know where to focus its energy.

DISTINCT COMPETENCE

The *how* refers to the skills and assets that a company uses to create its product or service. If a company has competitors (and almost all do), it is important that the company develop a strength that makes it better than competition. This is what we refer to as a *distinct competence*. A distinct competence is a firm-specific strength that allows a firm to deliver a more valuable product or service than its competition. Distinct competences arise in the form of resources or capabilities.

RESOURCES

Resources are the assets a company holds. The company has tangible assets, such as machinery and buildings, and intangible assets, such as knowledge or patents. Resources are a source of competitive advantage for a firm if those resources are valuable, rare, and difficult for competitors to imitate (Barney 1991; Mahoney and Pandian 1992; Amit and Schoemaker 1993; Peteraf 1993;

Wernerfelt 1994). For instance, many reservations have coal or uranium reserves, which are rare and nearly impossible for others to get. Therefore, a tribe that controls a rare earth mineral has a clear advantage in markets where that natural resource is important.

Unique knowledge is also an important resource. *Cultural capital* refers to knowledge and understanding of a specific culture. If that knowledge is seen as important, it is possible for an organization to capitalize on its cultural understanding. Stewart et al. (2014) refer to this strategy as the "culture-of-origin" strategy. This strategy is often used by American Indian businesses. For example, a Native American artist who markets his goods based on the authenticity of his indigenous identity is using the culture-of-origin strategy. It could be argued that the Made in Native America movement is based on the culture-of-origin strategy. This strategy works best for products or services in which indigenous knowledge is perceived to have value to a potential buyer. For instance, knowledge of traditional healing practices could lead to the development of marketable health-care products. Knowledge of traditional music could lead to the creation of an indigenous music label. In other industries the culture-of-origin strategy could be more difficult. For example, it might be difficult for a Native American–owned manufacturing firm to convince buyers that unique indigenous manufacturing practices (assuming such practices exist) are more valuable than standard nonindigenous manufacturing methods.

One resource that is highly valuable for American Indian tribes is the status of tribes as sovereign nations. Political sovereignty meets all the criteria for a distinct competence. Sovereignty is valuable, rare, and cannot be imitated within the US domestic market. As such, tribes have a unique and inimitable resource that could serve as a source of competitive advantage. A quick perusal of websites devoted to economic development shows that tribes have used their limited sovereignty in multiples ways, including the establishment of exclusive gaming venues, the creation of unique tax incentives, and the development of preferential tribal-member hiring policies. Many of these practices have emerged due to the freedom that tribal governments have in establishing their own commercial codes. Control over unique laws provides tribes with the ability to add value for those who wish to do business within the Native American community.

Another potentially valuable asset is certification or designation as a minority-owned business under various federal, state, and commercial certification programs. For example, certification under the federal SBA 8(a) program allows a certified firm to pursue contracts that have been reserved only for 8(a) designees. Many larger corporations have adopted their own internal programs that provide preferential treatment for minority-owned firms. These programs provide value to the sponsoring organization by helping them diversify their supply chains, which can be good for the development of new products or services that better match the needs of the company's diverse buyers.

CAPABILITIES

Unique resources are good to have, but they only work well if a company has the skills to use them. *Capabilities* are the organization's skills in exploiting the resources at its disposal. Capabilities can be an extremely effective source of competitive advantage because it is very difficult for competitors to know exactly *by what means* another organization produces its good or service (Nelson and Winter 1982; Eisenhardt and Martin 2000). As such, capabilities are difficult to observe and, more important, difficult for competitors to imitate. Instead of thinking of skills as generic activities, it is useful to pinpoint areas within an organization where activities can create value. These areas are referred to as the *value chain*—the chain of organizational activities or functions that contribute to the creation and delivery of a product or service. A typical value chain looks something like this:

Primary Chain: Research and Development → Production → Marketing → Customer Service

Support Activities: Information Systems, Logistics, Human Resources, Management

---

The Value Chain. Source: Hill and Jones 2012

The *primary chain* contributes directly to product development. Organizations research their ideas, then produce a good or deliver a service, market that good or service, and then take care of customers after the initial point of sale. The *support activities* can contribute directly, but these activities often contribute indirectly by ensuring that the primary chain activities can occur. The *value chain* is referred to as such because at any of these points it is possible for a company to use its skills to create value for the customer. For example, an artist might raise the perceived value of her art through clever marketing, thereby raising the value of the art. Or a timber company can increase the timeliness of its orders by using better information systems, thereby raising the value of its lumber.

GENERIC ORGANIZATIONAL COMPETENCIES

Competence	Meaning
Efficiency	Using fewer inputs per unit of output
Quality	*Excellence*: adding desired features into your product or service
	Reliability: ensuring your product or service does its intended job effectively and reliably
Innovation	*Product*: creating new and unique features in a product
	Process: developing new and better ways to produce the good
Responsiveness	Responding to unique customer needs through customization or being faster than others to respond to customer demands

In addition to thinking about *where* an organization has capabilities (the value chain), it is also helpful to think of *how* an organization uses its capabilities. Instead of simply saying an activity is "good," we can be more precise in defining "good" by using the generic competencies of efficiency, quality, innovation, and customer responsiveness. A company should be making an effort to compete in at least one of these areas. We refer to these as *generic competencies* because any organization in any industry can pursue them.

Thus a company should be able to identify its capabilities in terms of both *how* and *where* it has a unique skill set. For example, a casino might identify its distinct competence as quality marketing (quality=how, marketing=where). Or a drumming group that specializes in streaming its music online might identify its distinct competence as innovative information systems (innovative=how, information systems=where). Regardless, a company needs to be focused on developing a competence in at least one area. Otherwise, there is nothing distinct about the firm, giving potential buyers no particular reason to buy that company's goods or use its services.

BUSINESS STRATEGY

Once a firm develops a distinct competence through its resources or capabilities, it uses those strengths to position itself strategically in relation to its competitors. By *competitors* we mean firms that compete for the same sales or funding resources. Competition can be direct, such as casinos fighting for customers walking along the Las Vegas strip. Or competition can be indirect, such as multiple tribal agencies competing for a limited pool of federal government grants. By *position* we refer to a company's choice on how much to emphasize either low costs or differentiation (Porter 1980; Scherer 1980; Hambrick 1983).

COST LEADERSHIP

Cost leadership refers to the choice to compete on the generic competence of efficiency. By lowering the cost of producing a good or delivering a service, a company also has the ability to lower the price it charges its customers. Cost leaders will often find innovative ways to reduce their production costs and decrease production errors, typically through improvements in manufacturing methods or through improvements in supply-chain logistics. Many firms will also achieve cost reductions by spreading their costs over a larger volume of production. This is called *economies-of-scale*. By producing in large volume, the average cost of each unit decreases as the company learns more efficient ways to build the product. In addition, producing in volume allows the producer to buy necessary inputs and supplies in bulk quantities, often leading to discounted bulk prices for those inputs. For example, the Seneca Tribe has developed multiple Seneca One Stop convenience stores. Owning multiple stores instead of one allows the tribe more leverage over suppliers to lower the price it pays for fuel and other stock items.

DIFFERENTIATION

Companies that compete on quality, customization, and product innovation are following a differentiation strategy. When a company's products are unique, they are differentiated. Uniqueness can come from higher levels or quality or through innovative and unique features. When an organization uses the culture-of-origin strategy (discussed earlier), it is using a differentiation strategy. In other words, American Indian–branded goods are being marketed and sold because of their uniqueness. If there is nothing unique about an indigenous artist's work, the artist may struggle to find a sufficient number of buyers, especially if the art is being marketed as indigenous art.

FOCUS STRATEGY

A company that seeks to sell its goods or services to niche and specialty markets is following a focused strategy (Porter 1985). In other words, some organizations purposefully avoid selling to the generic mass market. This may be due to intense competition in the mass market, or it may be because the organization's skill set is too specialized to move into a mass market. For example, most Native American musicians do not record for a mass audience. A Native American drumming group's music is probably not going to sell well to a mass audience, not because it is not high quality (it is) but because the mass market audience isn't trained to appreciate the genre. Traditional indigenous drumming is a skill that currently has a limited niche audience. To make things even more difficult, it is not clear that all American Indian drum groups have the skills that would allow them to compete in the mass market, which is already saturated with high-quality percussionists from rock and other popular genres.

CHOOSE ONE STRATEGY, NOT MULTIPLE

A basic rule-of-thumb with strategy is that a company should not try to be both a cost leader and a differentiator. It is better to concentrate in one direction and be good at cost leading *or* differentiation. Companies that try to do both can easily end up being mediocre on both fronts, leading to an uncompetitive situation referred to as "stuck in the middle." One concept that helps us to visualize why it is that firms become stuck in the middle is the idea of Red Queen evolution (Barnett 2008). The Red Queen theory derives from the Lewis Carroll story *Through the Looking Glass* (aka the Alice in Wonderland tale). There is a scene in the story where the Red Queen tells Alice that she must run fast just to stay in the same place. In a competitive business environment, firms "run" a race with their competitors by investing profits back into their business, which allows each firm to continually improve and innovate. The dilemma is this: in most industries some firms are investing into cost leadership while others are investing in differentiation, which means that a company that wants to do both will need to invest equally in both directions.

Say, for example, three competitors each earn a profit of $100. Firm A, a cost leader, decides to reinvest all of its $100 profit into increasing its efficiency. Firm B, a differentiator, decides to reinvest all of its $100 profits into increasing quality. Firm C, which has no clear strategy, decides to invest $50 into efficiency and $50 into increasing quality. The risk is that Firm C's product or service will not be as affordable as Firm A's nor will it be as high quality as Firm B's, leaving consumers unsatisfied because consumer expectations regarding price and quality have now been altered by the new standards set by Firms A and B. The Red Queen race has diverged in two directions, forcing Firm C to choose one direction or become stuck in the middle.

WHY DOES IT MATTER TO TRIBES?

The simple answer is that organizations need to develop a distinct competence in order to gain a competitive advantage. Without a distinct competence, a firm may have a difficult time creating goods or services that are sufficiently high in quality or sufficiently low in price that potential customers will buy their product instead of similar goods from a competitor. In very basic terms, the organization must be good at *something* in order to develop cheaper or better products. Companies in the corporate world spend a lot of time and energy identifying and developing distinct competencies. Tribal organizations should do the same. A good exercise for Native American tribes would be for each tribe to ask, "What are we good at? What value do we add that our competitors cannot?"

SUSTAINABILITY

Organizations that have a distinct competence are more sustainable in the long term. By *sustainable* we mean that the organization is profitable enough to provide returns to its stakeholders over an extended time frame, usually years or decades, allowing it to survive and prosper. Organizations are expected today to provide returns of three sorts: financial, environmental, and social. Thus an organization needs to make enough financial profit that it can support the welfare of its employees while also being a good steward of the natural environment. These Three Ps (profit, people, and planet) work together to comprise the "triple bottom line," which is the new standard for measuring sustainable organizations. American Indian nations have long been interested in environmental and social sustainability. However, triple-bottom-line thinking suggests that tribes can only provide social and environmental returns *if* there is enough profit made in its businesses to support social and environmental programs. In essence, business profitability is the foundation that enables the development of socially responsible tribal communities.

INVESTING IN THE FUTURE

In a competitive environment a tribe does not have the luxury of investing all of its profits back into the community. Some of the tribe's profits (the money left over after all expenses have been paid) must be reinvested back into its business. One option is to reinvest some of the profit back into existing businesses. This makes sense because some of those businesses are running a competitive Red Queen race, which dictates that they must continue to improve at the same rate their competitors are. If the competition is improving, so must the tribe, or it will not be able to sell its service or product.

Once the tribe has reinvested back into its existing businesses at a sufficient level, another option is to diversify into other industries. There are two types of diversification. The first type, *non-related diversification*, is the choice to move into other industries that have no real connection to existing businesses. This is a strategy of *opportunity chasing*, which might be profitable but does not build a coherent internal skill set. In other words, if the capabilities and resources required to compete from industry-to-industry differ, then a tribe does not have an opportunity to build on its distinct competence. A second option, *related diversification*, is a strategy by which organizations diversify into other industries where their existing distinct competencies will be valuable. For instance, a tribe might leverage its knowledge of quality casino entertainment to diversify into professional sports, where its knowledge of entertainment will readily apply. Related diversification allows an organization to strengthen its distinct competence by applying it to new industries. However, in order to purse related diversification, a tribe must first understand its distinct competence. Again, the important question is, "What is the tribe good at?"

CONCLUSION

All businesses must have a good business model and Native American businesses are no exception. One path toward indigenous sovereignty is reservation capitalism and business ownership (Miller 2012). Tribes can end their dependence on others by creating their own profitable businesses. However, for tribes and tribal businesses to be competitive, a basic understanding of business strategy is necessary. It is clear that tribes have potentially valuable resources, such as tribal sovereign status and indigenous cultural capital (Stewart et al. 2014). But tribes must also become adept at building identifiable distinct competencies that allow them to understand how their *skills* add value in the marketplace. Tribes who understand their unique skill set will be better prepared for diversification, leading to a more purposeful approach toward investing in future new business ventures.

DISCUSSION

1. A *distinct competence* is defined as an organization-specific strength, based on unique resources or unique capabilities. Does your tribal organization have a distinct competence? Is it based on unique resources or unique capabilities? Is it difficult to imitate? Explain.

2. Do you think tribal organizations are in a better position to compete on low costs or by differentiation? Why?

3. The *culture-of-origin strategy* is the explicit use of traditional culture and identity in the marketing of American Indian goods and services. Do you think this is a good idea? Who owns the rights to tribal culture? Should individuals profit from a community-based culture?

4. Based on your tribal organization's distinct competence, what industries would be good industries for diversification? Discuss.

5. The *triple bottom line* is defined as sustainable performance in profits, people, and planet. Discuss your tribal organization's stance on the triple bottom line. Do you believe it makes the tribe and its community more sustainable? Why?

References

Amit, R., and P. J. H. Schoemaker. 1993. "Strategic Assets and Organizational Rent." *Strategic Management Journal* 14: 33–46.

Barnett, W. P. 2008. *The Red Queen among Organizations: How Competitiveness Evolves*. Princeton, NJ: Princeton University Press.

Barney, J. B. 1991. "Company Resources and Sustained Competitive Advantage." *Journal of Management* 17: 99–120.

Eisenhardt, K. M., and J. A. Martin. 2000. "Dynamic Capabilities: What Are They?" *Strategic Management Journal* 21: 1105–21.

Ghemawat, P. 1991. *Commitment: The Dynamic of Strategy*. New York: Free Press.

Hambrick, D. C. 1983. "High Profit Strategies in Mature Capital Goods Industries: A Contingency Approach." *Academy of Management Journal* 26: 687–707.

Hill, C. W., and G. R. Jones. 2012. *Essentials of Strategic Management*. Boston, MA: Cengage Learning.

Mahoney, J. T., and J. R. Pandian. 1992. "The Resource-Based View within the Conversation of Strategic Management." *Strategic Management Journal* 13: 363–80.

Miller, R. J. 2012. *Reservation "Capitalism": Economic Development in Indian Country*. Santa Barbara, CA: ABC-CLIO.

Nelson, R. R., and S. G. Winter. 1982. *An Evolutionary Theory of Economic Change*. Cambridge, MA: Belknap Press.

Peteraf, M. A. 1993. "The Cornerstones of Competitive Advantage: A Resource-Based View." *Strategic Management Journal* 14: 179–91.

Porter, M. E. 1985. *Competitive Advantage*. New York: Free Press.

————. 1980. *Competitive Strategy: Techniques for Analyzing Industries and Competitors.* New York: Free Press.

Scherer, F. 1980. *Industrial Market Structure and Economic Performance.* 2nd edition. Boston: Houghton Mifflin.

Stewart, D., J. Gladstone, A. Verbos, and M. Katragadda. 2014. "Native American Cultural Capital and Business Strategy: The Culture-of-Origin Effect." *American Indian Culture and Research Journal* 38, no. 4: 127–38.

Wernerfelt, B. 1994. "A Resource Based View of the Company." *Strategic Management Journal* 15: 171–80.

5 THE BUSINESS LAW OF THE THIRD SOVEREIGN

Legal Aspects of Doing Business in Indian Country

Gavin Clarkson, *New Mexico State University*

ABSTRACT

While a majority of business schools teach business law at either the undergraduate or graduate level, very few examine how the concepts taught apply when doing business in Indian Country. The first question for such an examination is seemingly quite basic: What is Indian law? The answer, however, is a complex legal framework that covers criminal law, civil law, and everything in between. Within that framework Indian law generally falls into two categories: *Federal Indian Law*, which governs interactions between Indian federal, state, and tribal governments; and *tribal law*, which governs activity among individuals and entities within Indian Country. Indian law is thus a highly specialized field with two fundamental principles that every manager and/or business owner should know before beginning any business interactions in Indian Country. First, Indian tribes are quasi-sovereign nations with their own bodies of law, and second, the *federal* in Federal Indian Law is there for a reason. These two principles encompass a convoluted history of interactions with the various tribal nations, and they are relevant to potentially any type of business or business transaction involving tribes, tribal members, or Indian Country generally.

KEYWORDS: Federal Indian Law, tribal law, tribal sovereignty, tribal courts

INTRODUCTION

WHILE A MAJORITY OF BUSINESS SCHOOLS TEACH BUSINESS LAW at either the undergraduate or graduate level, very few examine how the concepts taught apply when doing business in Indian Country. This chapter supplements the material typically covered in a undergraduate-level legal environment of business or business law course; it also provides additional material for legal principles and concepts unique to doing business in Indian

Country. Where possible, this chapter provides brief historical context behind the development of those legal principles and concepts.

A BRIEF HISTORY OF AMERICAN INDIAN LAW AND POLICY

The first question to be explored is seemingly quite basic: What is Indian law? The answer is a complex legal framework that covers criminal law, civil law, and everything in between. Within that framework, Indian law generally falls into two categories: *Federal Indian Law*, which governs interactions between Indian federal, state, and tribal governments, and *tribal law*, which governs activity among individuals and entities within Indian Country (Fletcher 2011). These two categories include laws that are not identical but are often related. For every general body of American law, there is (or soon will be) a corresponding Federal Indian Law and/or tribal law. Indian law is thus a highly specialized field with two fundamental principles that every manager and/or business owner should know before beginning any business interactions in Indian Country. First, Indian tribes are quasi-sovereign nations with their own bodies of law, and second, the *federal* in Federal Indian Law is there for a reason. These two principles encompass a convoluted history of interactions with the various tribal nations that could (and often do) require an entire textbook to adequately cover. Despite that, the following paragraphs attempt to provide a brief overview of this history.

As the newly formed United States began its inexorable march westward, it developed an insatiable appetite for more land that was already occupied by various Indian tribes. To satisfy Western expansion goals, the Indian lands usually were not taken by force but were instead ceded to the United States by treaty in return for, among other things, the establishment of a trust relationship (Clarkson 2007). The federal government thus assumed a guardian-ward relationship with the Indians. This relationship was assumed not only because of prevailing racist notions of Indian societal inferiority but also because the trust relationship often was consideration for the Indians' relinquishment of land. Notably, the Indians and the federal government entered into these treaties as government-to-government relationships among collective political entities. From the beginning of its political existence, the United States "recognized a measure of autonomy in the Indian bands and tribes. Treaties rested upon a concept of Indian sovereignty . . . and in turn greatly contributed to that concept" (Prucha 1994, 2).

While the formal existence of the United States began at a point in time when the prevailing policy of treaty-making recognized tribal sovereignty, such an orientation proved to be impermanent. In the 1870s, the US Congress ceased making treaties with the Indians and instead developed an Allotment Policy characterized as a "mighty pulverizing engine"—a policy that would destroy tribalism and force Indians to assimilate into dominant society as individuals (Clarkson 2007). This Allotment Policy devastated the tribes, and its consequences remain highly problematic.

The United States changed its policies toward tribal government structures again in 1928. In response to a report documenting the failure of federal Indian policy, Congress passed the Indian Reorganization Act of 1934 (IRA).[1] In an effort to reinforce tribal sovereignty, the legislation allowed tribes to adopt constitutions and to reestablish structures for governance (Clarkson 2007). Congressional policy had once again reversed itself—instead of destroying tribal sovereignty, the federal government was now encouraging it. As a result, many tribes began to thrive economically. The IRA "provided a powerful stimulus to tribal governmental organization and in many cases so strengthened that organization as to enable continued development despite fluctuation in administrative policy" (Getches et al. 2011).

Federal Indian policies would oscillate through one more cycle in the next half-century (Clarkson 2007). A 1949 report on Indian affairs by the Hoover Commission recommended " 'complete integration' of Indians [as a federal policy] goal so that Indians would move 'into the mass of the population as full . . . citizens' " (Clarkson and Sebenius 2012). As a result, in 1953 the official congressional policy changed to one of ending the Indians' status as wards of the United States. For the tribes that were "terminated" under this policy, the results were disastrous, and it was during this time that Congress passed Public Law 280, which extended state criminal and civil jurisdiction to Indian Country in five states and allowed other states to assume all or part of such jurisdiction, either by statute or by state constitutional amendment.

Just as Congress had reversed itself when it repudiated allotment and passed the IRA, however, the policy of termination also was short-lived (Clarkson 2007). Ironically, termination had the opposite effect in its attempt to detribalize: Indians finally recognized that federal policy too often was directed at destroying tribalism. From that perspective they concluded "that only tribal control of Indian policy and lasting guarantees of sovereignty could assure tribal survival in the United States" (Clarkson and Sebenius 2012). With the Kennedy and Johnson administrations' abandonment of the termination policy, "programs such as the Economic Opportunity Act [were passed, which] recognized the permanency of Indian tribes and the importance of social investment in reservation communities" (Clarkson and Sebenius 2012, 1055). President Richard Nixon was arguably the most ardent supporter of Indian sovereignty, and he issued a landmark statement calling for a new federal policy of "self-determination" for Indian nations (Clarkson 2007). Perhaps the greatest of Nixon's contributions to Indian tribal sovereignty was Public Law 638, the Indian Self-Determination and Education Assistance Act of 1975, which authorized the secretaries of Interior and Health and Human Services to contract with and make grants to Indian tribes and other Indian organizations for the delivery of federal services. Acting at times pursuant to federal court orders, the Bureau of Indian Affairs (BIA) assisted tribes in reconstituting their governmental structures.

During this period the US Supreme Court handed down *Morton v. Mancari*, one of the most important Indian cases of the modern era (417 U.S. 535 [1974]). The Court held that tribal Indians were members of "quasi-sovereign" tribal entities and that Indian status was thus "political" rather than "racial." *Mancari* involved the BIA's hiring preference for Indians, but the Court extended its holding to other areas of Indian policy as "long as the special treatment can be tied rationally to the fulfillment of Congress' unique obligation toward the Indians," and the policy "is reasonable and rationally designed to further Indian self-government" (*Mancari*, at 555) Thus, through acts of Congress and Supreme Court rulings, tribes are ensconced within the federalism framework. In the words of Justice Sandra Day O'Connor: "Today, in the United States, we have three types of sovereign entities— [T]he Federal government, the states, and the Indian tribes. Each of the[se] sovereigns . . . plays an important role . . . in this country" (O'Connor 1997, 1). Given this notion of three sovereigns, the two fundamental principles of tribal sovereignty and federal prominence in Indian law seem slightly more coherent.

LEGAL ENVIRONMENT

The outside perception of the legal environment in Indian Country often begins with a widely believed myth that no legal systems existed prior to European colonization of the New World. In reality, however, many tribes had highly developed systems of law and justice; their judges just didn't wear black robes and white wigs. Certain tribes, such as the Cheyenne, had a constitutional form of government that they maintained through oral tradition (Clarkson 2002). Other tribes had more sophisticated constitutional governments as well as written laws. The Iroquois Confederacy was founded before 1570, and the Choctaw first wrote down their constitution in 1825. In fact, the US system of federalism is based the Iroquois Confederacy. Usually the only reference to Indian Country in a standard legal environment of business textbook is the discussion of the Founders' explicit borrowing of the Iroquois notion of federalism.

Tribes have a long and robust legal tradition that in many ways, but not all mirror the legal system off-reservation. Noted First Nations scholar John Borrows (2010) has written that traditional rules for how to live in tribal communities have power and currency beyond their use in traditional societies and can inform contemporary issues in useful ways. Although that notion is an overarching theme throughout this entire book, a recognition of the values inherent in tribal legal systems can provide valuable lessons outside of Indian Country. A prime example is the peacemaker court of the Navajo Nation, which has served as a pattern for numerous alternative dispute resolution systems throughout the United States (Fletcher 2011).

TRIBES ARE NATIONS AND THEY HAVE THEIR OWN BODIES OF LAW

TRIBAL CONSTITUTIONS

Although most Indian nations did not have written constitutions prior to the passage of the IRA in 1934, most tribal nations today operate under some form of constitutional government. Some tribes continue to use versions of constitutions that were written for them by the BIA after 1934. A few tribes, must notably the Navajo Nation, operate without a constitution. Other tribes, such as the Cherokee Nation of Oklahoma, have held constitutional conventions to substantially revise their constitutions. In almost all cases, however, tribal constitutions bear some resemblance to the US Constitution, particularly in such areas as separation of powers.

TRIBAL STATUTES

Tribal legislative bodies, usually a Tribal Council, pass laws that govern the actions of those within a tribe's jurisdictional boundaries. While most tribal laws cover everyone in Indian Country, there are a few exceptions where non-Indians are not subject to tribal jurisdiction, particularly in the criminal context (Clarkson and Dekorte 2010). As with the laws of the states, federal laws preempt tribal statutes.

TRIBAL REGULATIONS

Just as with states and the federal government, tribal agencies implement tribal statutes and develop regulations to facilitate statutory implementation and enforcement. Sometimes tribal agencies can pass regulations on their own, while at other times the Tribal Council passes regulations based on recommendations from tribal agencies.

TRIBAL COURTS

While tribal laws, ordinances, regulations, and resolutions are often codified and published, either in book form or online (Fletcher 2011), as with the other two sovereigns, it is up to the courts to interpret the gaps, conflicts, and ambiguities of those laws when applied to particular situations. As discussed elsewhere in this edited volume, tribal economies are growing, and for both political and economic reasons, tribes have reclaimed their jurisprudential sovereignty by establishing or reestablishing vibrant judiciaries. Such reclamation has been politically important since tribal courts are "the primary tribal institutions charged with carrying the flame of sovereignty and self-government" (Pommersheim 1988, 71) and have been acknowledged as the cornerstone of tribal sovereignty. Such reclamation is economically important because the first key to economic development is sovereignty. This tribal jurisprudential resurgence has taken place within a broader framework of Indian law whose origins predate the founding of the United States. As a result, today's tribal courts have limited criminal jurisdiction over Indians but broader jurisdiction over civil matters involving Indians or tribal interests on lands owned or controlled by the tribe.

When courts borrow the reasoning from previous court decisions, they are applying common law and that notion is the same for tribal courts. Tribal courts not only look to their own prior decisions; they also look to how tribal courts in other tribes have handled similar situations, which is intertribal common law. In certain circumstances tribal courts will apply intratribal common law, or "customary" law. This latter category is perhaps the most difficult for those outside the community to gain awareness of, but it is nonetheless necessary for those doing business in Indian Country to be aware of customary law, either by direct acquisition of legal knowledge or by hiring attorneys with knowledge of the customary laws of a given tribe.

DISPUTE RESOLUTION

Disputes originating in Indian Country can be brought in tribal court, state court, or federal court depending on the specific circumstances and the tribal status of the various parties. Often outside parties attempt to avoid tribal court, but in many cases the federal courts require exhaustion of tribal remedies. As is the case off-reservation, some agreements involving business and transactions in Indian Country include arbitration provisions, and those agreements are enforceable by tribal, state, and federal courts.

When doing business with a tribe, however, it is critically important for counterparties, even if they are themselves tribal members, to be aware of tribal sovereign immunity. Just as neither the federal government nor state governments can be sued without their consent, tribal governments and their instrumentalities, including IRA Section 17 corporations, are immune from suit unless they have waived their sovereign immunity. Often the most challenging part of a negotiation over a transaction is the discussion of the scope of a waiver of sovereign immunity, yet that is an issue that must be addressed in advance by any counterparty doing business with a tribal entity.

THE *FEDERAL* IN FEDERAL INDIAN LAW IS SPECIFICALLY INDICATIVE

Federal Indian Law is separate and distinct from tribal law and is one of the earliest legal doctrines in the United States. In particular, one of the hallmarks of Federal Indian Law is the general exclusion of states. Article IV of the Articles of Confederation granted the Continental Congress the exclusive right of regulating trade and managing all affairs with the Indians. Later, that notion was incorporated into Article I, Section 8 of the Constitution: "Congress shall have the power [to] . . . regulate commerce with foreign nations, and among the several states, and with the Indian tribes." Thus the vast majority of Indian law encountered by those doing business in Indian Country is Federal Indian Law, which is the US Constitution, US Supreme Court judicial action, treaties between the tribes and the United States, federal legislation and regulations, all of which govern the relationships between tribes, states, and the federal government.

CRIME

Although both tribes and the federal government can pass criminal statutes that apply in Indian Country, Indian Country is the only location in the United States where the race of both the victim and the offender are relevant for purposes of jurisdiction and prosecution (Clarkson and Dekorte 2010). Table 5.1 offers some clarity on this jurisdictional maze.

CRIMINAL JURISDICTION IN INDIAN COUNTRY, BY PARTY AND CRIME

Crime by Party	Jurisdiction
Crimes by Indians against Indians	
"Major crimes"	Federal or tribal (concurrent)
Other crimes	Tribal (exclusive)
Crimes by Indians against non-Indians	
"Major crimes"	Federal or tribal (concurrent)
Other crimes	Federal or tribal (concurrent)
Crimes by Indians without Victims	Tribal (exclusive)
Crimes by non-Indians against Indians	Federal (exclusive)
Crimes by non-Indians against non-Indians	State (exclusive)
Crimes by non-Indians without Victims	State (exclusive)

TORTS

Most tribal nations have not adopted comprehensive tort statutes, nor do tribal courts have an extensive body of common law tort decisions. Tribal courts often use the legal standards of the surrounding state to determine the applicability of tort doctrines such as negligence (Fletcher 2011). Tribal legislatures have, however, started to enact statutes regarding the filing of tort claims against tribal entities, particularly as it relates to tribal sovereign immunity. When the defendant is a non-Indian, however, as with criminal jurisdiction, tribal court jurisdiction over non-Indians remains a contentious issue. In fact, in 2016 the Supreme Court deadlocked four to four on the issue of tribal jurisdiction in *Dollar General v. Mississippi Choctaw* (579 U. S. ____ [2016]), so it is likely that this issue will continue to be litigated.

CONTRACT LAW IN INDIAN COUNTRY

As is the case with tort law, tribal courts generally adapt and apply the law of the surrounding states when resolving contract disputes, as most tribal nations have neither comprehensive contract law codes nor an extensive body of common law decisions upon which to rely (Fletcher 2011). When contracting parties are operating under the jurisdiction of tribal courts, however, the recent trend has been to agree on choice of law provisions that detail which law the tribal court should apply in adjudicating contract law disputes. There are also instances where tribal customary law directly affects the outcomes, usually with exclusively tribal parties and involving agreements that are uniquely cultural in nature, such as a family agreement (Fletcher 2011).

CONTRACTUAL WAIVERS OF TRIBAL SOVEREIGN IMMUNITY

As mentioned earlier, when contracting with a tribe or tribal entity, it is critical for all counterparties to be fully aware of the implications of tribal sovereign immunity. As is the case with states, tribes cannot be sued without their consent, even when they are parties to a contract. Obviously, counterparties to the tribe want to be able to have any grievances heard in a court of competent jurisdiction and collect any judgments to which they are entitled, so the negotiations over potential waivers of sovereign immunity are just as important as the provisions of the contract itself. A sample waiver of sovereign immunity follows:

> Given the long-standing tradition in Indian Country of resolving disputes through restorative justice methods such as "peacemaking," the parties agree to, first, directly confer if there are disputes; second, to use a mediator or peacemaker if the Parties are unable to resolve disputes directly within thirty days; and third, to submit any lingering disputes arising from this agreement to final and binding arbitration under the commercial arbitration rules of the American Arbitration Association. Should the Chief Judge of the ___ Tribal Court be empowered to appoint a special Tribal Court judge to serve as an arbitrator, such arbitration proceedings may be conducted under the auspices of the ___ Tribal Court so long as the special Tribal Court judge appointed to adjudicate any disputes shall have no less than five years' experience in [relevant subject matter] arbitration and shall be mutually agreed upon by the Parties.
>
> For purposes of resolving any such disputes, the Tribe, on behalf of itself and the ___ Tribal Entities, waives the sovereign immunity of the ___ Tribal Entities to the extent necessary to initiate proceedings in arbitration, and agrees to permit the commencement, maintenance and enforcement of an arbitration action by [Counterparty] to interpret or enforce the terms of this Agreement, and to enforce and execute any arbitration judgment against any ___ Tribal Entity or the assets or rights of any ___ Tribal Entity, provided, however, that the sole recourse against any ___ Tribal Entity shall be against the Transaction, excluding the real property interests

of any ___ Tribal Entity in the Transaction. Without limiting the generality of the foregoing, the Tribe waives the immunity of the ___ Tribal Entities from unconsented arbitration proceedings to: (1) enforce and interpret the terms of this letter agreement and award and enforce the award of damages owing as a consequence of a breach hereof; (2) determine whether any consent or approval of a ___ Tribal Entity has been improperly granted or unreasonably withheld; (3) enforce any judgment prohibiting a ___ Tribal Entity from taking any action, or mandating or obligating any of the ___ Tribal Entities to take any action; and (4) adjudicate any claim under the Indian Civil Rights Act of 1968 or any successor statute. While the Parties may mutually agree to seek the assistance of tribal mediators or peacemakers from the Tribe or other tribes, to the extent permitted by law, the Tribe hereby irrevocably waives, on behalf of itself and each of the other ___ Tribal Entities, all rights to require the subject matter of any Action to be heard by or presented to any court or other adjudicatory or dispute resolving body of the Tribe, whether such right arises because of the doctrine of exhaustion of tribal remedies, principles of comity, or otherwise. This waiver shall not, however, preclude the Parties from mutually agreeing to have a special Tribal Court judge act as arbitrator if the Chief Judge of the ___ Tribal Court is empowered to appoint a special Tribal Court judge.

THE TRIBAL UNIFORM COMMERCIAL CODE (UCC)

Another area of concern when contracting in Indian Country involves loans and extensions of credit that include collateral. Off-reservation, these issues are handled by the Uniform Commercial Code (UCC). In 2005 the drafters of the UCC developed the Model Tribal Secured Transaction Act (MTSTA; www.uniformlaws.org/shared/docs/mtsta/mtsta_aug05_final.pdf). Secured transactions in Indian Country jurisdictions with a version of the MTSTA operate similarly to transactions off-reservation. In tribal jurisdictions that have yet to pass a variation of the MTSTA, contracting parties may find it difficult to seize collateral on-reservation.

BANKRUPTCY

Although it was potentially an open question as to whether tribal entities could file bankruptcy, that question was definitively settled in 2012, at least for tribes, when the Santa Ysabel tribe was denied access to bankruptcy

protection. Tribal corporations, however, may be eligible for bankruptcy protection, as Sa' Nyu Wa, the economic development corporation owned by the
Hualapai tribe, was able to argue that it was a corporation separate from
the tribe and thus eligible as a "corporation" to file under Chapter 11 of the
Bankruptcy Code. That case settled without a final determination as to
the eligibility of tribal corporations to file bankruptcy.

EMPLOYMENT AND LABOR LAW

Although the legal landscape is unsettled in terms of the applicability of federal employment law to tribal governments and enterprises, it is generally
good practice for tribal entities to adhere to the legal standards that would
apply to off-reservation businesses. For private businesses, whether or not
they are Indian-owned, many tribal governments have passed additional
regulations that govern employment practices. Most notable are Tribal
Employment Rights Ordinances (TERO), which usually require that all on-
reservation employers give preference to qualified Indians in all aspects of
employment, contracting, and other business activities. Such preferences are
legal not only because tribes are exempt from Title VII of the Civil Rights
Act and several other employment laws but also because of the holding in
Morton v. Mancari that Indian status is political and not racial.

Finally, tribal governments are not covered by the National Labor Relations Act (NLRA), although recent decisions have reversed this exemption
when applied to tribal gaming operations, even though they are operated by
tribal governments. The applicability of the NLRA on-reservation continues
to be a contentious and political issue as this book goes to press.

BUSINESS ORGANIZATIONS

Chapter 6 on legal forms of organization, by Amy Klemm Verbos, provides
a comprehensive overview of the various corporate forms available for businesses in Indian Country.

PROPERTY
REAL PROPERTY

One of the major challenges in Indian law is determining whether such
law applies in a given location. This challenge is made more complicated
because of the variations of real property that constitute Indian Country.

The most commonly referenced definition of Indian Country actually comes from the federal criminal code (18 U.S. Code § 1151), which defines Indian Country as

(a) all land within the limits of any Indian reservation under the jurisdiction of the United States Government, notwithstanding the issuance of any patent, and, including rights-of-way running through the reservation,

(b) all dependent Indian communities within the borders of the United States whether within the original or subsequently acquired territory thereof, and whether within or without the limits of a state, and

(c) all Indian allotments, the Indian titles to which have not been extinguished, including rights-of-way running through the same.

Within that definition there are two primary types of lands: individually owned lands and tribally owned lands. There are two types of individually owned lands: trust land (where the federal government holds legal title but the beneficial interest remains with the individual Indian) and restricted fee land (where an individual Indian holds legal title but with legal restrictions against alienation or encumbrance) (Clarkson and Murphy 2016). There are three types of tribally owned lands: trust land, which have the same federal ownership but with a tribal beneficiary rather than an individual; restricted fee land, where the tribe holds legal title but with the same legal restrictions against alienation or encumbrance as with individual ownership; and fee simple land owned by the tribe outside the boundaries of the reservation, which can be alienated without restriction absent any special circumstances. If this categorization was not complicated enough, there are additional nuances in the cases of lands in Oklahoma as well as pueblo land holdings.

Lands held in trust are highly restricted in terms of their use, and often the beneficial owners must get the permission of the BIA before the lands can generate economic benefit. This trust status has been continually identified as an impediment to economic development in Indian Country (Clarkson and Murphy 2016).

INTELLECTUAL PROPERTY

Indian nations have significant interests in intangible resources that may be legally protected under existing intellectual property law (Cohen 2012). Such resources include stories, songs, dances, and artwork that may be protected by copyright law; plants and herbs that have medicinal or commercial uses that may be protected by patent law; and tribal names and symbols that may be protected by trademark law (Clarkson 2003).

Indian nations face unique challenges beyond the usual difficulties in defining intellectual property (Cohen 2012). Tribal interests may differ in several ways from other holders of intellectual property: rights may be collectively held rather than individually held; rights may be held in trust for the benefit of others in the tribe; there may be religious or other interests in keeping the information secret; the tribe may prefer to prevent rather than exploit commercial use of the resources; and the interests may be intertwined with sacred ceremonies or religious traditions requiring special treatment. The most current example of tribal interests conflicting with established intellectual property rights involves the professional football team in Washington, DC. The cancellation of that trademark is ongoing as this book goes to press (*Blackhorse v. Pro-Football*, TTAB Cancellation No. 92046185, 2014), but the legal maneuvering has been ongoing since 1992.

International instruments and organizations recognize some protections for indigenous intellectual property, although US law has not always followed those international approaches. For example, the United Nations Declaration on the Rights of Indigenous Peoples states that "indigenous peoples have the right to maintain, control, protect and develop their cultural heritage, traditional knowledge and traditional cultural expressions, as well as the manifestations of their sciences, technologies and cultures, including human and genetic resources, seeds, medicines, knowledge of the properties of fauna and flora, oral traditions, literatures, designs, sports and traditional games and visual and performing arts. They also have the right to maintain, control, protect and develop their intellectual property over such cultural heritage, traditional knowledge, and traditional cultural expressions."

Under current intellectual property regimes, however, there are few existing mechanisms to protect the knowledge derived from traditional indigenous practices and indigenous genetic material. The root of the problem is that current intellectual property regimes are designed to protect and reward prospective inventive activity. Under "Western standards," neither traditional knowledge that has been maintained within a community and passed down through generations nor genetic knowledge that is transmitted through one's own body fulfill the elements of current IP standards. Consequently, current IP regimes are not designed to award legally recognizable property rights to the actual owners of traditional knowledge.

ENVIRONMENTAL LAW

Tribal environmental authority in Indian Country stems from the same two fundamental principles of tribal sovereignty and federal oversight. Tribal sovereignty allows tribes to pass environmental laws and regulations to ensure environmental protection to the full limits of their inherent governmental authority to act (Cohen 2012). Tribes may enact tribal laws and regulations that establish standards, permit requirements, and penalties for violations, and provide for enforcement in tribal court and through tribal regulatory proceedings.

From a federal standpoint, Congress has authorized Indian tribes to assume primary regulatory authority, or primacy, for administering most of the federal environmental programs in Indian Country (Cohen 2012). In addition, the Clean Water Act, the Safe Drinking Water Act, and the Clean Air Act all contain language authorizing tribes to be treated the same as states by the Environmental Protection Agency (EPA) for purposes of program administration. This treatment of tribes as states (known as TAS) has resulted in several instances where tribes have passed stricter environmental regulations than their surrounding states, which were then in turn binding on non-Indians as if a neighboring state had passed the regulation.

INDIAN GAMING

Chapter 8, by Gavin Clarkson and James K. Sebenius, provides an overview of the origins of Indian gaming, the current regulatory framework, and unique issues in that highly regulated industry.

CONCLUSION

Although this chapter has only briefly covered the wide range of business law topics that relate to Indian Country, I hope the reader has gained a deeper appreciation of the complexities of Indian law. As is the case with business law generally, the need to hire competent legal counsel is just as great, if not greater, when dealing with tribes, tribal businesses, or any other entity within Indian Country.

DISCUSSION

1. Identify and describe the two categories of Indian law.
2. How has Indian law changed over time?

3. Compare and contrast tribal courts to state or federal courts.

4. Identify and describe the legal areas that organizations need to be aware of when doing business in Indian Country.

Note

1   See Indian Reorganization Act (Wheeler-Howard Act) of 1934, Pub. L. No. 73-383, 48 Stat. 984 (codified as amended at 25 U.S.C. §§ 461–94 (2006)).

References

Borrows, J. 2010. *Drawing Out Law: A Spirits Guide.* Toronto: University of Toronto Press
———. 2003. "Racial Imagery and Native Americans: A First Look at the Empirical Evidence Behind the Indian Mascot Controversy." *Cardozo Journal of International and Comparative Law* 11: 393.
———. 2002. "Reclaiming Jurisprudential Sovereignty: A Tribal Judiciary Analysis." *University of Kansas Law Review* 50: 473.
Clarkson, G., and D. DeKorte. 2010. "Unguarded Indians: The Complete Failure of the Post-Oliphant Guardian and the Dual-Edged Nature of Parens Patriae." *Illinois Law Review* 1119.
Clarkson, G., and A. Murphy. 2016. "Tribal Leakage: How the Curse of Trust Land Impedes Tribal Economic Self-Sustainability." *Journal of Law, Economics, and Policy* 12: 177.
Clarkson, G., and J. Sebenius. 2012. "Leveraging Tribal Sovereignty for Economic Opportunity: A Strategic Negotiations Perspective." *Missouri Law Review* 76: 1046.
Cohen. 2012. *Cohen's Handbook of Federal Indian Law.* LexisNexis
Fletcher, M. L. M. 2011. *American Indian Tribal Law.* New York: Aspen Publishers.
Getches, D., et al. 2011. *Cases and Materials on Federal Indian Law (American Casebook Series).* 6th edition. Saint Paul, MN: West Academic Publishing.
O'Connor, S. D. 1997. "Lessons from the Third Sovereign: Indian Tribal Courts." *Tulsa Law Journal* 33: 1.
Pommersheim, F. 1988. "The Contextual Legitimacy of Adjudication in Tribal Courts and the Role of the Tribal Bar As an Interpretive Community: An Essay." 18 *New Mexico Law Review* 49: 71.
Prucha, F. P. 1994. *American Indian Treaties: The History of a Political Anomaly.* Oakland: University of California Press.

6 LEGAL FORMS
OF ORGANIZATION

Amy Klemm Verbos, *University of Wisconsin–Whitewater*

ABSTRACT

American Indian businesses may be formed in several different organizational structures: as a sole proprietorship, a general partnership, a limited liability company, or a corporation. Although businesses are most often formed to produce and provide goods and services at a profit, some organizations that undertake business activities may be formed as nonprofit, hybrid, or government organizations. Certain types of business organizations may be created under state law, federal law, or tribal law. This chapter briefly identifies and describes these available forms of organization and discusses the management implications for tribal and citizen-owned American Indian businesses.

KEYWORDS: tribal organizations, tribal law, limited liability company, corporation

INTRODUCTION

EVERY BUSINESS OWNER MUST DECIDE HOW TO ORGANIZE THE business before commencing business operations. By default, this organization can be very informal and requires nothing more than simply commencing business as a sole proprietor. When two or more people or entities do this, it is a partnership. A tribe may also begin business without forming a separate entity. However, there are important legal advantages to adopting an organizational form that provides a business owner with limited liability for the actions done by and on behalf of a business. Other important considerations are the tax implications of the organizational form and the legal limitations on what a certain type of organization is permitted by law to do. A special consideration that applies to tribes is the issue of whether a business enterprise will fall within its sovereign immunity, shielding the tribe and its assets from being sued by anyone with a grievance against the business enterprise.

There are several options to choose from in making a decision about the best type of organization form to select. The most common are a corporation or a limited liability company. There are other specialty types of entities, such as nonstock corporations incorporated for nonprofit purposes, limited liability partnerships, service corporations, benefit corporations (corporations that also have social purposes), and cooperatives, but these are not covered in depth in this chapter. When a tribe seeks to form or buy a business, it has the option to create the legal infrastructure within its own tribal law, form a federally chartered corporation under Section 17 of the Indian Reorganization Act (IRA), administered by the US Department of the Interior Bureau of Indian Affairs (BIA), or proceed under state laws (for more information, see Atkinson and Nilles 2008). This chapter discusses these legal forms of organization and some of the positive and negative aspects of each. The discussion is limited to organizations and tribes located within the United States. Please see chapter 5 on Indian law for other important issues to consider when selecting a form for a business organization. Nothing contained in this chapter should be construed as legal advice. Readers considering forming a business enterprise should seek legal advice from an attorney and accounting advice from a CPA to best weigh their options for organizational formation under the specific facts and circumstances at issue.

OVERVIEW OF FORMS OF BUSINESS ORGANIZATIONS

This chapter offers a brief overview of the most common forms of organization: sole proprietorships, general partnerships, limited partnerships, corporations, and limited liability companies. This overview provides basic information on each organizational form. The actual selection of a type of organization for business creation should be done in consultation with a lawyer and an accountant, who can advise the owner on the available organizational forms in that particular jurisdiction as well as help to find the most suitable business structure under a particular situation.

SOLE PROPRIETORSHIPS

Sole proprietorships are the most common form of small business entity. An individual simply begins providing goods or services in commerce. If you have ever sold a piece of art or craftwork, resold a textbook, car, or other item, you have engaged in this most basic form of business. The main benefit of sole proprietorship is its simplicity. There are no filings to make or paperwork to fill out (unless you employ others, in which case you would need to file employee tax paperwork). Many businesses begin this way. The main drawback is that the sole proprietor is personally liable for the debts of the business. This includes any bank loan or credit cards used in the business, contract liabilities (such as a liability if the business does not deliver goods on time), and liabilities if anyone is injured on the premises of the business or by one of its employees. To reduce or mitigate this risk, a sole proprietor may obtain insurance that will cover some of these risks. Many people do not wish to personally take on the risk of debts and other business liabilities, especially because new businesses often fail. A sole proprietor has to use his or her personal savings and other nonbusiness assets to pay off business debts. For this reason attorneys often recommend that businesses be formed as limited liability companies or corporations.

GENERAL AND LIMITED PARTNERSHIPS

General partnerships occur when two or more individuals or entities (such as limited liability companies or corporations) go into business together. Partnerships range from informal to those that are governed by complex written agreements. General partnerships do not require formalities such as filing with a state. General partners are jointly and severally liable for the debts of the partnership's business. That means that either of the partners could be sued for all of the partnership's debts. That partner could then seek contribution from the other partner(s). If a tribal business intends to enter into a general partnership, the best way to proceed is to develop and negotiate a partnership agreement so that it will be clear how the partnership will operate its business. A partnership agreement is also important to decide how or if partnership interests can be transferred to others, how contributions may be required of the partners, how the business will be managed, how income will be distributed, and what could happen to dissolve the partnership and wind up its business.

Unlike general partnerships, limited partnerships are required to make state filings. State law requires that there is at least one general partner who actively manages the business of the limited partnership and is liable for its debts (see, e.g., Wis. Stat. §179.01 et. seq.). The general partner does not need to be an individual; rather, it can be a corporation or a limited liability company. Limited partners are often called *passive investors* because they are not permitted to be active in the business. Limited partners are not liable for the debts of the partnership. Limited partnerships are often used in real estate investments. The agreements between the general partner and limited partners are usually written into a partnership agreement. The terms of these complex agreements are usually negotiated by the parties through their attorneys.

CORPORATION

A corporation is an entity that is formed under statutory law to act as a legal person. For example, the *Merriam-Webster Dictionary* defines a corporation as a "business or organization authorized by law to carry on an activity with the rights and duties of a single person." Since it is a legal person, it can sue and be sued, enter into contracts, and it has *perpetual existence*, which means that it continues to operate as a legal person after the person who organized it dies. A corporation is created by filing articles of incorporation with the appropriate state, federal, or tribal governmental office. Most corporations are formed under statutes that allow a corporation to engage in "any lawful business" (see, e.g., Wis. Stat. §180.0301). The articles of incorporation may, but are not required to, restrict its purpose further. Other state and federal statutes may restrict what a corporation's "lawful business" can be. For example, corporations cannot be banks (those are created under other enabling state or federal statutes). Corporation statutes allow a corporation's profits to be reinvested in the business or paid as dividends to shareholders. The decision to reinvest or pay dividends is generally made by its management, but sometimes corporations issue special classes of stock that have rights to periodic dividends. These shares are usually nonvoting shares of stock. Under federal securities laws a corporation that follows the legal requirements can sell its shares to the public and be listed on a securities exchange.

Corporations also adopt bylaws, which indicate how the corporation will be run, including the number of directors and any qualifications, how directors are elected by the shareholders, where and when directors meet, where and when the annual meeting of shareholders will be held, and the officers that the corporation will have. A corporation is often thought of as "owned" by its shareholders but this is not exactly correct. Shareholders *invest equity* into a corporation in the hopes of receiving increased stock value and/or dividends from the corporation. Also, if a corporation is dissolved, its shareholders are the residual claimants for its assets, which means that once all its debts and obligations are resolved, if there is anything left over, the shareholders receive it. So shareholders have rights but not the ability of an owner who is a sole proprietor to manage, sell, buy, make contracts, and otherwise operate the business. Instead, shareholders vote to elect a board of directors to oversee the managers of the business. The directors do not operate the business of the corporation either. Rather, they hire the chief executive officer (CEO) of the corporation, often called its president or sometimes chair.

The CEO is responsible for managing and overseeing all of the operations and finances of the corporation and reports to its board of directors. He or she may be fired by a majority vote of the directors at a duly called meeting attended by a quorum of the directors. The number of directors needed to constitute a quorum is stated in the bylaws. A corporation is required to file an annual report with the appropriate government office. Failure to do so can result in administrative dissolution, which means that it ceases to exist as a legal person. Shares of stock in a corporation can be bought and sold, but there are legal restrictions on this in securities laws. Sometimes a corporation's assets are sold to another party. Management winds up the corporation's business, paying off its debts and paying the excess to shareholders, and then dissolves it. Other times, a corporation will merge with another corporation, and shares of the surviving corporation will be issued to replace the shares in the acquired corporation.

State laws also allow formation of nonprofit or nonstock corporations. A *nonprofit corporation* does not have shareholders and cannot distribute any surplus it may have (see, e.g., Wis. Stat. § 181.0103 et. seq. [2015]). Most nonprofit corporations are created for social, arts, health, educational, religious, or other nonbusiness purposes. However, nonprofit corporations can create enterprises (often considered to be *social enterprises*), which may create a surplus over its expenses.

In recognition that many investors want corporations to behave in socially responsible ways and to engage in socially responsible businesses, a majority of states have enacted laws that permit so-called hybrid entities such as *benefit corporations*. Benefit corporation statutes indicate that the business is for profit but also has a social purpose (see, e.g., Cal. Corp. Code §§ 14600–14631 [2015]). There is a third-party evaluator required to certify the benefits provided, in many cases a nonprofit corporation, B Lab (https://www.bcorporation.net/what-are-b-corps/about-b-lab). Since "any lawful purpose" for which a business corporation may be formed does not preclude having social aims in addition to profitability, André (2012) has suggested that benefit corporations are unnecessary, create the potential for officer and director liability, and that it is inappropriate for state governments to delegate certification to a private entity that is paid by the corporation it serves. Farmer (2014) disagrees, predicting a positive future for benefit corporations. This is a very new form of entity, and whether it will spread to all fifty states and become a popular business form is yet to be determined. Until courts resolve questions surrounding these hybrid organizational forms, tribal enterprises and citizen entrepreneurs should proceed cautiously.

LIMITED LIABILITY COMPANIES

Although corporations have been around for centuries, limited liability companies (LLCs) came to be in the last quarter of the twentieth century, with Wyoming adopting the first enabling statute in 1977 (W. S. 1977 §§ 17-15-115 to 17-15-135, subsequently repealed and replaced in 2010). However, it was not until 1988 when the US Internal Revenue Service issued Revenue Ruling 88-76 that LLCs as a preferred choice of business entity took off (Bishop and Keatinge 2009). Under Revenue Ruling 88-76, LLCs gained the tax benefits of a partnership. In LLCs this favorable tax treatment, the limited liability of a corporation, and fewer formal requirements to meet than corporations combine to make this legal form of organization very popular for business creation. An LLC is created by filing articles of association with the appropriate state or tribal governmental office.

LLCs may be member-managed or manager-managed. In a manager-managed LLC, a manager is named in the articles of association to operate the business. This arrangement is formalized in an operating agreement. Manager-managed LLCs allow the members of the LLC to be passive investors and leave its management to a professional manager, usually either a corporation or another LLC. Member-managed LLCs may also have an operating agreement. However, when there is just one member, sometimes an LLC will forego the formality of such an agreement. This is a very popular organizational form and is often used by small businesses, startup businesses, and tribal enterprises.

THE LAW GOVERNING BUSINESS FORMATION

Business organizations outside of Indian Country are most often formed under state law, including common law (which is created through court rulings). Since this body of law is well developed, there can be some advantages to use a well-recognized organizational form. However, under some circumstances there are distinct benefits to forming a Section 17 corporation through the BIA. In other circumstances a tribe may wish to look to its own laws, having adopted its own corporation code or LLC code that allows it (or its tribal citizens) to form an entity under tribal law. Let's look at each of these circumstances in turn.

STATE LAW

Tribally owned businesses are sometimes created as state corporations or limited liability companies, usually under the law of the state where the business's main office is located. A tribe may choose state law for entity formation when it owns only some rather than all of the shares of the corporation or there are one or more additional members if it is an LLC. Non-Native businesspeople are sometimes uncomfortable with tribal law and may resist forming the entity under a tribal corporation or LLC code. However, it is unlikely that a tribally owned and operated corporation under state law will be afforded sovereign immunity by state or federal courts that have jurisdiction over its disputes (Pierson 2015). The argument for the extension of immunity increases when the business is conducted on a reservation or trust land (see, e.g., McCoy 2010). However, even if sovereign immunity does not apply, the tribe itself will, under most circumstances, be insulated from the debts, obligations, and lawsuits of its separately organized business operations due to the general limits on liability that corporations and LLCs enjoy under the law. Nevertheless, sovereign immunity can be a significant benefit to a tribal enterprise, so a tribe should consider its other options for how to form a business enterprise.

FEDERAL LAW

Tribal gaming enterprises are generally formed as federally chartered Section 17 corporations under the IRA (25 U.S.C. §477), because federally chartered corporations are not subject to federal income taxes. According to Atkinson and Nilles (2008), the BIA regional offices have some latitude in the formalities required to incorporate as a federally chartered tribal corporation, but generally five steps are required. First, the tribal council must pass a resolution authorizing the formation of the corporation. Second, the tribe must draft a charter, which is comparable to articles of incorporation but contains more information about how it will be separate and distinct from the tribe itself. Atkinson and Nilles (2008) recommend drafting this document broadly since there are no statutory procedures to amend the charter once it has been approved. The third step depends on the constitution of the tribe, which will either delegate authority to form corporations to the tribal council, or it will require a majority vote of the tribal members. Fourth, the appropriate documents must be filed with the local BIA office. Once the BIA approves the charter, the tribal council or other governing body of the tribe must ratify it (25 U.S.C. §477; Atkinson and Nilles 2008). This process can take some time because there are many formalities. Interestingly, the charter can only be revoked or dissolved by an act of Congress (25 U.S.C. §477).

Once the Section 17 corporation has been formed, the tribal council appoints a board of directors to oversee its operations (Atkinson and Nilles, 2008). Just as in state corporations, the board of directors hires a chief executive officer or manager to run its business. One restriction is that it must be wholly owned by the tribe (25 U.S.C. §477), so if the business enterprise will have other owners, another type of entity must be chosen.

TRIBAL LAW

A tribe must put the legal infrastructure in place to allow the tribe to engage in business enterprises. Most tribal lawyers and consultants, including the Harvard Project on American Indian Development, recommend that business enterprises be separate from tribal politics to increase the likelihood of smooth operations of its businesses, to gain the confidence of the business community in which it will operate, and to avoid the potential for political corruption squandering the assets of or otherwise interfering with the enterprises (see, e.g., Atkinson and Nilles 2008; Harvard Project on American Indian Economic Development 2008). This means setting up a separate board to oversee business enterprises. This entity may be incorporated or a separately chartered but unincorporated instrumentality of the tribe. For example, Mno-Bmadsen, the nongaming economic development arm of my tribe, the Pokagon Band of Potawatomi Indians, is an unincorporated, chartered instrumentality of the tribe (see mno-bmadsen.com/). The Winnebago Tribe of Nebraska has separately incorporated its economic development arm, Ho-Chunk, Inc., which presently owns over thirty subsidiaries in ten states and four foreign countries, in several different industries (see www .hochunkinc.com).

Additional tribal laws are required for the tribe or its tribal citizens to form corporations or limited liability companies under tribal law. This generally means that the legislative branch of the tribe (often the tribal council) must adopt a corporation code and/or an LLC code. A tribe's lawyers will generally recommend that the tribe also adopt a commercial code to provide the basic laws that will govern the commercial relationships entered into by tribal corporations or tribal LLCs. In general, tribal courts have jurisdiction over all disputes involving a tribal corporation or tribal LLC, unless the organization has entered into a contract that assigns jurisdiction and choice of law to state courts and state law and/or requires the parties to the contract to submit to arbitration. The BIA has put model codes for corporations and LLCs on its website to assist tribes that may be interested in adopting these statutes (see www.bia.gov/WhoWeAre/AS-IA/IEED/DEMD/TD/index.htm).

American Indian businesses are formed under tribal law by filing articles of incorporation for a corporation or articles of association for an LLC, with the appropriate tribal governmental office designed in the tribe's corporation code or LLC code, as the case may be. The information about how they operate is much the same as entities under state law. However, the tribal codes will govern how the stock or membership interests may be sold, how mergers may occur, and how to dissolve the business entity. Tribal enterprises formed under these codes provide the highest degree of self-determination. The sovereign immunity of commercial tribal enterprises has been called into question, but these questions have not yet been resolved.

IMPLICATIONS FOR AMERICAN INDIAN BUSINESS

There are important management implications of the form of enterprise that is selected. Much depends on the particular situation of the business and its founders. For example, a tribal citizen may choose to form an LLC to enter into a restaurant business on her tribe's reservation. This will permit the member of the LLC to operate the business with little personal risk to her other assets. The business will have "pass through" taxation, which means that the owner will claim the income from the business as ordinary income on her income taxes. Claims against her business must be brought in tribal court.

Tribal gaming enterprises have a special status under federal law (see chapter 8 in the edited volume), making a Section 17 corporation under federal law the best choice for this type of entity. Other business enterprises may take a variety of forms. For example, a gas station and convenience store that sells liquor will need a license from the state to operate and, depending on the state, it might prove to be most expeditious to form a state law corporation or an LLC to operate this enterprise to avoid lengthy issues about licensing a tribal corporation for such purposes. Another scenario is when a tribe forms a joint venture with another tribe. A *joint venture* occurs when two or more entities go into business with a common purpose. Suppose, for example, that two tribes decide to invest in a commercial real estate venture, building a strip mall in a city near one of the tribes. Each tribe will generally form an entity to act as owner of its share in the joint venture, this might be under tribal law, or if tribal law is not available, state law. Then the joint venture may be formed as a general partnership, corporation, or LLC.

Partnership and LLC forms have certain tax advantages to the members. It is very important in the agreements entered into at the time the joint venture is formed that the parties limit what business the entity may undertake, create a clear process as to how the joint venture will be managed and how profits will be distributed, and provide a way of resolving disputes between the tribes relative to the business.

CONCLUSION

Every business enterprise has an organizational structure. American Indian businesses have additional options for formation over non-Native businesses. These include Section 17 corporations under federal law, when a business is formed by a tribe, and under tribal law when the tribe has adopted the appropriate legal infrastructure to support the formation of the business. When deciding what form to adopt, the business owners should consider the type and size of the business, the business risk that accompanies less formal means of doing business (such as being a sole proprietor or general partnership), how the business will be taxed, and, in the case of tribally owned enterprises, the best case for sovereign immunity. This is a very fact-specific determination and will be dependent on who is to own the entity, how the entity will be managed, and what law is best suited to govern the operations of the business. It is important to consult a lawyer and an accountant to assist in making these determinations.

DISCUSSION

1. What is the most common form of business organization? What are the advantages and disadvantages of this organizational form?
2. Kara and Ashley decide to start a restaurant business together. Would it be better to form a general partnership or an LLC? If the restaurant is to be located on their tribe's reservation, should they form it under state law or tribal law? Might it make a difference if only one of the owners is a tribal citizen?
3. Which forms of organization allow a business owner to reduce his or her personal liability for the debts of a business?
4. What options does a tribe have in forming its tribally owned business enterprises?
5. What options for forming an organization does a tribe have if it enters into a business venture that will be partially owned by a nontribal entity?

References

André, R. 2012. "Assessing the Accountability of the Benefit Corporation: Will This New Gray Sector Organization Enhance Corporate Social Responsibility?" *Journal of Business Ethics* 110, no. 1: 133–50. doi:http://dx.doi.org/10.1007/s10551-012-1254-1.

Atkinson, K. J., and K. Nilles. 2008. *Tribal Business Structure Handbook*. US Department of the Interior, the Office of Assistant Secretary—Indian Affairs. Washington, DC. Online at www.bia.gov/cs/groups/xieed/documents/document/idc-022678.pdf. Accessed on December 27, 2015.

Bishop, C. G., and R. R. Keatinge. 2009. "An Introduction." *Suffolk University Law Review* 42: 455–57.

Farmer, K. 2014. "Benefit Corporations Are Rapidly Expanding To Provide Legal Protection for Firms Seeking To Be Socially Responsible As Well As Profitable." *Rocky Mountain Law Journal* 3: 35–45.

Harvard Project on American Indian Economic Development. 2008. *The State of Native Nations: Foundations under U.S. Policies of Self-Determination*. New York: Oxford University Press.

McCoy, P. I. 2010. "Sovereign Immunity and Tribal Commercial Activity: A Legal Summary and Policy Check." *Federal Lawyer* 57 (March–April): 41–48.

Pierson, B. L. 2015. "The Precarious Sovereign Immunity of Tribal Business Corporations." *Federal Lawyer* 62 (April): 58–61.

7 TRIBAL FINANCE AND ECONOMIC DEVELOPMENT

The Fight against Economic Leakage

Gavin Clarkson, *New Mexico State University*

ABSTRACT

When $1 million is invested in most communities, it generates approximately $10 million of cash flow. In Indian Country, however, a $1 million investment typically generates just $1 million of cash flow. The largest Wal-Mart on the planet, in terms of dollar sales per square foot is in Gallup, New Mexico, on the edge of the Navajo Nation. The second largest is in Billings, Montana, otherwise known as the "Crow-Mart," on the edge of the Crow reservation. Why is economic leakage so pervasive on reservation communities and yet the towns bordering those communities consistently see a net monetary inflow from tribal members? One possibility is the federally imposed restriction of reservation land that makes it nearly impossible for on-reservation entrepreneurs to secure startup financing, as they cannot borrow against the equity they have in their homes. As a result, fewer entrepreneurial ventures occur on reservations and thus fewer options exist for on-reservation consumers to spend their money on the reservation. The inevitable consequence of such a lack of consumer spending options on-reservation is leakage.

Indian Country is America's domestic emerging market, and as in other emerging markets, many successful businesses in Indian Country are starving for expansion capital, while other businesses cannot even obtain startup capital. The US Treasury estimates that the private-equity deficit in Indian Country is $44 billion. Tribal leaders and those wishing to do business in Indian Country need to develop strategies using a variety of tools to increase the level of on-reservation business activity, particularly entrepreneurial activity. This chapter discusses overall economic conditions in Indian Country, presents an economic development toolkit focused on tribal entrepreneurship, and examines the opportunities for tribes to access the capital markets for larger projects and ventures.

KEYWORDS: tribal finance, tribal economic development, economic leakage, tribal economics

INTRODUCTION

GALLUP, NEW MEXICO, IS A BORDER TOWN JUST OUTSIDE THE Navajo Nation reservation with an estimated twenty-two thousand residents; however, that number nearly triples on the first of the month. Social Security checks are distributed to the elders and veterans on that day, and most tribal members have neither access to a local bank nor sufficient consumer-spending options on the reservation. Most Navajos therefore end up driving for an hour or more to purchase much needed groceries, lumber, auto parts, and children's school clothes in border towns such as Gallup. According to a 2006 study conducted by the University of New Mexico Bureau of Business and Economic Analysis, significant competition for retail dollars from the Navajo Nation is spread among several surrounding non-Indian communities, including Gallup, Grants, Farmington, Show Low, and Winslow (Mitchell 2006). The Diné Policy Institute report on food sovereignty (2014) found that 60 percent of respondents needed food items that were not available locally. The Navajo Nation Department of Economic Development reported that 71 percent of Navajo dollars are spent off-reservation (Choudhary 2003), and nearly 80 percent of tribal consumers purchased their groceries off-reservation. This economic leakage happens despite the long drives off-reservation to the grocery store, some as far as 240 miles. These startling statistics demonstrate the magnitude of the economic leakage that pervades the Navajo Nation and also explains why the Wal-Mart in Gallup is one of the world's largest.

Such leakage is not unique to the Navajo Nation, however. The former chairman of the Crow Nation in Montana suggested to the *Billings Gazette* that if "anyone doubts that money flows into Billings [from the Crow Nation], go to Wal-Mart today after members receive their per-capita check from the tribe. 'We don't call it Wal-Mart, we call it Crow-Mart'" (Shay 2007). The Crow Nation and the six other federally recognized tribes in Montana conducted a study that found that tribal and BIA salaries pump more than $200 million directly into the state economy, and "since every dollar turns at least five times in a local economy, the total annual contribution may reach $1 billion" (Selden 2001). When private sector wages as well as goods and services purchased by tribal and BIA entities are considered, the contribution to the state of Montana ranges between $3 billion and $5 billion a year. In his 2012 book *Reservation Capitalism*, Robert Miller identifies several studies on leakage from various reservations in addition to the Montana tribal study. Research on the Zuni Pueblo economy found that 84 percent of all individual income was spent off-reservation (Miller 2012). Former commissioner of Indian Affairs, Robert L. Bennett, perhaps best summarized the problem of leakage: "When a million dollars is invested in most communities, it generates approximately ten million dollars of cash flow. But in Indian communities, one million dollars generates just one million dollars of cash flow" (Bennett 1986).

But why is economic leakage so pervasive on reservation communities, yet the towns bordering those communities consistently see a net monetary inflow from tribal members? Clarkson and Murphy (2016) argue that a primary cause for the lack of on-reservation consumer options is the cumbersome and onerous policy of the US government holding tribal land in trust. An artifact of a long since discredited congressional policy called *allotment*, federally imposed restrictions on trust land make it nearly impossible for on-reservation entrepreneurs to secure startup financing, as they cannot borrow against the equity they have in their homes. As a result, fewer entrepreneurial ventures occur on reservations, and thus there are fewer options for on-reservation consumers to spend their money on the reservation. The inevitable consequence of such a lack of consumer spending options on-reservation is leakage. Any potential solution to the trust land issue faces an uphill climb, so tribal leaders and those wishing to do business in Indian Country need to develop strategies using a variety of tools to increase the level of on-reservation business activity, particularly entrepreneurial activity. The first part of this chapter provides an overview of economic conditions in Indian Country. The second part presents an economic development toolkit focused on tribal entrepreneurship. The last part examines the opportunities for tribes to access the capital markets for larger projects and ventures.

AN ECONOMIC OVERVIEW OF INDIAN COUNTRY

While discussions of emerging markets usually focus on economic development in third world countries, most Indian tribes have an economy on par with those same countries. Extensive land bases, spread-out communities, and homesteads mired in one long-standing poverty cycle characterize most reservations. Just as with other emerging markets, the need for economic development in Indian Country remains acute and affects nearly every aspect of reservation life. Federal Indian policy over the past two centuries bears significant responsibility for the lack of economic progress in Indian Country. Allotment Era policies can be seen as an effort to place control of tribal economies, including tribal resources, in the hands of federal agencies or officials (Harvard Project on American Indian Economic Development 2002) and resulted in the loss of two-thirds of tribal lands and resources (Getches et al. 2011). Although the Indian Reorganization Act (IRA) sought to reverse this trend and improve tribal economic conditions by bolstering tribal governments and supporting tribal business entities that would engage in economic development (Cohen 2015), the federal government continued its oppressive control of tribal businesses, thereby limiting the effectiveness of the IRA in promoting and supporting tribal economies. After the disastrous Termination Era of the 1950s and 1960s, federal Indian law and federal policy finally began to meaningfully foster tribal economic growth, but tribal entrepreneurship still lags in Indian Country (Clarkson 2009).

Contrary to popular belief, gaming does not provide a sufficient economic or social recovery for most tribal economies. A majority of the more than 560 federally recognized Indian tribes do not have any significant gaming operations (Spilde and Taylor 2013), and of those that do, only a small handful generate substantial revenues (Clarkson 2009). Although a few tribes near major metropolitan centers operate successful gaming enterprises, hundreds of tribes have no gaming industry, and many operate small casinos located far from population centers. Thus the economic benefits of gaming are not universally distributed throughout Indian Country. For example, the unemployment rate still hovers around 50 percent for Indians who live on reservations (nearly ten times that for the United States as a whole), and more than one third of American Indian children live in poverty.

On-reservation tribal businesses are vital to the sovereignty and welfare of tribal governments and American Indians/Alaska Natives nationwide. In 2014 the US Supreme Court, in the case of *Michigan v. Bay Mills Indian Community* (134 S. Ct. 2024, 2043 [2014]), reiterated that "(a) key goal of the Federal Government is to render Tribes more self-sufficient and better positioned to fund their own sovereign functions, rather than relying on Federal funding." With dwindling federal funds, tribal communities face significant challenges in establishing steady revenue streams and attracting external investors. While not exclusively linked to location, these challenges to tribal economic development are often entrenched because a majority of reservation lands are geographically isolated, historically disadvantaged, and poor. The vast majority of tribal communities struggle with long-standing cycles of poverty, and as with other developing nations, the need for economic development on tribal lands remains acute, affecting nearly every aspect of reservation life. Large portions of Indian Country lack basic infrastructure, which poses a daunting barrier to tribal leaders' attempts to develop their economies.

Such realities highlight the importance of stimulating economic development for tribal community social and economic recovery. Research from the 2006–10 American Indian Community Surveys indicates that the pace of reservation economic growth slowed between 2000 and 2010. Although economic growth on reservations outpaced the United States during the recession, the income gap between reservations and the rest of the United States remains large, with the real per capita income for American Indians on reservations at $10,963, compared with $26,648 for all races in the United States. Economists now speculate that current growth rates on reservations have slowed the pace for closing the gap until at least the year 2080 (Akee and Taylor 2014).

All too many tribal governments lack the ability to provide the basic infrastructure most US citizens take for granted, such as passable roadways, affordable housing, and the plumbing, electricity, and telephone services that come with a modern home (Clarkson 2009). Approximately 20 percent of American Indian households on reservations lack complete plumbing facilities, compared with 1 percent of all US households. About one in five American Indian reservation households dispose of sewage by means *other than* public sewer, septic tank, or cesspool. The Navajo reservation is the same size as West Virginia, yet it only has two thousand miles of paved roads while West Virginia has eighteen thousand miles. Investors and employers, even in the most distressed inner cities of the United States, take roads, telephones, electricity, and the like for granted. The absence of such basic infrastructure from large portions of Indian Country poses a daunting barrier to tribal leaders' attempts to attract new private-sector investment and jobs. Although tribal leaders have acknowledged and attempted to reduce these problems for decades, they have not had the resources to create a more hospitable business environment. A vicious cycle has consequently developed: businesses avoid establishing a presence on reservations because of the lack of infrastructure, while tribal governments are left unable to improve their infrastructure because on-reservation commerce is woefully insufficient.

THE CHALLENGE OF ECONOMIC LEAKAGE

Miller has listed three reasons why economic leakage in tribal communities leads to disastrous economic situations for Indian reservations. First, the lack of community development "[l]eads to more poverty and overall lower Indian family incomes. Second, having so few employers and jobs available in Indian Country leads to high unemployment rates. And, third, the absences of thriving economies, characterized by a sufficient number of privately and publically owned businesses in Indian Country, adds to the impoverishment of Indians and their families" (Miller 2012, 113). Without entrepreneurship a tribal economy cannot be self-sustaining, yet tribal members still must meet their basic consumption needs. As Miller has pointed out: "[T]he money Indians spend does not circulate on their reservations between various public and private business opportunities and jobs. Clearly, if there are no businesses on reservations where residents can buy necessary and luxury goods, they will make those purchases off reservation. The lack, then, of small businesses on reservations leads to many negative economic impacts" (Miller 2012, 114).

THE CURSE OF TRUST LAND

Both Clarkson and Murphy (2016) as well as Morgan (2005) focus on trust land as a primary impediment for entrepreneurs who want to start small businesses or pursue entrepreneurial endeavors in Indian Country. As Clarkson and Murphy have pointed out, selling and leasing tribal land, even for community development, must be approved by the United States. Morgan puts it more bluntly: "Trust status hurts individual American Indians. It prevents us from using our land as collateral, which has effectively killed Native-owned agriculture. This system left us with almost no choice but to lease out our land, primarily to non-Indians. That's why we are land rich, but still dirt poor" (Morgan 2005).

Miller has echoed this sentiment: "[T]ribes and Indian owners cannot sell, lease, develop, or mortgage [trust land] for loans without the express approval of the federal government. Needless to say, having the United States looking over the shoulders of tribal governments and requiring federal approvals of most economic decisions, and the time it takes to gain these bureaucratic approvals, adds enormous costs and inefficiencies to tribal and Indian economic endeavors. The inefficient and non-business-oriented federal bureaucracy creates serious obstacles for tribal governments and Indians in using trust assets for economic purposes and for non-Indian companies who want to work in Indian Country" (Miller 2012, 40). The policy of restricting tribal land as trust land means that potential entrepreneurs do not have access to a prime source of capital for business startup.

THE ECONOMIC DEVELOPMENT TOOLKIT

Although the challenges standing in the way of meaningful economic development are daunting, they are not insurmountable. Many tribes have wholly owned corporate entities that enjoy many of the same legal protections and advantages as the tribe itself (Thompson 2016). In addition, there are a number of federal financial incentives to encourage investment in projects in economically distressed areas in general—and on tribal lands specifically.

LEGAL INFRASTRUCTURE

As discussed in chapter 5, under tribal law or federal law (in the case of IRA Section 17 corporations), tribal governments can charter their own tribal government–owned corporations. These corporations hold the same status as the tribe itself for purposes of federal income tax exemptions and sovereign immunity from suit. While tribal corporations are subject to federal law, tribal governments and their tribal corporations are generally not subject to state laws. Furthermore, as discussed in chapter 5, tribes can pass their own laws and make their own regulations regarding economic activity on their lands. This same legal infrastructure can also support the business formation by individual tribal members. While tribal member-owned businesses do not have sovereign immunity, they still enjoy the same exemptions from state law and regulation as tribally owned corporations.

For tribal, tribal member, and even nontribal businesses operating in Indian Country, Thompson (2016) identifies a number of potential advantages in terms of legal infrastructure. Indian Country has a flexible regulatory environment that can provide a number of advantages. Because tribes regulate their own lands, those lands are generally not subject to local, county, and state zoning/land use restrictions or state permitting requirements. State environmental restrictions generally do not apply in Indian Country, therefore tribes can issue environmental licenses and permits in conformance with tribal and federal EPA requirements. In addition, tribes can structure product liability laws for tribal courts to limit liability in instances that might require this type of protection.

ADVANTAGES OF DOING BUSINESS IN INDIAN COUNTRY

With the appropriate legal infrastructure in place, properly structured businesses in Indian Country enjoy a number of advantages, not least of which are tax advantages. Tribes and tribal enterprises are exempt from federal and state income taxes just like any other government-owned entity. For businesses jointly owned by the tribe and either a tribal member or a nontribal entity, the portion owned by the tribe (or tribal corporation) is generally exempt from federal and state income taxes. Most tribes do not have their own sales taxes. In addition, most states provide state sales tax exemptions for sales to governmental entities. Although trust land has a number of disadvantages, it does provide at least one benefit in terms of profitability, as land held in trust is not subject to state property taxes. Once a business is operational, additional tax incentives exist for Indian Country employers. They can receive a tax credit of up to 20 percent of wages and health insurance for qualified employees living on Indian reservations (Thompson 2016). Those businesses can also claim depreciation at twice the normal rate for locating equipment and buildings on tribal land.

Many tribes and tribal entrepreneurs focus their efforts on government contracting because of the substantial preferences available. Under the Buy Indian Act, for example, many federal agencies give preference to Indian and tribally owned companies in procurement contracts. The Small Business Administration's 8(a) program authorizes preferences for minority-owned small businesses in bidding for federal contracts. Tribally owned corporations, however, receive additional benefits, such as the ability to pursue larger contracts without the contract size restrictions imposed on other 8(a) companies. In addition, if a small business is located on Indian lands and 35 percent of its employees reside on the reservation, the company is eligible for HUB Zone preferences in the awarding of federal contracts. Benefits include competitive and sole source contracting and a 10 percent price evaluation preference in full and open contract competitions (Thompson 2016).

FINANCING TRIBAL ENTREPRENEURSHIP

Tribal corporations and tribal member-owned businesses need both startup and expansion capital, yet Indian Country is the most underbanked territory in the United States (Clarkson 2009). According to the Native CDFI Network (2016), 86 percent of Indian Country communities lack a single financial institution within their borders to access affordable financial products and services. Certain institutions, however, are attempting to address the lack of access to financing in Indian Country, particularly those entities that are certified as a community development financial institution (CDFI). There are currently more than seventy certified Native CDFIs located in eighteen states across the country, serving Indian Country, Alaska, and Hawaii. Native CDFIs have entered markets normally considered "high risk" and have had a significant role in creating businesses, jobs, homeowners, and serving as the catalyst for developing local economies. Their unique programs and services are designed to build financial assets in the low-income populations they serve and to provide access to economic opportunities by offering a range of financial products—from individual "credit builder" loans and small business startup loans to larger investments such as New Market Tax Credits (NMTC). CDFIs that can obtain an NMTC allocation can then use those tax credits to attract outside investment for Indian Country projects. NMTCs provide investors with a tax credit of up to 39 percent of the entire amount of the investment. The tax credit is spread over seven years: 5 percent of the investment for the first three years, and 6 percent of the investment amount can be claimed the next four years (Thompson 2016).

There are other federal programs that either provide partial guarantees for banks who make loans in Indian Country or provide direct financial assistance to Indian Country entrepreneurs. Although not specifically focused on Indian Country, the SBA's 7(a) Loan Guaranty Program helps small businesses, including businesses owned or controlled by federally recognized Indian tribes, obtain loans from private lenders (Cohen 2015). The BIA's Indian Loan Guaranty, Insurance, and Interest Subsidy Program provides a guaranty or insurance coverage for up to 90 percent of a loan to a tribe, a tribal business enterprise, one or more individual Indians, or a business entity that is at least 51 percent Indian-owned (OIEED 2008). Individuals can receive guarantees of up to $500,000, and tribal corporations have received guarantees of more than $20 million. The borrower must have at least 20 percent equity in the business, and the loans may be used for a variety of purposes, including operating capital, equipment purchases, business refinance, building construction, and lines of credit (Thompson 2016). All loans guaranteed under the program must contribute to a tribal economy, and guarantees are not available for loans that would be made without the program.

The US Department of Agriculture (USDA) is also a potential source of capital, providing low-interest loans (and some grants) for tribal governments to build essential community facilities in rural areas (Thompson 2016). Eligible facilities include hospitals, clinics, airport hangars, child care centers, fire departments, police stations, prisons, schools, and local food systems. The USDA also has a loan guarantee program, although the guarantee amount is less than that available from the BIA.

THE TRIBAL FINANCE TOOLKIT

For many years tribal access to capital was limited to grants and other assistance from the federal government (as discussed in the previous section).
Although these sources are still available, and the number of sources has
expanded, in recent years tribal access to the capital markets has broadened
substantially to include a wide variety of lenders. As tribal economies have
expanded, so too has the ability of tribes to incur debt to finance economic
development activities and infrastructure improvements. Perhaps the most
important issues to consider in tribal debt financing is how the tribe will service the debt and how the debt will be secured. Depending on the source of
funds used to repay the debt, tribal borrowing can take a number of forms
(Clarkson 2007), including:

- A *general obligation bond*, which can be either secured or, more
  commonly, unsecured. In the latter case the issuer will generally
  promise to repay principal and interest from any of the issuer's available
  funds. In both secured and unsecured general obligation bonds, the
  general credit of the issuer is pledged.
- A *revenue bond*, which differs from a general obligation bond in that the
  debt obligation is limited in terms of recourse to a specifically identified
  source of revenue that is pledged to secure the debt. The issuer does not
  pledge its general credit. In contrast to general obligation bonds,
  revenue bonds pledge only the earnings from revenue-producing
  activities, usually to project being financed.
- A *private activity bond* (PAB), which provides financing for private
  businesses or individuals, and the revenues from the financed activities
  are usually pledged to cover the debt service for the bonds. For example,
  state and local governments often issue tax-exempt PABs for the benefit
  of nonprofit corporations for projects such as charity hospitals or to
  finance low-income residential rental property or mortgage loans for
  first-time low-income homebuyers. Private activity bonds are also
  issued for airports, docks and wharves, solid waste facilities, sewage
  facilities, and certain other facilities.
- *Asset-backed obligation*, which refers to debt that is secured primarily or
  solely by one or more specific assets that are pledged as collateral. In the
  event of default, the lender may seize the collateral and sell it to help
  repay the debt. The ability to pledge certain types of assets as collateral,

particularly real property or a gaming operation, may be limited by
tribal or other applicable law.

- *Lease-purchase obligation*, which refers to a form of debt very common
  for equipment financing. It typically involves a capital lease. Recourse is
  usually limited to the equipment that is being financed.

Other considerations that affect the nature of tribal debt financing are the
size, nature, and purpose of the debt. Smaller amounts can usually be borrowed from a single lender, such as a local bank. For larger amounts, however, the tribe will likely borrow from multiple sources, such as a group of
banks or bondholders in the capital markets. The nature of the debt obligation can also affect the borrowing structure. For example, bank debt often
has a shorter term than bond debt, and taxable bonds have shorter terms
than tax-free bonds. Similarly, the amount that can be borrowed will be a
function of the sources pledged to repayment, particularly for revenue obligations. Tribal assets and revenue streams can be aggregated to create a larger
pool of assets to use as collateral in order to borrow larger amounts. Finally,
the purpose of a borrowing plays a significant role in determining the structure of the transaction, as certain activities are more conducive to long-term
bond financing while others are more appropriate for a bank loan.

The issue of tribal sovereign immunity will almost always come up in the
context of tribal debt financing. Lenders or bondholders are unlikely to loan
money to a tribe if they are unable to enforce the obligation to repay. Tribes
can grant limited waivers of sovereign immunity in response to the commercial realities of the capital markets. Although bank debt and bond indentures
represent a promise to pay a specific sum of money (principal amount) at a
specified date or dates in the future (maturity date) together with periodic
interest at a specified rate, each type of debt has unique attributes and estab-
lishes a relationship with a different set of lenders. In addition, given the
same level of earnings, an issuer will likely be able to borrow larger amounts
for longer periods by issuing bonds rather than by borrowing from a bank
(Clarkson 2007).

BANK DEBT

Commercial banks typically lend money to governmental borrowers as part
of an ongoing business relationship. For larger amounts a group of banks,
often called a *syndicate*, will collectively lend money to the borrower. A
borrower can usually borrow up to two times its annual earnings from a

bank or bank syndicate, and the term of a bank loan (or note) is generally three to five (and sometimes up to seven) years. Bank debt can be used as temporary financing when a borrower plans to subsequently issue more debt through a bond offering to finance a larger project. A portion of the bond proceeds are then used to pay off the bank note.

BOND DEBT

Unlike bank debt (which generally has a single lender holding the note), a bond indenture provides for negotiable instruments—that is, bonds that can be bought and sold in the capital markets. Thus the lenders, or bondholders, often have no direct relationship with the issuer. While issuing a bond is typically a more complex transaction than obtaining a bank loan, issuers can generally borrow larger amounts for longer terms. An issuer can borrow as much as three to four times its annual revenues by issuing bonds, and the payments can be stretched over ten, fifteen, or even thirty years in some cases. Bond transactions often involve a financial intermediary, usually an investment banking firm that assists issuers in finding buyers for the bond. By marketing to a larger audience in the broader capital markets, the financial intermediary attempts to obtain the best possible interest rate and terms for the issuer, which may often be better than those available from commercial banks.

An important distinction between bank debt and bond indentures is that unlike bank loans, bonds are classified as "securities" and are therefore subject to a variety of securities laws. Note, however, that Section 103(c) of the Tax Code treats all obligations as "bonds" even if they are bank loans, finance leases, installment purchases, or actual bonds issued under bond indentures. Thus, while the debt markets differentiate substantially between bank debt and bond indentures, the Tax Code does not. For purposes of clarity, subsequent use of the term *bonds* in this chapter refers to bonds issued under bond indentures in the capital markets and does not include the other forms of governmental debt considered to be "bonds" under Section 103.

TAX-EXEMPT DEBT

Tax-exempt debt is debt where the interest paid to the debt holder is not subject to taxation. Because the interest is tax-free, investors are able to generate the same after-tax return with a lower interest rate as they would from a similar taxable investment that pays a higher interest rate. In addition to the availability of lower interest rates, sometimes as much as 300 basis points lower, longer terms are available in the tax-exempt market. Unlike taxable bonds, tax-exempt bonds can be issued only for certain purposes. Indian tribes face two additional restrictions that do *not* apply to state and local governments: Indian tribes cannot issue private activity bonds similar to those issued by state and local governments (Clarkson 2007). Equally significant, Indian tribes can issue tax-exempt bonds "only if such obligation is part of an issue substantially all of the proceeds of which are to be used in the exercise of any essential governmental function" (26 U.S.C. § 7871[c][1]).

This additional essential governmental function (EGF) requirement is not imposed on states. Furthermore, 26 U.S.C. § 7871(e) states that "the term 'essential government function' shall not include any function which is not customarily performed by State and local governments with general taxing powers," but does not provide any guidance as to when a particular activity becomes "customary" for a municipal government. EGF bonds can be used to finance roads, parks, water and wastewater treatment systems, government buildings, and schools, among other purposes. However, as Clarkson (2007) has noted, the Internal Revenue Service (IRS) has prohibited the use of such bonds to finance a golf course and a hotel facility connected to an Indian casino. As the federal government holds most tribal land in trust, those lands are not available for property taxes, and thus the tax base of a tribe is usually insufficient for a tribe to issue general obligation bonds (Clarkson 2007). Since the revenue from a revenue bond is usually linked to the project being financed, both the prohibition on tribal private activity bonds and the additional restriction to "customary" governmental activity place tribes at a significant disadvantage relative to state and local governments in the capital markets and is inequitable when compared to other forms of municipal debt.

The narrow interpretation of this language by the IRS has had a stifling effect on tribes' tax-free bonding authority. These restrictions on the scope of what can be financed with tax-exempt debt in particular deny poor tribes the opportunity to address their glaring infrastructure and economic development needs. Tribes with substantial natural resources or significant gaming operations have the option of financing certain activities on a taxable basis even if the restrictions in the Tax Code prevent them from financing those activities on a tax-exempt basis. Poorer tribes do not have that luxury, however, and upwards of $50 billion in annual capital needs go unmet in Indian Country (Clarkson 2007), in part because the debt service required to finance the projects to meet those needs is too expensive at taxable rates.

The IRS's interpretation of tribal tax-exempt bonding authority has meant a substantially higher audit risk for tribal bonds, as tribal governments are also victims of a demonstrably disproportionate number of IRS enforcement actions. Fewer than 1 percent of the tax-exempt municipal offerings are audited by the IRS each year, but direct tribal tax-exempt issuances are thirty times more likely to be audited within four years of issue. In all of these cases, the tribes financed activities that state and local governments had previously financed without any challenge from the IRS. While the National Congress of American Indians and the National Intertribal Tax Alliance have worked for years to remove these inequities, even the venerable Wall Street firm of Merrill Lynch is on record decrying the inequity of the tax treatment of tribes relative to municipalities (Clarkson 2007). This high rate of tribal audits becomes even more troubling when one realizes that tribal tax-exempt issuances make up only 0.1 percent of the tax-exempt bond market. The situation for tribal tax-exempt debt has improved slightly, as Congress authorized $2 billion of "Tribal Economic Development Bonds" as part of the American Recovery and Reinvestment Act of 2009 using a more flexible standard than the IRS had allowed for the essential government function bonds. The $2 billion was quickly allocated in two separate tranches, but market conditions made it difficult for tribes to issue the bonds, and Congress has thus far declined to change the EGF test permanently for all tax-exempt bond financings (Cohen 2015).

Even with the EGF test still required, many tribal projects may contain some elements that qualify for tax-exempt financing. For example, if a tribe is developing a project that will require a variety of infrastructure improvements, the tribe could likely issue a separate set of tax-exempt bonds to finance the qualifying portion of the overall project. If a tribe has already incurred expenses on a project that qualifies for tax-exempt treatment, it can use bond proceeds to reimburse those expenses (Hyatt, Israel, Benjamin 2005). Whenever a tribe considers financing a project that might qualify for some level of tax-exempt financing, the tribal council should adopt a reimbursement resolution early in the process.

CONCLUSION

Although Indian Country is still a domestic emerging economy, entrepreneurs and tribal ventures have more opportunities and better tools to pursue those opportunities than ever before. Although access to capital remains a significant challenge, as more Indian Country entrepreneurs succeed, more capital will flow into Indian Country. In turn, more economic activity in Indian Country will cycle multiple times within Indian Country, thereby reducing the amount of economic leakage.

DISCUSSION

1. What is economic leakage and why is it a problem in Indian Country?
2. What are some advantages of doing business in Indian Country?
3. Discuss the various debt and equity financing options for entrepreneurial ventures in Indian Country.
4. What challenges do tribal governments face when issuing tax–exempt debt?
5. What are the major differences between tribal government–owned businesses and tribal member–owned businesses?
6. What kind of business would you like to start in Indian Country, and why?

References

Akee, R K.Q., and J. B. Taylor. 2014. *Social and Economic Change on American Indian Reservations: A Databook of the US Censuses and the American Community Survey 1990–2010*. Sarasota, FL: Taylor Policy Group.

Bennett, R. L. 1986. "The War on Poverty." In K. R. Philp, ed., *Indian Self-Rule: First Hand Accounts of Indian-White Relations from Roosevelt to Reagan*. Boulder, CO: Utah State University Press.

Choudhary, T. 2003. *Comprehensive Economic Development Strategy of the Navajo Nation*. Window Rock, AZ: Navajo Nation.

Clarkson, G. 2009. "Accredited Indians: Increasing the Flow of Private Equity into Indian Country as a Domestic Emerging Market." *Colorado Law Review* 80: 285.

———. 2008. "Wall Street Indians: Information Asymmetry and Barriers to Tribal Capital Market Access." *Lewis and Clark Law Review* 12: 943.

———. 2007. "Tribal Bonds: Statutory Shackles and Regulatory Restraints on Tribal Economic Development." *North Carolina Law Review* 85: 1009.

———. 2003. "Racial Imagery and Native Americans: A First Look at the Empirical Evidence Behind the Indian Mascot Controversy." *Cardozo Journal of International and Comparative Law* 11: 393.

Clarkson, G., and A. Murphy. 2016. "Tribal Leakage: How the Curse of Trust Land Impedes Tribal Economic Self-Sustainability." *Journal of Law, Economics, and Policy* 12: 177

Cohen, F. 2015. *Cohen's Handbook of Federal Indian Law*. Newark, NJ: LexisNexis.

Diné Policy Institute. 2014. *A Report on the Navajo Nation Food System and the Case to Rebuild a Self-Sufficient Food System for the Dine People*. Window Rock, AZ: Navajo Nation.

Fletcher, M. 2011. *American Indian Tribal Law*. New York: Aspen Publishers.

Getches, D., et al. 2011. *Cases and Materials on Federal Indian Law (American Casebook Series)*. 6th edition. Saint Paul, MN: West Academic Publishing.

Harvard Project on American Indian Economic Development. 2002. *Native America at the New Millennium*. Cambridge, MA: Harvard University.

Hyatt, T., P. E. Israel, and A. Benjamin. 2005. *An Introduction to Indian Tribal Finance*. Portland, OR: Orrick, Herrington & Sutcliffe.

Miller, R. 2012. *Reservation Capitalism*. Santa Barbara, CA: Praeger.

Mitchell, J. 2006. *Gallup Mainstreet Community Economic Assessment*. Albuquerque: University of New Mexico.

Morgan, Lance. 2005. "Ending the Curse of Trust." *Indian Country Today*. March 18. Online at https://indiancountrymedianetwork.com/news/ending-the-curse-of-trust/.

Native CDFI Network. 2016. Online at http://nativecdfi.net/about/native-cdfis/.

Office of Indian Energy and Economic Development (OIEED). 2008. OIEED Brochure. Online at http://bia.gov/cs/groups/public/documents/text/idc-001933.pdf.

Pommersheim, F. 1988. "The Contextual Legitimacy of Adjudication in Tribal Courts and the Role of the Tribal Bar as an Interpretive Community: An Essay." *New Mexico Law Review* 18, no. 49: 71.

Selden, R. 2001. "Economic Development Attitudes Must Change." *Indian Country Today*. June 13.

Shay, B. 2007. "Crow Leader Outlines Plan for Fuel Plant." *Billings Gazette*. December 6. Online at http://billingsgazette.com/news/local/crow-leader-outlines-plan-for-fuel-plant/article_d0207741-ec01-51a6-9596-c2a3bacd2f1f.html.

Spilde, K., and J. B. Taylor. 2013. "Economic Evidence on the Effects of the Indian Gaming Regulatory Act on Indians and Non-Indians." *UNLV Gaming Research and Review Journal* 17: 1.

Thompson, H. D. 2016. "Doing Business with Tribal Government–Owned Corporations: Some Competitive Advantages." *Tribal Business Journal* (March): 52–54.

8 HIGH-STAKES NEGOTIATION

Indian Gaming and Tribal-State Compacts

Gavin Clarkson, *New Mexico State University*
James K. Sebenius, *Harvard Business School*

ABSTRACT

Although Indian tribes and the surrounding states were often bitter enemies throughout much of US history, tribes and states have recently been able to work cooperatively in a number of areas. In some instances Congress has mandated such cooperation, and at other times the cooperative activity has arisen between the parties themselves as a matter of pragmatism. In either instance, tribes and states have often found themselves at the bargaining table. The negotiation dynamics of tribal-state compacting can be incredibly challenging. The parties may have experienced centuries of animosity. The "shadow of the law" relevant to the substance of the negotiation may be ill defined or easily misunderstood. Finally, significant cultural differences may obscure common ground that could facilitate a successful negotiation.

Although the range of tribal-state compacts includes a wide range of areas, Indian gaming has probably generated the greatest amount of activity in recent years. In particular, the negotiations that led to the immense success of the Pequot gaming operation have become almost mythical in nature, with states often misunderstanding the lessons of the Foxwoods story. The true story is one of strategic negotiation and the leveraging of tribal sovereignty into economic opportunity. This chapter presents a case study of the actual negotiations and also discusses the sovereign nature of tribal governments as well as the complex regulatory environment that governs Indian gaming.

KEYWORDS: Indian gaming, negotiation, regulation, tribal sovereignty

INTRODUCTION

THE 1886 SUPREME COURT CASE *UNITED STATES V. KAGAMA* (118 U.S. 375, 384) wrote that for Indian tribes "the people of the states where they are found are often their deadliest enemies." Recently, however, tribes and states have found sufficient common ground to work cooperatively in certain areas, particularly as state budget deficits continue to worsen. In some instances Congress has mandated such cooperation. In other instances the cooperative activity has risen between the parties themselves as a practical matter. However tribes and states have found themselves at the bargaining table, the negotiation dynamics of tribal-state compacting can be quite challenging (Clarkson and Sebenius 2012). The parties have experienced centuries of animosity. The "shadow of the law" relevant to the substance of the negotiation is ill defined or easily misunderstood, as is often the case with Indian law. Questions about the boundaries of Indian Country may be unsettled and subject to litigation. Finally, significant cultural differences obscure common ground that may facilitate a successful negotiation. While the range of tribal-state compacts is large, Indian gaming has generated the greatest amount of attention in recent years. Although Indian tribes have conducted gaming operations since the 1970s, the advent of large-scale tribal casinos dramatically increased the economic impact of Indian gaming. In order to appreciate the lessons of Indian gaming, it is critical to understand tribal-state gaming negotiations in the context of Indian law. The very existence of the Indian gaming phenomenon grew out of a core tenet of Indian law: Indian tribes are sovereign governmental entities. This concept, along with a brief history of Indian law, is covered in chapter 5 of this book.

The primary objectives of this chapter are, in addition to offering an in-depth examination of Indian gaming, covering basic negotiation concepts in the context of gaming and discussing the regulatory framework that governs Indian gaming. Assuming a basic familiarity with the Indian law concepts covered in chapter 5, the first part of this chapter examines the origins of Indian gaming, focusing on the development of the legal framework that governs tribal gaming activities and necessitates the negotiation of tribal-state gaming compacts. Given the need for tribal-state negotiations, the second part of the chapter presents a framework for structuring and analyzing negotiations. The third part applies that framework in the retelling of one of the first tribal-state gaming compacts between the Mashantucket Pequots and Connecticut. The fourth part of the chapter evaluates the change in the negotiation landscape subsequent to the Pequot negotiations and assesses the impact of technological changes on Indian gaming. This chapter concludes by arguing that, although the relative tribal-state positions may have changed, much of the fundamental negotiation dynamic remains the same. Therefore, many of the same lessons are applicable today.

A BRIEF HISTORY OF INDIAN GAMING

Legend has it that commercial gaming on Indian reservations in the United States began as a response to 1975 fire that destroyed two trailers on the Oneida Indian reservation in Verona, New York (Clarkson and Sebenius 2012). The reservation had neither a fire department nor firefighting equipment, and two Oneidas perished in the blaze. To prevent such tragedies in the future, the Oneidas decided to do what other fire departments had done: raise funds through bingo. The Oneidas launched a bingo game in a double-wide trailer, offering prizes in excess of the limits permitted by New York law. The Oneidas maintained that because they were an Indian nation, they were not bound by state bingo regulations. Tribe members claimed that their right of sovereignty entitled them to run their own game and to offer a large jackpot so as to draw non-Indians—and their money—to a place they otherwise might never visit. Subsequently, according to one Oneida tribal member, "the Seminoles got wind of it" and began their own high-stakes bingo game in Hollywood, Florida, in 1979 (Clarkson and Sebenius 2012). The Seminole tribe contracted with a non-Indian organization to build and manage its bingo hall. The agreement called for the managers to receive 45 percent of the profits after repayment of a $1 million construction loan. The enterprise was a success, and the Seminoles repaid the loan in fewer than six months.

As tribal bingo operations grew more successful, states demanded a cut. States unsuccessfully sought to extend their laws to tribal lands so as to prohibit, regulate, and/or tax tribal bingo operations. Whereas the district attorney in Madison County, New York, successfully shut down the Oneidas' game, the Seminoles fought the state in the courts when Florida authorities tried to close the Seminoles' bingo hall in 1981. The Seminoles argued that Florida did not have the authority to prohibit gaming on their reservation, and the Fifth Circuit agreed, relying on an earlier US Supreme Court case. The Court held that if a state regulates but does not prohibit an activity, it may not prohibit that same activity in Indian Country. Thus the Seminoles secured the right to run their game and pay out unrestricted prizes.

CALIFORNIA V. CABAZON BAND OF MISSION INDIANS, 480 U.S. 202 (1987)

The Oneida reservation in New York may have been Indian gaming's modern birthplace, but the first case to reach the US Supreme Court came from California. The Court held that states cannot ban or regulate the conduct of

Indian gaming operations on reservations without explicit congressional consent. In applying an earlier decision, the Court found that although Public Law 280 granted certain states civil and criminal jurisdiction over Indian lands, Public Law 280 did *not* grant total civil jurisdiction. Instead, it granted jurisdiction to adjudicate civil disputes in Indian Country. The crucial test was whether the regulation at issue was civil and regulatory or criminal and prohibitory. In applying this test, the Court held that because California allowed some forms of gambling, extending that state's laws over the gaming operations of the Cabazon and Morongo Bands of Mission Indians would amount to an exercise of power that was civil and regulatory, rather than criminal and prohibitory. As such, California's bingo laws were not applicable to the gaming operations on Indian lands in California. The Supreme Court found that the intent of Congress was to apply the state's rules of decision in Indian Country, not to confer total jurisdiction over Indian lands.

Although California had an interest in preventing unscrupulous persons from participating in gambling, the federal and tribal interests in tribal self-determination and economic self-sufficiency were stronger: determination and economic development are not within reach if the tribes cannot raise revenues and provide employment for their members. The tribes' interests obviously parallel the federal interests. The tribes have long needed a method of economic development, and gaming provided it. Faced with the alignment of the interests of the tribes and the federal government, the state's interests had to give way.

THE INDIAN GAMING REGULATORY ACT (IGRA), 25 U.S.C. §§ 2701 ET SEQ.

Congress was not content to sit still as the Indian gaming phenomenon took shape, particularly after *Cabazon*. During the 1980s declining federal financial assistance had motivated many tribes to pursue new revenue sources that they could control, and high-stakes bingo was an obvious choice for tribes after the *Seminole Tribe v. Butterworth* decision. By 1988 tribes were sponsoring over one hundred gaming operations generating in excess of $100 million annually. In 1986 the House of Representatives passed a bill in an attempt to control some types of gambling on reservations. The bill died in the Senate, but congressional efforts to regulate Indian gaming continued. The two primary legislative approaches illustrated the split between the Department of the Interior, favoring gaming as an engine of economic development, and the Department of Justice, favoring those states hoping to subject tribal gaming to their authority.

Following *Cabazon*, many states, as well as non-Indian gaming interests, feared a rapid expansion of Indian gaming. Therefore, they applied pressure on Congress to impose additional regulatory control over Indian gaming. States that relied on gaming for revenue feared competitors that did not have to pay state taxes. Other states feared that Indian gaming operations, free of the requirements faced by non-Indian concerns, enjoyed too great a competitive advantage. States that prohibited gaming altogether feared the social consequences of widespread gaming. Indian Country lobbied to protect this important economic development opportunity for tribes and to protect Indian gaming from state regulation and taxation. Several pressures, including the immediate response of the states to *Cabazon*, combined to maneuver Congress toward a legislative compromise in the form of the Indian Gaming Regulatory Act (IGRA).

Today IGRA regulates all Indian gaming and provides the framework for the agreements that tribes and states negotiate to facilitate gaming. Meant to achieve a principal goal of federal Indian policy, which is to promote tribal economic development, tribal self-sufficiency, and strong tribal government, IGRA mirrors the Supreme Court's holding in *Cabazon* that Indian tribes have the exclusive right to regulate gaming activity on Indian lands if the gaming activity is not specifically prohibited by federal law and is conducted within a state that does not, as a matter of criminal law and public policy, prohibit such gaming activity. Created under Congress's Indian Commerce Clause power, IGRA preempts state prohibition or regulation of Indian gaming on Indian land. Although IGRA seems to have settled many matters, states, tribes, and the federal government often still disagree over its application.

The act's purpose was to provide the framework for gaming on Indian reservations, to regulate Indian gaming, and to allay concerns that organized crime would find a haven on Indian reservations, which some viewed as lawless enclaves. Importantly, Congress has recognized that gaming is "an economic activity that Indian tribes can develop and that [the tribes] should be the primary beneficiary of their efforts." IGRA's "Declaration of Policy" reflects the three major concerns behind its adoption. First, Congress wished to relieve the federal government of some of its financial obligations to tribes by promoting economic development and self-sufficiency through gaming revenues. Second, Congress believed federal regulation of Indian gaming was required to "shield it from organized crime" and to ensure that tribal members were the primary beneficiaries of gaming revenue. Third, Congress desired to establish an independent regulatory agency, the National Indian

Gaming Commission (NIGC), with oversight authority to define and enforce national standards. Part of that standardization involved the classification of gaming operations:

- Class I gaming encompasses traditional games used in ceremonial and social settings that are outside the scope of any but tribal regulation and control.
- Class II gaming includes bingo and bingo-like games. Also included in class II are card games not explicitly prohibited by the state, provided they are otherwise in conformity with all state laws and regulations.
- Class III gaming consists of all gaming that is not class I or II. This class is the area of most contention since it is the most profitable class of gaming. This class includes so-called "Vegas-style" games, such as house-banked card games, roulette, slot machines, and the like. Under IGRA, class III gaming operations must be conducted under a tribal-state compact. IGRA notes that such compacts may provide for the assessment by the state of such activities in such amounts as are necessary to defray the costs of regulating such activity. Nothing in this section shall be interpreted, however, as conferring upon a state or any of its political subdivisions' authority to impose any tax, fee, charge, or other assessment upon an Indian tribe or upon any other person or entity authorized by an Indian tribe to engage in a class III activity.

The tribe initiates the compacting process by requesting that the state in which the casino is to be located negotiate a tribal-state compact outlining the terms of such gaming. If the state agrees to negotiate, the parties have sixty days to come to an agreement. The compact is then submitted to the secretary of the interior for approval. If the parties cannot reach an agreement, mechanisms exist for developing procedures to regulate gaming operations on a given reservation, even in the absence of a compact. As originally enacted, IGRA required that the states bargain in good faith regarding the content of gaming compacts and gave tribes a federal cause of action to compel negotiation once 180 days had passed from the original request.

A FRAMEWORK FOR ANALYZING TRIBAL-STATE NEGOTIATIONS

Whenever a tribe's success depends on the decisions and actions of other governmental parties who have different interests, negotiation or negotiation-like processes may be inevitable. Although gaming compacts garner most of the headlines, negotiated agreements between tribes and states that resolve jurisdictional or substantive disputes and recognize each entity's sovereignty can cover a wide range of issues. The processes of interaction range from formal to informal and from explicit to tacit. The goal of the processes may be reaching a legally binding compact or arriving at a temporary mutual understanding subject to renegotiation. Broadly speaking, negotiation is a process of potentially opportunistic interaction aimed at advancing the full set of one's interests by jointly decided action. To be effective at negotiating, the tribe must persuade the state to say yes to a proposal that meets all of the tribe's real interests and mean it. Of course, the state is trying to accomplish the same objective. Basically, each side is trying to solve its *basic negotiation problem*, which is how best to advance one's full interests, either by improving and accepting the available deal or opting for its best no-deal alternative.

Three core elements make up each side's basic negotiation problem: (1) the importance of underlying interests as the raw material for negotiation; (2) the implication that negotiation is a means for advancing interests, rather than an end in itself, implying that other noncooperative means compete with negotiated possibilities; and (3) the fact that negotiation seeks jointly decided action and thus inherently is a process of joint problem solving. Essentially, to advance the tribe's real interests, tribal negotiators must assess what "yes" they want from the state and why the state might say it rather than opt for no-deal. The tribe's approach should influence how the state sees its basic negotiation problem such that what the state chooses—for the tribe's reasons—is precisely what serves the tribe's interests. The fundamental principle of effective negotiation is the art of letting them have *your* way for reasons that they perceive to be their own.

INTERESTS: THE RAW MATERIAL FOR NEGOTIATION

The concept of *interests* is foundational to effective negotiation. Tribal interests in a negotiation are whatever the tribe cares about that is at stake in the process. Socrates' admonition to "know thyself" lies at the core of effective deal making, along with its worthy twin to "know thy counterpart." Since negotiation requires at least two parties to say yes for a deal, the tribe must probe the full set of the other parties' interests and also examine its own tribal interests. The best negotiators are clear on their ultimate interests as well as other side's interests. They also know their possible trade-offs among lesser interests and are flexible and creative on the means. Interests visible at the surface may hide deeper interests that could be critical to a successful negotiation, so good negotiators also probe negotiating positions to identify and understand those deeper interests. *Issues* are on the table for explicit agreement. *Positions* are each party's stands on the issues. *Interests* are the underlying concerns that resolution ultimately affects.

Consider an example involving a power company that proposed building a significant dam to bring electricity at lower rates to the area's consumers and to demonstrate to the financial community that it could get large projects completed despite having been repeatedly stymied in these efforts. Predictably, environmentalists opposed the plan, claiming that it would damage the downstream habitat of the endangered whooping crane. Farm groups also lined up against the project, fearing that the dam would reduce waterflow in the area, yet the power company needed results and a greener image. The issue was the dam; positions on that issue were "absolutely yes" and "no way." Yet incompatible positions masked compatible interests. Although years of negotiations among these groups focused on their conflicting positions, the parties ultimately reached an agreement for a smaller dam, streamflow guarantees, and a trust fund for preserving the downstream and other endangered habitats of the whooping crane. Rather than a convergence of positions, this agreement represented a reconciliation of interests.

While neglecting to think through the perspective of the other side is an error, a related problem is to assume that one side's interests are the opposite of the other side's interests. Psychologists who have studied negotiating behavior have discovered this assumption to be a pervasive tendency and dubbed it the "mythical fixed pie" (Bazerman and Neale 1992). Yet in looking for a richer set of interests of all sides behind their incompatible positions, the differences of interest point the way to mutual advantage, thereby expanding the pie. In a simple example, two siblings quarrel over where to cut an orange (the issue), with each demanding three-quarters of it (their incompatible positions). If one turns out to be hungry while the other sibling needs flavoring for a recipe (their underlying interests), however, the siblings can devise a creative solution that meets both interests: the orange can be peeled with the fruit going to the hungry one and the rind to the cook. By discovering that one sibling was hungry while the other sibling needed flavoring, both siblings can be made better off because of the difference in their underlying interests.

In short, interests constitute the raw material for negotiation. Tribal negotiators should assess and attach priorities to the full set of tribal interests, not a narrow subset. Similarly, they should assess not only tribal interests but also the full set of the other side's interests, including relevant internal parties. Furthermore, the underlying interests of each side must be distinguished from the issues on the table for negotiation and the positions the parties take on those issues. Rather than asking, "What's your position?" and asserting, "Here's our position," negotiators should instead seek directly and indirectly to understand what real interests lie behind those positions. Finally, the parties should not stop with shared interests but instead seek complementary *differences* that can be dovetailed into joint gains.

NEGOTIATION AS A MEANS OF ADVANCING INTERESTS

Apart from what different tactics and approaches may yield at the bargaining table, a crucial question involves what Fisher and Ury (2011) have dubbed each side's Best Alternative To Negotiated Agreement (BATNA). The BATNA, or no-agreement alternative, reflects the course of action a party would take if the proposed deal were not possible. Depending on the situation, one party's BATNA may involve walking away without any agreement or going to court rather than settling. It may involve forming a different coalition or alliance, going on strike, or any number of other contextual alternatives to negotiation. If asked to agree to a particular deal, assessing the BATNA sharpens the decision by asking "as compared to what?"

The value of the BATNA to the tribe sets the threshold of the full set of its interests that any acceptable agreement must exceed. Similarly, the state will have its own BATNA. Doing "better" in terms of each party's interests compared to the BATNA is a necessary condition for an agreement. As such, BATNAs imply the existence or absence of a Zone of Possible Agreement (ZOPA) and determine its location (Mnookin et al. 2000). Of course, each side knows only its own limits and must assess and update its assessment of the other side's BATNA. And in practice many negotiators have a hazy sense of their own BATNAs. Improving one's own BATNA or worsening the other side's BATNA often influences the outcome of the negotiation. The better one side's BATNA appears to it and the other party, the more credible the threat is to walk away unless the deal is improved. Instead of further refining tactics at the table, parties sometimes should act away from the table to improve their BATNA. Thus an analysis of BATNAs furnishes an important guide to the potential role for negotiation as well as the extent to which each side should spend scarce resources at the table trying to improve a potential deal or away from the table seeking a better one.

NEGOTIATION AS A JOINT PROBLEM-SOLVING PROCESS

Many problems are single decision-maker situations where the judgments or actions of others should not affect an individual's judgments or actions. Yet negotiation distinguishes itself from such problems by the parties' interdependence. The actions of each side leading to agreement have the potential to affect the outcome; thus their interaction leads to a joint decision-making process. Each side faces the same basic negotiation problem: given the choice of agreement or no agreement, how can one best advance the full set of his or her own interests relative to the best no-agreement alternative? The other party's problem is a mirror image: by the choice of agreement or no agreement, how can they best advance the full set of their interests relative to their BATNA? Since they will say yes for their reasons and not for their counterpart's reasons, agreement means joint problem solving, addressing their problem as a means to solving one's own. In these terms, the essential task is getting the state to see the basic elements of their problem such that the tribe's preferred agreement is what the state chooses for its own reasons. In this sense, negotiation is a form of "selfish altruism," or using the solution to the state's problem as the route to solving the tribe's problem.

Remembering that negotiation is the art of letting them have *your* way, the challenge is to try to shape how the other side sees their problem such that they choose what *you* want. To change the other side's mind, it is important to know where their mind is *now*. Then it is possible to build what classic Chinese strategist Sun Tzu called a "golden bridge" from where they are now to where you want them to be. The fact that negotiation is inherently a joint problem-solving exercise should ensure that solving one side's problem—as they see it or can be induced to see it—is a part of solving the problem of the other side. Having assessed the full set of each side's interests, as distinct from their positions, and having estimated their BATNAs, the fundamental principle of effective negotiation points to the essential strategy: shape how the other parties see their basic problem such that, for their reasons, they choose what your side wants.

DEVELOPING A NEGOTIATION STRATEGY

The core concepts—interests, BATNAs, and joint problem solving—play roles within a larger framework of negotiation analysis. Solving the joint problem requires both creating and claiming value on a sustainable basis. "Creating value" means "expanding the pie" or increasing the worth of the agreement to each side beyond what was otherwise available. "Claiming value" means distributing or apportioning that value among the parties. By being "on a sustainable basis," an agreement is more valuable to the extent it endures and remains healthy. Moreover, the bargaining techniques employed should not damage the party's reputation and undercut its capacity to negotiate in the future.

To facilitate this goal, Lax and Sebenius (2006) have developed a "3-D negotiating strategy," which involves acting in a mutually reinforcing way among three core dimensions of the joint problem: (1) during the interpersonal process "at the table"; (2) with respect to the substance of value creation; and (3) "away from the table" to change the game so it is most likely to yield optimum results. This strategy is not a recipe or a sequential approach whose "dimensions" are independent of one another. Instead, the approach involves cycling through these factors on a provisional basis to determine the most relevant and promising opportunities. Then, as analysis deepens and the process unfolds, the negotiator needs to update his or her assessments and overall negotiating approach. A framework leading to an effective 3-D negotiating strategy starts with an overview of the relevant context and then assesses both the opportunities for and the barriers to creating and claiming value. Barriers and opportunities arise as a function of the structural, personal, and ordered aspects of the situation.

THE CASE OF THE MASHANTUCKET PEQUOTS: NEGOTIATING SLOTS AT FOXWOODS

Although the Lax and Sebenius (2006) framework gives prescriptive advice for approaching a negotiation, it also provides useful tools for analyzing a concluded negotiation, such as the negotiations between the Mashantucket Pequots and Connecticut.

ROUND 1: THE INITIAL CASINO NEGOTIATIONS

In early 1989, after the passage of IGRA, the Pequots announced that they intended to build a casino alongside their bingo hall. The tribe sought to negotiate a compact with Connecticut, but officials declined. The attorney general took the position that Connecticut law did not allow casino gambling, and thus the state could not grant the tribe's request for a compact. Connecticut law, however, did allow "Las Vegas nights"—that is, play-money fundraisers run by nonprofit or charitable organizations that featured such casino games as blackjack and roulette. The Pequots argued that if the state permitted other organizations to run casino-type games, the tribe had the legal right under IGRA to do so. To force the state government to the negotiating table, the Pequots filed suit against Connecticut on November 3, 1989. The stage was set for the first battle for the Foxwoods casino.

Context of the initial negotiations

When approaching a negotiation, the parties must address its relevant context. A nonexclusive list of contextual factors includes economic, competitive, historical, political, institutional, and organizational matters. A good assessment of the setting is neither complete nor exhaustive but gives a useful sense of the involved and potentially involved parties, perceptions of their interests, and the nature of the process by which they are interacting. In short, assessing a negotiation's relevant context entails looking at the setting to see its implications for structure and psychology as well as the elements available for efforts to change the game.

In March 1989 the Pequots requested that state officials negotiate a gambling compact with them. When Connecticut officials refused, the Pequots sued the state in US District Court in Hartford. They claimed that the state had failed to negotiate in good faith with the tribe. Judge Peter Dorsey ruled in the Pequots' favor in May 1990 and ordered the state to negotiate a compact with the tribe within sixty days. Connecticut officials appealed the ruling to the Second US Circuit Court of Appeals in New York but lost again. Bound by Dorsey's ruling, state officials began to negotiate a compact with the Pequots. Outside gaming interests, particularly from Nevada and Atlantic City, lurked in the background, fearful that a Pequot victory would open the floodgates for Indian casinos in other parts of the country. Furthermore, the local towns near the reservation, bitter over being "blindsided" by the initial Pequot land claims litigation, were hostile toward tribal interests. They argued that allowing the tribe to expand its gaming operations beyond bingo by opening a casino would negatively impact them, regardless of whether that casino included slot machines. While the Pequots wanted to expand their gaming operations, they also wanted to ensure that the state of Connecticut respected them as a separate sovereign. Another goal was to prevent the state from taxing their gaming revenues. While the tribe's sovereignty meant that it could control liquor-use policies, the degree of state police presence, and any procedures for licensing casino employees on the reservation, those interests were subordinate to the primary objective of running a casino that was as profitable as possible.

Opportunities and barriers of the initial negotiations

Similar to the example explained earlier of squabbling sibling peeling the orange, the Pequots saw an opportunity to create and claim value by focusing on differences. The state's top priority was to prevent crime from infiltrating the casino and the Ledyard area, while the Pequots' primary objective was to run a successful casino. Michael Brown, the lead negotiator for the Pequots, decided he could offer the state the authority to regulate drug and alcohol use and implement crime-control measures at the Ledyard casino. In exchange, Brown demanded that the Pequots have control over the casino's business aspects, unrestricted by limits on the number of gaming tables, square footage of floor space, or operating hours.

Brown opened the negotiations by suggesting that in running the casino the Pequots would comply voluntarily with all state liquor laws. He made it clear that the tribe would be willing to make additional concessions if the state would yield on regulating the casino's business operations. State negotiators agreed to an unlimited number of gaming tables, unconstrained floor space, and unrestricted operating hours. In return, Brown and the Pequots agreed to allow state police to patrol the casino and to require that all employees be approved and licensed by the State Department of Special Revenue. The Pequots would retain all casino profits after reimbursing the state for money spent on regulation.

Although a number of issues had been resolved, the two sides failed to complete an agreement by Dorsey's August 6 deadline. Dorsey brought in a federal mediator, retired state superior court judge Henry J. Naruk, to expedite the process of drafting a compact. By October negotiations differed on only one major issue. The Pequots wanted to operate slot machines, often a casino's most lucrative revenue source. The state claimed that the tribe could not operate slots because state law prohibited slot machines. As an interim measure, Brown successfully pressed to negotiate a hundred-page appendix to the compact—approximately one-third of the entire agreement—which addressed future regulation of slot machines. The Pequots and the state agreed to a moratorium on the use of slot machines at the casino.

In mid-October the Pequot legal team suggested to Naruk that he accept the state's version of the compact. The state, meanwhile, had appealed Dorsey's decision to allow gambling on the reservation to the US Supreme Court. With its appeal pending, Connecticut refused to sign the compact it had submitted to Naruk, who nonetheless delivered the unsigned compact to Manuel Lujan Jr., secretary of the Department of the Interior. After making several minor changes, Lujan approved the agreement that the Pequots and Connecticut had negotiated and that Naruk had delivered. Because Connecticut had refused to sign the document, it did not qualify as a tribal-state compact. Instead, Lujan promulgated it as a federal procedure governing the operation of a casino on the Ledyard reservation. Thus the state and the Pequots had no compact; gambling on the reservation was governed exclusively by the procedures of the agreement. The Supreme Court refused to hear Connecticut's appeal, and Dorsey's decision stood. The state would have to endorse a compact with the Pequots or accept gambling regulations for the Pequot reservation that Lujan created. Connecticut had taken its legal battle as far as it could and lost. Almost immediately, the tribe broke ground for its forty-six-thousand-square-foot casino.

Strategic activities of the initial negotiations

In this first round each side chose its BATNA instead of reaching an agreement. As a result, the Pequots could initiate gaming operations but could not install slot machines, which would be the most lucrative component to a gaming operation. Both sides realized that more rounds were to come, however, and each party took steps away from the table to improve its own BATNA while attempting to weaken the other side's BATNA. After Judge Naruk submitted the compact to Secretary Lujan, but before the casino opened, the general election in Connecticut changed the players at the table, and a new governor, opposed to gambling in general and slots in particular, now sat at the table. Governor Lowell Weicker made it clear that his top priority, given the sordid history of Connecticut gaming, was to prevent crime from infiltrating the casino and the surrounding area.

Weicker's first effort to thwart the Pequots' casino involved moving the fight against reservation gambling from the federal court system to the state legislature. In early 1991, shortly after he took office, Weicker drafted a bill calling for the repeal of the state law permitting "Las Vegas night" fundraising events by charities. If passed, the bill would strip the Pequots of the legal basis for their casino. To galvanize opposition to the bill, the Pequots hired lobbyists to work the corridors of the state senate and house of representatives to create support for the tribe among lawmakers. Also siding with the Pequots and speaking out against the measure were civic groups, parochial schools, and charities, which together raised over $80,000 through "Las Vegas night" events in 1990. In addition, business leaders in southern Connecticut opposed Weicker's proposal, arguing that a Pequot casino would provide a welcome boost to the regional economy that was reeling from defense-industry cutbacks and a national recession. In a University of Connecticut survey of state residents, 68 percent of those polled supported the Pequots' right to open a casino on their Ledyard reservation.

Out-of-state gambling interests feared that Indian casinos might expand beyond Connecticut, so they deployed powerful lobbyists of their own to support Weicker's bill. In May 1991 the state senate approved the measure in an eighteen to seventeen vote; the house later voted eighty-four to sixty-two to reject the governor's proposal. Without the support of a majority in both the senate and the house, the bill was dead. During all of the legislative maneuvering, the Pequots enhanced their position by building their casino and hiring and training employees. Foxwoods opened for business in February 1992 with twenty-three hundred employees. The fifty-one poker tables were kept busy with out-of-town visitors because Foxwoods was the only casino in the eastern United States that accommodated poker players. Slot machines were still conspicuously absent, however.

Ten months later, the casino had not yet spent a single hour closed; customers were gambling twenty-four hours a day. Each day approximately thirteen thousand people flocked to Foxwoods to place off-track bets and to play blackjack, craps, roulette, baccarat, bingo, and poker. Foxwoods was often so crowded that patrons had to wait hours for a seat at the gaming tables. To service the crush of eager gamblers, the Pequot tribe had to augment its casino workforce. Within ten months the casino had ballooned to thirty-five hundred employees, constituting a $60 million payroll. In its first year in operation the booming casino was on its way to generating significantly more than the $100 million in gross revenue that had been projected. Demand was so great that in July of 1992, only five months after Foxwoods opened, the Pequots embarked on a $142 million expansion of the complex.

ROUND 2: NEGOTIATING SLOTS AT FOXWOODS

Context of negotiating slots at Foxwoods

When Governor Weicker took office in 1991, he inherited a financial crisis. Projections indicated that for the 1990–91 fiscal year ending June 30, Connecticut would incur a deficit between $800 million and $1 billion, its fourth consecutive year of deficits. Furthermore, revenue and spending estimates for the 1991–92 fiscal year suggested that unless the state took corrective action, it faced a deficit of approximately $2.7 billion in its $7.8 billion budget, the largest shortfall for any state in the country. In large measure a deep national recession had caused significant fiscal woes for Connecticut. The state had historically derived more than half its revenue from an 8 percent sales tax and taxes on corporate income. Now Weicker—after one month in office—proposed a personal income tax, which was enacted into law.

Although the state expected the personal income tax would eliminate much of the budget shortfall, it was an unproven source of revenue, and estimates of the amount it would generate varied. Most agreed, though, that the new tax alone would not be enough to close the gap in Connecticut's finances. To balance the budget, the state would have to make deep and unpopular cuts in government expenditures. The combination of a new income tax and severe spending cuts enabled Connecticut to achieve a budget surplus in 1991–92 for the first time in five years. Feeling optimistic and sensing that the public was weary of sacrifice, Weicker promised legislators in the spring of 1992 that he would not raise taxes for the remainder of his term. Despite the 1992 budget surplus, however, economic conditions in Connecticut continued to deteriorate. In January 1992 the state's unemployment rate reached 7.5 percent, the highest it had been in a decade. That year, both General Dynamics and Pratt & Whitney announced significant layoffs, which resulted in thousands of additional job losses at the Connecticut companies that supplied materials to those companies.

As layoffs continued unabated around the state, Connecticut budget officials pared back their tax-revenue forecasts. Estimates of tax collections fell so sharply that by December 1992 the legislature's Office of Fiscal Analysis projected a shortfall of $424 million for the 1993–94 fiscal year on a budget of approximately $8 billion, assuming existing programs were maintained and expenditures were adjusted only for inflation. Having promised not to raise taxes and aware that lawmakers had little appetite for further spending cuts, Weicker and the General Assembly had no choice but to produce a balanced budget for the 1993–94 fiscal year. Meanwhile, in the southeast corner of the state, the Pequots were building a casino that looked as if it would become a goldmine. Unfortunately for Weicker and Connecticut legislators, the state could not tax profits the casino earned. For all the excitement the Pequots' casino generated, the state would not share in the spoils, but the Pequots' success quickly attracted other gambling interests to the state.

By the fall of 1992, Weicker, who remained opposed to legalized gambling, faced mounting political pressure kindled by commercial gambling heavyweights. Trump, Bally, Harrah's, and Mirage lobbied state legislators to secure licenses for non-Indian casinos. Mirage owner Stephen Wynn made particularly aggressive overtures to the state, promising to create jobs and provide attractive tax benefits. Wynn pointed out that the state treasury was missing out on the gambling boom at Foxwoods because the Pequots were neither required to pay taxes on their casino's profits or their personal earnings nor were non-Indian employees paying a significant portion of the state income tax. In March 1992, Wynn treated four Connecticut lawmakers to an all-expenses-paid weekend at his opulent Mirage resort and casino in Las Vegas. There he unveiled an architectural blueprint for the $350 million casino he hoped to open in Hartford, and he discussed the possibility of opening a second casino in Bridgeport. Harrah's and other gambling concerns followed suit, revealing their own plans for Connecticut casinos.

The movement to legalize casino gambling in Connecticut gathered steam. With many Connecticut residents supportive of casinos, introduction of a bill during the upcoming legislative session permitting expanded gambling in the state seemed almost certain. To Weicker, gambling on the Pequot reservation no longer posed the greatest threat to a healthy social environment in Connecticut. Foxwoods, after all, had not given rise to drugs, prostitution, or other crime problems in Ledyard. The real threat, in the governor's view, was the corporate-sponsored movement to legalize casinos throughout the state. Casino operators from Las Vegas and Atlantic City continued to woo state and local officials, hoping to win the right to build gambling and entertainment complexes in Hartford and Bridgeport. They promised jobs and revenue for Connecticut and its two largest cities. The state's legal jai alai frontons and dog track, which were struggling financially, also lobbied for slot machines. A specially assembled State Casino Gambling Task Force scheduled a vote in early January 1993 on whether to recommend that the legislature legalize casino gambling.

Opportunities and barriers of negotiating slots at Foxwoods

In late 1992, Michael Brown, the Pequots' lead negotiator, learned that Connecticut was facing a $424 million budget shortfall for the 1993–94 fiscal year. The governor and the legislature were required to agree on a balanced budget by July 1, 1993. In response, Brown suggested that the Pequots could help the state make up the budgetary shortfall in exchange for the right to operate slot machines at Foxwoods, but with a twist. The Pequot payments would be conditional on tribal exclusivity for the operation of slot machines in the state. By granting the Pequots exclusive slot machine operation in exchange for voluntary payments from the tribe to the state the governor would simultaneously be able to contain the spread of gambling while sharply and relatively painlessly reducing the budget gap. The tribal council supported Brown's proposal.

Although the governor was intrigued, he was unwilling to sign a state budget partially funded by a percentage of the uncertain revenues of a casino. Weicker insisted that the Pequots guarantee a minimum annual payment of 25 percent of annual slot machine revenues or $100 million, whichever was greater. Even then concerns remained, but over the next few weeks the Pequots' legal counsel and the governor's office drew up a seven-page memorandum of understanding that would permit the Pequots to operate slot machines exclusively in exchange for guaranteed payments to the state. On January 5, the eighteen-member State Casino Gambling Task Force voted in favor of recommending that the state legislature approve non-Indian casinos in Hartford and Bridgeport. The task force also recommended that the state legalize video slot machines at casinos, jai alai frontons, dog tracks, and off-track betting parlors.

On January 13 the governor invited the media to a press conference to witness the signing of the memorandum of understanding he had negotiated with the Pequots. The agreement was a surprise to the public. Many legislators were stunned by the governor's unilateral action that preempted pro-corporate gambling measures they were about to undertake. The agreement permitted the Pequot tribe to install an unlimited number of video slot machines at the Foxwoods casino. In return, the Pequots would pay the state $30 million by the end of Connecticut's fiscal year on June 30, 1993. In subsequent years the tribe would pay the state $100 million or 25 percent of slot machine revenues, whichever was greater. If the state ever permitted any other organization to operate slot machines in Connecticut, the Pequots would no longer be required to make payments to the state. With the agreement in place, legalization of slot machines anywhere in Connecticut other than Foxwoods would cause the state to lose at least $100 million in guaranteed annual revenue, and even more if Foxwoods's slot machine revenue projections proved accurate. On January 16, 1993, the Pequots installed the first one hundred video slot machines at Foxwoods. In the first week that slot machines were operational, casino attendance increased by 60 percent.

Strategic activities of negotiating slots at Foxwoods

Having built Governor Weicker a "golden bridge," the Pequots enticed him to join their side of the table. Implementation of the agreement was far from certain, and the newly realigned sides continued efforts to improve their respective BATNAs while weakening those of their opponents. Legislators who liked the idea of expanded gambling in the state would be reluctant to sanction new casinos, for doing so would put an end to guaranteed payments from the Pequots. After installing more than a thousand slot machines at Foxwoods, on June 30, 1993, the Pequots delivered $30 million to Connecticut's Department of Special Revenue, pursuant to the agreement. The tribe's slot machines had been in operation since February and were one of the primary reasons that revenue at Foxwoods grew from $120 million in the casino's first year to nearly $1 billion in its second year.

Meanwhile, the state legislature still haggled over a budget for the 1993–94 fiscal year. The state constitution required that the legislature submit a balanced budget for the approaching fiscal year by midnight on July 1. On that morning, however, the budget reflected a shortfall of $13 million, and legislators were no longer willing to compromise on spending. Desperate, the speakers of the house and senate called Michael Brown, pleading with him to persuade the Pequot tribe to increase its minimum guaranteed payment to the state from $100 million to $113 million for the next fiscal year only. In the afternoon Brown met tribal leaders and convinced them that by voluntarily increasing their guarantee payment by $13 million in a time of fiscal crisis, the Pequots could lock up the support of the legislative branch. In a discussion that lasted fewer than five minutes, the tribal council agreed to pledge an additional $13 million to the state. The legislature prepared a bill documenting this special, onetime arrangement and passed a balanced budget before the midnight deadline. The Pequots demanded nothing in return for the increased payment guarantee. Over the course of the next year, the Pequots undertook massive expansion projects at the newly renamed Foxwoods Resort Casino. By the end of 1993, Foxwoods had 234 table games, 3,108 slot machines, and 139,000 square feet of gaming space. By 1995 more than thirty thousand people were visiting the casino every day. It was reported to be the world's largest and most profitable casino.

MAJOR SHIFTS IN THE NEGOTIATION LANDSCAPE

Given the enormous success of Foxwoods, tribes from all over the United States began to push for gaming compacts. Sometimes those compacts came easily, and other times the states were obstructionist. Each side made moves "away from the table" either to improve their position or to worsen the other side's BATNA. One portion of IGRA that gained scrutiny and created immediate conflict between states and tribes was the good-faith bargaining provision. Since that section of IGRA forced states to the negotiating table, altering that requirement was a logical area for a state to focus its strategic efforts.

SEMINOLE TRIBE V. FLORIDA (517 U.S. 44 [1996]):
THE STATES ADJUST THEIR BATNAS

In September 1991 the Seminole Tribe of Florida sued the state of Florida, alleging the state had refused to enter into any negotiation for inclusion of certain gaming activities in a tribal-state compact, thereby violating IGRA's requirement of good-faith negotiation. Florida responded by arguing that the suit violated the state's sovereign immunity from suit in federal court. After procedural battles in the lower courts, the parties appealed the case to the US Supreme Court. After finding that Congress had abrogated the state's Eleventh Amendment immunity from suit, the Court held in a five-four decision that Congress had acted beyond its Constitutional power when it made states subject to suit for bargaining in bad faith with tribes over gaming compacts.

Commentators have criticized the *Seminole Tribe v. Florida* decision on a number of theoretical grounds (Clarkson and Sebenius 2012), but from a practical standpoint the decision disrupted IGRA's compromise, as states were now immune from suit even if they were lacking good faith in the negotiation of gaming compacts. This shift in the negotiation landscape allowed states to demand a large share of tribal gaming proceeds, which was not IGRA's intent. Former NIGC general counsel Kevin Washburn noted the difficulty of reconciling the intention of Congress and the resulting compacting process designed "to give states a voice in Indian gaming" and not a "cut of the profits" (Washburn 2002, 7–8). In addition, *Seminole Tribe* defanged IGRA by removing the only tool tribes possessed to ensure the exercise of their right to force states to sit at the negotiating table. The economic consequences were obvious with states negotiating fewer compacts and taking a much tougher line (Brietzke and Kline 1999).

ADJUSTMENTS TO TRIBAL BATNAS

Subsequent attempts have tried to rebalance the situation. In response to *Seminole Tribe v. Florida*, the secretary of the interior promulgated regulations permitting tribal gaming in the absence of state agreement. In addition, the Department of Interior implemented a policy of refusing to approve compacts that incorporate revenue sharing if the state does not provide a substantial level of exclusivity to the tribe. This policy gives the tribes an additional bargaining angle if the state gets too greedy in asking for a percentage of Indian gaming revenues. Perhaps more influential on the tribal BATNA is the technological progression of gaming machines. Although class II gaming originally was conceived of as bingo, enterprising tribes and gaming equipment developers worked to simulate the "class III experience" but used technology that fell within the scope of class II gaming. The inner workings of such equipment were based on a bingo-style simulation, but the user interface attempted to approximate a slot machine or other video gaming device that ordinarily would fall under class III. This development was possible because the definition of class II allowed such games to be played using a computer, an electronic device, or other technological aid.

As class II gaming technology becomes more sophisticated, the distinction between these machines and true class III machines diminishes. Such machines can be considered "class II.9" machines, and their profitability approaches that of true class III machines. Since class II gaming does not require a tribal-state compact, a tribe could open a casino with exclusively class II.9 machines and cut the state out of any revenue share whatsoever if a state refused to negotiate in good faith on class III machines. Thus, while the relative bargaining strength may have shifted toward the state after *Seminole Tribe v. Florida*, the Code of Federal Regulations and the technological advancement of gaming equipment have caused the pendulum to swing back toward the tribes.

ECONOMIC EXIGENCIES: THE SENECA COMPACT

New York faced an acute budget situation in 2001, which prompted Governor George Pataki to enter into gaming compact negotiations with the Seneca Nation of Indians of western New York. By the summer of 2001 negotiators for both sides agreed to a memorandum of understanding establishing the broad parameters of a deal. The governor's Democratic opponents in the Assembly sought to impose labor regulations on the Seneca Nation's gambling operations, sidetracking early agreements. This intrusion on sovereignty was unacceptable to the Seneca, who appealed to the governor to work for the deal they had struck. The aftermath of the terrorist attacks on September 11, 2001, exacerbated the budget situation, and the governor became even more interested in a deal. He needed revenue for his budget as well as economic development in upstate New York for his popularity. He indicated his belief that he would "need a Connecticut deal" to drive a compact through Albany. Leaders and lobbyists for the Seneca realized they faced a closing window of opportunity to secure a major gambling compact for western New York.

Asked by the governor for a substantial revenue share, Seneca negotiators indicated the state would, like any other equity partner, have to contribute something to make the compact feasible. Seneca negotiators, using language in the Seneca Land Claims Settlement Act authorizing repurchase of land-into-trust, negotiated to get the state to sell for one dollar the downtown Convention Center and thirteen surrounding acres in Niagara Falls, to agree to use eminent domain to help secure another fifty acres, to support the Seneca's efforts to transfer these lands into trust, to establish a fifty-mile zone of exclusivity for the life of the compact, and to assume in its entirety the burden of satisfying county and municipal governments. Furthermore, tribal negotiators demonstrated that a 25 percent revenue share would cripple the deal, proposing instead a graduated schedule of increasing revenue share averaging around 17.5 percent for the life of the compact, with years eight through fourteen at 25 percent. The Seneca Nation also had the right, by the terms of the compact, to open and operate two additional class III gaming operations. Finally, as with Foxwoods, should the exclusivity provisions be breached, all revenue sharing obligations would disappear.

In her letter authorizing the compact, Secretary of the Interior Gale Norton pointed to the substantial financial concessions offered to the state as justifying the state's substantial share of the revenue. Unlike other compacts negotiated by cash-strapped states, which the secretary rejected under IGRA, the provision of real assets by the state helped convince Secretary Norton to permit the high state revenue share. All parties demonstrated their good faith in negotiations, and both parties to the compact gained substantial economic rewards.

CONCLUSION

Although the *Seminole Tribe* decision eviscerated IGRA's mechanism for balancing tribal and state interests, tribes are still able to negotiate gaming compacts that advance tribal interests. The agreement concluded between the Seneca Nation and New York is an example of a post-*Seminole* agreement where the tribe applied the lessons from Foxwoods. Although a successful outcome may have required a heightened level of strategic negotiation acumen on the part of the tribe, the Seneca Nation was able to negotiate a deal to open a casino on the shores of Niagara Falls on land essentially given to them to build the casino. Although much of this chapter has focused on the negotiation dynamics surrounding gaming compacts, the strategic lessons from these negotiations are nonetheless applicable beyond the gaming context. For example, the most recent bargaining challenge for the Pequots is not with Connecticut but instead with the bondholders who have lent money to the tribe's gaming operations. While Foxwoods remains one of the largest casinos in the United States, it was nonetheless hit by the economic downturn in 2008 just like the rest of the gaming industry. As a result, the tribe sought to restructure nearly $2 billion in debt.

Unlike traditional corporate gaming companies, however, Foxwoods and its bondholders do not have the complete set of restructuring tools at their disposal. Because of the sovereign status of the tribe and the prohibition of nontribal ownership of tribal casinos, Foxwoods could not do a debt-for-equity swap or raise additional capital by selling off assets on tribal trust land. While corporate gaming creditors may have the option of operating a gaming facility after the gaming operator seeks protection in bankruptcy, tribes are not eligible for relief under the bankruptcy code, in part because IGRA mandates that the tribe has the "sole proprietary interest and responsibility for the conduct of any gaming activity," thus preventing bondholders from assuming control of an Indian gaming facility (25 U.S.C. §2710[b][2][A]). In addition, as mentioned in chapter 5 on business law, tribes do not fit into any of the categories of debtor under Section 109 of the Bankruptcy Code, and thus reorganization under bankruptcy is not an option. The only option is a negotiated restructuring with the various classes of bondholders.

The Pequots and their creditors are not the first to face this challenge. The Poaque Pueblo and Little Traverse Bay Band of Odawa Indians also had to negotiate a restructuring of their bond obligations. Although a detailed analysis of the respective BATNAs of the various parties in these restructuring negotiations is beyond the scope of this chapter, the underlying negotiation principles remain the same. In fact, in a post-*Seminole* world where tribes cannot force states to the bargaining table, gaming compact negotiations arguably have become more like nongaming negotiations, where advancing the full set of one's interests requires jointly decided action. The story of Foxwoods provides excellent examples of both types of negotiations.

DISCUSSION

1. Identify and describe the three categories of Indian gaming, including which require a compact.
2. Describe the basic negotiation problem present in the Pequots' negotiations with Connecticut.
3. Is negotiating on behalf of a tribe different than negotiating on behalf of a non-Indian organization, and if so, how?
4. Is Indian gaming a good thing, and if so, why? If not, why not?

References

Bazerman, M. H., and M. A. Neale. 1992. *Negotiating Rationally*. New York: Free Press.

Brietzke, P. H., and T. L. Kline. 1999. *The Law and Economics of Native American Casinos*. *Nebraska Law Review* 78: 263.

Clarkson, G., and J. Sebenius. 2012. "Leveraging Tribal Sovereignty for Economic Opportunity: A Strategic Negotiations Perspective." *Missouri Law Review* 76, 1046.

Fisher, R., and W. Ury. 2011. *Getting to Yes*. 3d edition. New York: Penguin Books.

Lax, D. A., and J. K. Sebenius. 2006. *3-D Negotiation*. Brighton, MA: Harvard Business Review Press.

Mnookin, R. H., S. R. Peppet, and A. S. Tulumello. 2000. *Beyond Winning: Negotiating to Create Value in Deals and Disputes*. Cambridge, MA: Belknap Press.

Washburn, K. K. 2002. "Indian Gaming: A Primer on the Development of Indian Gaming, the NIGC, and Several Important Unresolved Issues." A.B.A. Center for Continuing Legal Education National Institute, Criminal Justice Section, Gaming Enforcement.

9 AMERICAN INDIAN LEADERSHIP PRACTICES

Stephanie Lee Black, *University at Albany*
Carolyn Birmingham, *Florida Institute of Technology*

ABSTRACT

American Indian leadership practices are influenced by cultural values and the roles they undertake within internal (i.e., the tribe) as well as the external environments. Although it is difficult to make generalizations for all American Indian tribes, this chapter seeks to provide a better understanding of American Indian leadership practices and how they are embedded in tribal culture. It also gives a comparison of American Indian leadership with Western traditions and leadership. We discuss some of the roles and challenges American Indians leaders face when managing the demands of their own tribes and that of the dominant Western culture.

KEYWORDS: leadership, American Indian leaders, Western traditions, cultural values

INTRODUCTION

THE CONCEPT OF LEADERSHIP IS OF KEY IMPORTANCE WITHIN the management and organizational behavior literature. Although there are many definitions of leadership, for purposes of this chapter *leadership* is defined as "the ability to influence people toward the attainment of goals" (Daft 2007, 422). Also, we can define leadership more broadly to include influencing task objectives and strategies, influencing commitment and compliance in task behavior to achieve these objectives, influencing group maintenance and identification, and influencing the culture of an organization (Yukl 1989, 253).

Leadership is vital to organizations, and the success of the organization is dependent on the quality of the leadership and the ability of the individual to communicate his or her vision and motivate others. According to Daft (2007, 422), "the concept of leadership evolves as the needs of organizations change, and the technology, economic conditions, labor conditions, and social cultural mores of the times all play a role." Moreover, the environmental context in which leadership is practiced influences which approach might be most effective as well as what kinds of leaders are more admired by society (Daft 2007). While concepts of leadership have yet to develop into one universal theory on leadership, we have continued to work on a better understanding of leadership traits, behavior, power, and situational factors (Yukl 1989). There are several major themes in leadership (Yukl 1989), which are discussed in this chapter comparing Western concepts of leadership to those of American Indians.

AMERICAN INDIAN BUSINESS LEADERS

History provides many examples of great American Indian leaders who have been honored for their leadership qualities. For example, Osceola is popular in Florida for his efforts to protect his territory from colonists (Hatch 2012). Crazy Horse is well known for his bravery in battle and his diligence in protecting his cultural identity (Marshall 2005). Geronimo is well recognized for his ability to use deep knowledge of his homeland geography to confuse the US cavalry and delay foreign settlement into his tribal lands (Debo 1976). Sitting Bull is famous for his political and military prowess (Utley 2014). Chief Seattle of the Duwamish was known among the settlers for showing others the need to respect the environment (Furtwangler 2012). Nez Perce leader Chief Joseph was well known as a distinguished speaker who promoted racial equality and freedom for American Indians (Gunther 2010) and who encouraged tribal loyalty (Humphreys, Ingram, and Kernek 2007).

AMERICAN INDIAN BUSINESS LEADERS AND CULTURE

When we look specifically at American Indian leadership, we must also look at the context in which these individuals are culturally embedded and recognize that culture plays a significant role. Hofstede (1980) describes the importance of national culture with respect to management leadership; he defines *culture* as the "collective programming of the mind which distinguishes the members of one group or category of people from another" (Hofstede 1991, 5). The primary differences between different national cultures stem from national values, thus an individual's national culture influences societal rules for behavior (Hofstede and Hofstede 2005). National cultural identity and societal demands affect how people from that culture think about leadership style, and cultural beliefs and values influence a society's definition of effective leadership (Dorfman et al. 2012; House et al. 2004; House et al. 2002). National cultures create different views on desired leadership qualities, and these differences rather than being universal are tightly coupled to cultural characteristics (Dorfman et al. 2012). For example, a study by Redpath and Nielson (1997) found that Canadian Native cultures are very different than the dominant Canadian culture and tend to be more collectivist, tolerant, egalitarian, and adaptive.

American Indian cultural values affect leadership style, especially when practiced in an American Indian business context because even though the organization uses dominant cultural management, accounting and legal structures, systems, and procedures, the traditional cultural values need to be taken into consideration (Stewart et al. forthcoming). With over five hundred federally recognized American Indian tribes in the United States, each acting as its own sovereign nation, these tribes may have different cultural traditions and practices that influence how individuals lead within their own tribes. The roles vary greatly from region to region and from tribe to tribe, and in some cases even from band to band within a tribe or people—all of which is reflected in their various management leadership behaviors. Although it is difficult to make generalizations for all tribes, within this chapter we discuss some of the different practices of leadership behavior in several contexts and compare to Western traditions to provide a better understanding of what it means to be a leader within the American Indian context.

LEADING IN AMERICAN INDIAN COUNTRY

There have been few empirical studies of American Indian leaders. Part of the challenge is that American Indians are geographically dispersed throughout the United States, linguistically diverse, and culturally varied. These hundreds of tribal nations are politically distinct and separately recognized as sovereign nations by the federal government (Stewart et al. forthcoming). Thus American Indian tribal nations have to "build bridges across linguistic, cultural, regional, class, and even color differences" (Nagel 1997, 8) to interact with the dominant US culture. As such, American Indian community leaders need to exhibit flexibility to create synergies between their tribes' and the dominant US culture, especially when their businesses often need to operate in both contexts. Moreover, as tribes strive for more tribal sovereignty, a tribal community's ability "to control its own political, social, economic, and religious life" (Edmunds 2004, 6), new American Indian leaders have emerged. They respond to these challenges by trying to create better lives for their people. American Indian leadership today has evolved to reflect contemporary challenges faced by Native people who have been confined to rural enclaves, controlled by federal government agencies, and subjected to policies aimed at destroying their cultures (Edmunds 2004).

THE AMERICAN INDIAN CONCEPT OF LEADERSHIP

Most management concepts are derived from Western business practices and the concept of leadership uses a Western lens when examining the role of the business leader in the development of human capital, implementation of change, and organizational performance (Deming 1992). Western culture has influenced the terms we have bestowed on American Indian leaders. For example, the term *chief* is a European term for *leader*, which dates back prior to 1794, when Europeans appointed tribal leaders to represent each tribe or clan so that they would have a designated leader to negotiate with them. Before this, American Indians were based on clans, which appointed various leaders for different roles depending on the function. With the arrival of Europeans, however, the range of indigenous leaders was often translated into one common English word: chief. Especially in colonial times, European-defined "chiefs" were often used as instruments of indirect rule and/or convenient alternatives to elective institutions. For example, the title of *principal chief* was created when the Cherokee formalized their political structure to establish the Cherokee nation and enter into talks with the Europeans. Since this time, the term *chief* has been given to many early American Indian leaders, but it was traditionally not a name used by their own people (Conley 2008).

Many individuals believe that most northern American Indians tribes are patriarchal and follow a hierarchical form of leadership. While some American Indian tribes are patriarchal in nature, most are matriarchal and collective, tracing lineage through the mother with women holding revered positions in society. Moreover, in some tribes leadership is considered a shared role depending on context and job function. Among the Cherokees, for example, it was the Women's Council that decided whether men were worthy of performing sacred duties, going to war, or holding public office. The chief may have the power, but he or she is typically not free to wield that power without obtaining consent from a council or tribal elders of some kind. Among the Iroquois or Haudenosaunee, the chief has traditionally been male but elected by women. In many of the tribes, people are considered equal regardless of gender. Other tribes, such as the Osage, are considered patriarchal but do not have defined gender roles (Young 2005; Meyer and Bogdan 2001).

It is important to recognize that leadership among indigenous people takes many roles. In traditional Western approaches, leadership is associated with an individual person whose traits and accomplishments propel him or her to positions of authority where power and authority is based on a hierarchical structure. In Western management the organizational leader is the one held responsible for the vision and key decision-making within the organization. In contrast, American Indian leadership traditions are often related to the requirements of the community. In fact, American Indians tend to define *leadership* less as a position and more as a sphere of influence that must be contextualized to be understood (Warner and Grint 2006). Leadership tends to be dispersed throughout the community, focused on situations rather than individuals (Lawson 2013). American Indian models of leadership tend to be concerned less with positional roles and more on context. Rather than having a more rigid hierarchical structure, many of them are flexible with changing patterns of authority (Lawson 2013), whereby leadership roles are transitional or shared. Also, American Indian perspectives are often based on a collectivist approach over an individualistic culture. Among American Indians, leadership therefore tends to be more concerned with how different forms of leadership in different circumstances can serve the community rather than enhance one's own financial gain and reputation.

WESTERN LEADERSHIP VERSUS AMERICAN INDIAN LEADERSHIP

In a discussion of American Indian organization and leadership, Wakshul (1997, 26) contends that American Indian leadership is distinct from Western business practices in the following ways: "(a) American Indian leaders need to know both their own community (values and history) as well as the Euro-American community because they must function in both societies; (b) American Indian leaders need to be holistic because Indian communities are small, Indians value interconnectedness, and Indians work on a wide variety of issues; (c) American Indian leaders belong to communal societies that must accommodate both tribal values and Euro-American systems in which Indians and non-Indians coexist." This was also echoed in a recent study (Stewart et al. forthcoming) in which American Indian CEOs and other executive team members discussed the need to balance both American Indian and Western needs and expectations for their businesses they ran.

COMMUNITY ORIENTATION AND SHARED LEADERSHIP

Under Western management concepts—that is, Taylor (1913)—leadership within organizations is based on the concept that one individual should be placed in charge of decision-making and strategic choices for the firm. This leadership style is based on a *vertical* leadership that emphasizes a hierarchy, the external role of the manager, and the formal authority as well as the influence over the team's process and outcomes (Carson, Tesluk, and Marrone 2007). However, American Indians tend to practice a *shared* leadership—a collective leadership by the team members and consisting of collaborative decision-making and shared responsibility for outcomes (Hoch and Dulebohn 2013). In a tribal context, each individual has an important role to play within the community, and each person makes a unique contribution. The total contribution is an organic whole that can only be understood over several life cycles. Moreover, no single individual acts in a hierarchical supervisory fashion. This type of decentralized leadership is like a flock of swallows that move together but never have the same leaders (Resnick 1997).

Traditionally, from a Western perspective, organizational leaders are valued for strong individualistic skills and being performance oriented. However, for many American Indian leaders the indigenous community values leaders who are community oriented and look toward the welfare of the community even over performance benchmarks. "American Indian models are more concerned with how different forms of leadership in different circumstances can serve the community rather than enhance the reward and reputation of their individual embodiment" (Warner 2016, 225). When chosen as a leader, he or she does not seek to stand out or self-aggrandize, but rather he or she is honored for the recognition and accepts the role with humility (Bryant 2003). These leaders are influenced by a respect for others within the tribe as well as the environment.

This is exemplified in the Seven Grandfather Teachings taught to tribal members through an ancient story that is a part of the oral tradition of certain tribes. These concepts teach human responsibilities about how to behave toward others and all of creation (Verbos and Humphries 2014). The concept of seven generations, found throughout indigenous North America, refers to decision-making that encompasses both the past and the future. American Indians envision life as one great, interconnected web whereby they strive to achieve harmony, unity, and a basic oneness. This concept of connectedness between various parts makes the traditional top-down structure of most organizations seem inappropriate, and tribal leaders must be aware of how their cultural belief in the interconnectedness of the world affects their leadership (Coyhis 1995). These cultural beliefs drive many Native American leaders to create sustainable organizations, with strong corporate social responsibility agendas as well as environmental stewardship.

AUTHENTIC LEADERSHIP

As a result of this collective orientation, a top-down management structure is ineffective because it conflicts with traditional American Indian values (Coyhis 1995). The philosophy of American Indian leadership is oriented around servant leadership where the needs of a leader's employees, customers, constituents, and community influence his or her behavior. Leaders nurture both the institution and those affected by the institution (Spears 1994). This turns the hierarchical pyramid upside down (Spears 1994). Within American Indian communities, leaders are considered servants of the people, and in tribal organizations all people are expected to act as leaders when their specialized knowledge or abilities are needed at a particular time.

The American Indian view of leadership is consistent with the Peloton management model of servant leadership, which emphasizes interconnectedness (McLure and Stanco 1996). As such, American Indian leadership is often rotated among tribal members., which allows various members to share responsibilities. Rotation empowers future leaders to take on various roles of both leading and following simultaneously. Therefore, rather than using a centralized leadership approach, this model of leadership is decentralized (Wheatley 1992). For example, in one tribe the closest word for *leader* means "one who goes first"—"indicative of the transient position of the leader in some contemporary images of decentralized systems" (Bryant 1998, 12). These differences are reflected in shared leadership; more inclusive, participative, and collectivist decision-making practices; and in decision-making priorities that are focused far more on long-term goals versus the typical Western focus on short-term goals.

There are other differences as well. Indian leaders often see themselves as students who are continually learning, who have a responsibility for the welfare of others. Western leaders frequently put their own interests first and behave strategically to achieve those ends. In contrast, in many Indian cultures, Western-style individualism and self-promotion are not respected behaviors. When there is a mix of Western and Indian leadership of a company, this can lead to conflict. Unlike in the dominant Western context, in an Indian context it is often hard to determine who the Indian leaders are because it is often a shared role whereby no single individual stands out.

The American Indian water carrier is used as a metaphor for this decentralized leadership style whereby "the tribal water carrier within a corporation is a symbol of the essential nature of all jobs, our interdependence, the identity of ownership" (DePree 1989, 65). The water carriers do what needs to be done, when it needs to be done, regardless of his or her position or authority role and is representative of the essential nature of all jobs and their interdependence on one another (DePree 1989). Moreover, authority is tied to the particular situation and ends when the need for it has ceased (Bryant 1998, 13).

NATIVE AMERICAN WOMEN AND LEADERSHIP ROLES

It should be noted that leadership roles for Native American women are as diverse and varied as the tribes they represent. However, Bernita Krumm describes the roles of several female tribal college presidents and how "models of leadership generally have common elements: They define a leader as one who possesses vision and focuses on mission, serves as a role model for others, and enables others to take action or perform their roles. These figures emphasize vision and mission as well as work with tribal culture members and governments. The style of successful women leaders tends to be participatory and consultative" (McLeod 2002, 10). Miller (1978) refers to women leaders as constant caregivers who respect others and are seen as holders of wisdom by the community. These women leaders tend to emphasize the importance of common values with the tribe as defined by its culture. In this capacity the leader is a facilitator and a promoter of group values and interests (Krumm and Johnson 2011), and leadership acts are seen as expressions of culture that build unity and order among the tribe.

COMMON THEMES IN INDIAN LEADERSHIP

In the context of Indian values, common themes emerge in the Indian approach to leadership, including decentralization of the leadership role, power and authority, all things have immanent value, deflecting one's image as a leader, preferring not to interfere, time is less important, and decisions are made collectively (Bryant 1998). In many respects the Indian approach is one of empowerment, one that Western leadership theories have long recognized as important. When leaders empower subordinates, both leaders and subordinates do better (Follett 1942; White and Lippet 1953; Stogdill and Coons 1957; McGregor 1960; Likert 1961). An Indian leader doesn't just have responsibility for his or her employees, however. Rather, they are responsible for the welfare of the entire collective (family, tribe, and people). This philosophy is often reflected in HR policies and practices that honor cultural values. As many reservation companies have outside (i.e., non-Indian) management, there can be conflict between Indian and outside leadership with respect to which set of practices (Western or Indian or a blend of both) dominate any particular situation. The outside leadership often needs to become familiar with the Indian leadership with respect to important cultural and values-based needs of the company, its employees, and the greater tribal community (Stewart et al. forthcoming).

Native Americans tend to use a more *distributed leadership* process, which refers to leadership being distributed through a group or network of interacting individuals. In this manner people work together to pool their initiative and expertise, whereby the outcome is a product that is greater than the sum of what one could accomplish individually (Woods et al. 2004). At the center of distributed leadership is the notion that leadership is the property of the group rather than the individual. American Indians have been known to describe the traditional decision-making context as a circle (Stewart et al. forthcoming). The circle, symbolizing relationships and interconnectedness, is a positive part of cultural and spiritual American Indian traditions (Marshall 2001; Mattern 1999; Verbos, Gladstone, and Kennedy 2011). "The significance of the circle from a Native perspective is discussed as a symbol and framework for group process" (Garrett, Garrett, and Brotherton 2001, 17). Therefore, rather than one individual being the decision maker (as is the case in most Western cultures), among many American Indian tribes, when an important decision needs to be made, they gather people together and allow everyone to participate and have a voice in the decision-making process. This conjunctive decision-making process brings together the participants, allows equal participation rights, and removes all hierarchical relationships.

The concept of time is also different among many Native Americans and tends to mirror a sense of reflectivity. Many American Indians tend to have a more flexible concept of time than other cultural groups (DuBray 1985), whereby time is of little importance in the grand scheme of things (Cleary and Peacock 1998). Instead, rather than reaching a rapid conclusion about a problem, Native Americans may prefer to take into consideration all the available data before reaching a decision (Pewewardy 2002). Moreover, decision-making may be done as a collective rather than by one individual, which may require a longer process.

Another management practice that differentiates Western culture from American Indian cultures is the concept of nepotism. In Western culture, particularly within the business community, nepotism and the notion of doing things that benefit family and relatives is viewed as unethical. In fact, some states have laws forbidding nepotism. Yet in American Indian cultures, taking care of family and relatives is one of the first obligations of a leader (Bryant 1998). Friends, family, and reservation members are hired not because they are the most skilled for the job (a Western approach) but because they need jobs. Also, Indian and tribal preferences in hiring exist and may even be tribal laws, which give preference to tribal members and other Indians over non-Indians (Stubben 2001). This practice presents unique problems for a manager. On the one hand, a job needs to be done; on the other hand, significant training may be required before the employee can actually do the job because the individual who was hired often lacks specialized training and higher levels of education (i.e., MBAs).

The practice of hiring family members influences the human resource management within the organization. For example, if a tribal council member has a relative who needs to be (or was) disciplined at work, that council member may interfere with the organization's internal HR practices. In addition, usually these companies are a major employer on reservations and complex interdependent relationships exist in the tribal/community context, which makes managing these businesses more complicated. Overall, Indian companies are far more intertwined in the community. As a result, there is not just a leadership employer/employee relationship; instead, leadership is embedded in the community and that community stakeholder is critical to the company. This in turn affects the decisions that are made far more than community stakeholders do in a more traditional Western-focused company (Whiteman and Cooper 2000; Stewart et al. forthcoming).

The structure of Indian organizations also influences how they are managed, and Indian companies often differ significantly from traditional Western businesses. In Western management theory (Weber, Henderson, and Parsons 1947; Scott 1981), organizations are viewed as instruments, and organizational decision-making is portrayed as a rational process where the goal is to maximize profits. Rather than being purely profit driven, American Indian entities are often hybrid companies that are both for profit and have a social welfare mission. This is reflected in the mission of, management of, and profit distribution of Indian companies. Part of the profits usually support tribal government and otherwise money-losing but necessary reservation-based companies (gas stations, grocery stores, etc.). A portion of the profits usually support social services as well as other initiatives on the reservation. For example, the Yavapai-Apache Nation's tribal leaders focused on using their Cliff Castle Casino revenues for tribal empowerment, cultural awareness, and sustainable economic development (Piner and Paradis 2004). In addition, Indian companies along with tribal government and its programs are typically the primary reservation employers. Thus the focus of many tribal enterprises is not profit driven but job creation within a self-sustaining enterprise (Smith 1994). This impacts decisions leaders make about the distribution of a firm's resources (Stewart et al. forthcoming).

The governance structure of American Indian businesses and traditional Western business is generally different as well. Although many tribes have created a quasi-independent development company to oversee tribal businesses, the separation of politics and business remains problematic. Part of the difficulty lies in the structure of tribal organizations. Whereas most mainstream corporations use a governance structure in which a single board directs a CEO who assumes responsibility for the enterprises held by the firm, a typical tribal organization uses a structure similar to the diagram below.

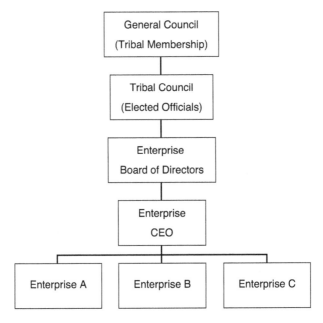

Governance Structure. Source: Stewart et al. forthcoming

This structure can result in a conflict of interest because tribal members and the tribal council oversee the board of directors. This mix of tribal leadership (with a vested interest in distribution of profits to the tribe and hiring tribe members regardless of their skill and experience) and more Western-style board members (with an interest in the for-profit side, where decisions focus on profit making, ensuring that profits are invested back into the company, hiring employees based on their skill set, etc.) can sometimes lead to a balancing act by company leadership. They need to satisfy both the social mission of the company (the tribal needs) and the profit-generating needs. The political overtones that this type of governance structure might generate can affect employer/employee relationships, discipline, and so on.

These many differences mean that understanding Indian leadership requires understanding Indian culture and values. Indian leaders straddle two worlds and need to adapt how they do what they do to satisfy two (sometimes conflicting) approaches to leadership—Western and Indian. A skilled Indian business leader needs to be competent in both Western and Indian approaches, know when to use each approach and when to use a blended approach, and know how to prioritize which approach to use when there are conflicts. These differences affect all levels and divisions of the company and how they operate. When leaders demonstrate the ability to navigate this divide successfully, both the company and the tribe benefit.

CONCLUSION

Leadership among Native American Indians can be a culturally specific phenomenon that varies by tribal customs and practices. As such, generalizations should not be made. However, what we have learned from studying Native American leadership practices is that there is no best type of leadership model. Instead, the skills for certain embodiments of leadership are different and dependent on the situation. Some of the common themes of Native American leadership show us that it can embrace both an individualistic but also a collective approach to decision-making, depending on the circumstances. The model is neither hierarchical nor authoritative, which makes it differ significantly from traditional Western business management concepts of leadership. Overall, decision-making is undertaken with an approach to balancing the community's needs and welfare, not only for the present generation but for future generations to follow (Warner and Grint 2006).

GROUP OR INDIVIDUAL EXERCISES
EXERCISE 1

Purpose of exercise: To practice effective disciplining skills

Scenario: You are a middle manager at a tribally owned construction company that does commercial development projects. Your administrative assistant, Marcie, is a good worker as well as a relative whom you hired. You have come to rely on her because she is loyal, has good clerical skills, and provides good insights with respect to your job duties and assignments. Marcie is willing to go the extra mile, including staying late to work on projects. However, she seems to have a recurring problem. Specifically, Marcie is habitually late . . . sometimes five minutes, other times up to two hours. You know that Marcie is frequently tardy because she is a single parent with two small children, ages three and five. You don't personally mind when she is tardy because she always calls when she is going to be late, and she has never let you down by not being there when you have needed her. The problem is, however, the other workers you supervise complain that you play favorites by not disciplining Marcie for her frequent lateness. Although many of your other employees are not as hard working or as conscientious as Marcie, you know that you must do something about the situation.

ASSIGNMENT: ANSWER THE FOLLOWING QUESTIONS

1. Outline the steps you would take to address this situation.
2. Please explain why you think your suggestions are the best choice.

EXERCISE 2

Apply your skills: Case for critical analysis

Scenario: Tribal member Gloria Blackstone was recently hired by the tribe to evaluate some of the tribal entities to see if she can make suggestions on improving the profitability of various companies. The first businesses that Gloria has examined are the tribal gas stations, which appear to be running at a loss. These gas stations are popular for Indians as well as non-Indians because they are located next to the freeway and have good access but also because these stations are exempt from state fuel taxes. Fuel prices are consistently 7 to 12 cents per gallon lower than at other gas stations primarily because of the state rebate.

However, upon analyzing the revenues, it appears that the gas stations run at a loss because many of the tribal members believe that the gas stations belong to the tribe and as such should be shared by everyone. Thus many of the members of the tribe do not pay for their gas or other convenience store purchases because they perceive that it is something owed to them. Gloria must take into consideration the tribal culture but still provide suggestions about how the tribe might institute new policies to make these businesses profitable so the tribe can keep these businesses.

QUESTIONS

1. If you were Gloria, what type of suggestions would you make to the tribal council to improve the profitability of these gas stations?
2. How would you take the culture into consideration and incorporate the tribal customs into your suggestions?
3. Can you think of particular problems that might arise in implementing your suggestions?

EXERCISE 3

Apply your skills: Case for critical analysis

Scenario: Harvey Ross, not a tribal member, has recently been appointed as president of the tribes' new lumber company. The tribe has significant acreage of prime pine forest that it has chosen to harvest and is looking to either develop or contract with outside companies to log tracts of the forest. Harvey knows that the tribe is looking for employment for some of the tribal members, but at present none of the members have experience in logging and the tribe will also have to spend considerable dollars to purchase logging equipment. Moreover, relations will have to be developed with lumber companies and other entities to purchase the lumber. Another consideration for Harvey is the fact that some of the tribe's elders have expressed concern with harvesting the lumber, which is considered to be a precious natural resource of the tribe. They are concerned that the resources may be exploited, which conflicts with their cultural beliefs. Harvey must provide a business plan to the tribal council regarding his plans for this new business, taking into consideration all these issues.

QUESTIONS

1. What suggestions would you make if you were Harvey?
2. How do you plan to create jobs for tribal members but also take into consideration the possibility of using outside vendors?
3. How should Harvey take into consideration the tribe's concern over exploiting the tribe's natural resources and create a sustainable company?

EXERCISE 4

Apply your skills: Difficult decision-making when company and tribal needs conflict

Scenario: You are the chief financial officer of your tribe's major business, one that supports many social and tribal government programs for the tribe. The tribal council wants to take 85 percent of the company's profits for the next five years (well above the usual percentage used by the tribe in the past) and invest that money into expanding several of the critical tribal social initiatives, ones that company profits already financially support. As a tribal member, you agree that the social program expansions are needed; in fact, some of your relatives benefit from them. The problem is that the impact of taking this amount of money from the company's profits would be damaging to the company. The company needs critical infrastructure improvements to replace necessary equipment that is reaching the end of its useful life. This won't be possible if most of the company profits are invested in tribal needs rather than company needs. An outcome of this decision by the tribal council would eventually result in a decline in company profits due to failure to invest in the necessary improvements, likely resulting in layoffs that would include tribal employees.

QUESTIONS

1. How do you balance your obligations to run the company using fiscally sound principles, addressing company needs *and* your obligation to the tribal council to meet tribal needs?
2. What criteria do you use when attempting to balance tribal and company needs for use of company profits?
3. How do you go about convincing the tribal council that there is a need to keep reinvesting a higher percentage of the company profits back into the company than they propose to reinvest?

EXERCISE 3

Apply your skills: Dealing with nontribal management

Scenario: This scenario raises similar issues, to some extent, as Exercise 1, but looking here at policies inside a company. You are the HR director of the tribe's casino, resort, and golf course, although you are not part of the executive management team. Because of a lack of tribe members with the skills and education, the tribe subcontracts much of the upper-level management of this large operation to an outside (i.e., nontribal) company. This outside company just appointed a new CEO to the tribe's company. This person is focused on making changes to increase profitability—a goal the tribe welcomes. The new CEO, without consulting the tribe or yourself, announced that HR policies are changing to decrease employee absenteeism, as it is excessive compared with the companies the CEO has run in the past. Some of these policies conflict with tribal religious practices and other customs. The one that has tribal employees the most upset restricts bereavement leave to immediate family for a maximum of three days. This would not allow employee tribal members to be able to participate in their tribe's customary month-long religious practices surrounding the death of a family member, including extended family members.

QUESTIONS

1. How should and how can a tribal company balance tribal and dominant culture business practices? Which should take priority under which conditions? Are compromises possible with specific issues? If yes, which issues?
2. What could you do in your role of HR director to increase the sensitivity of the new CEO to tribal needs and practices with respect to company policy?
3. How do you handle your upset employees while these issues are being worked out?

References

Bryant, M. 2003. "Cross-Cultural Perspectives on School Leadership: Themes from Native American Interviews." In *Effective Educational Leadership*, edited by N. Bennett, M. Crawford, and M. Cartwright, pp. 216–28. London: Paul Chapman Publishing.

Carson, J. B., P. E. Tesluk, and J. A. Marrone. 2007. "Shared Leadership in Teams: An Investigation of Antecedent Conditions and Performance." *Academy of Management Journal* 50, no. 5: 1217–34.

Cleary, L. M., and T. D. Peacock. 1998. *Collected Wisdom: American Indian Education.* Boston: Allyn and Bacon.

Conley, R. J. 2008. *The Cherokee Nation: A History.* Albuquerque: University of New Mexico Press.

Coyhis, Don. 1995. *Wisdom of the People.* Colorado Springs, CO: White Bison.

Daft, R. L. 2007. *Organization Theory and Design.* 9th ed. Mason, OH: Thomson South-Western.

Debo, A. 1976. *Geronimo: The Man, His Time, His Place.* 1st ed. Vol. 142. Norman: University of Oklahoma Press.

Deming. W. E. 1992. *Out of the Crisis.* Cambridge: Massachusetts Institute of Technology, Center for Advanced Engineering Study.

DePree, M. 1989. *Leadership Is An Art*. New York: Doubleday.

Dorfman, P., M. Javidan, P. Hanges, A. Dastmalchian, and R. House. 2012. "GLOBE: A Twenty Year Journey into the Intriguing World of Culture and Leadership." *Journal of World Business* 47, no. 4: 504–18.

DuBray, W. H. 1985. "American Indian Values: Critical Factor in Casework." *Journal of Contemporary Social Work* 66, no. 1: 30–37.

Edmunds, R. D., ed. 2004. *The New Warriors: Native American Leaders since 1900*. Lincoln: University of Nebraska Press.

Follett, M. P. 1942. *Dynamic Administration: The Collected Papers of Mary Parker Follett*. London: Harper & Brothers.

Furtwangler, A. 2012. *Answering Chief Seattle*. Seattle: University of Washington Press.

Garrett, M. T., J. T. Garrett, and D. Brotherton. 2001. "Inner Circle/Outer Circle: A Group Technique Based on Native American Healing Circles." *Journal for Specialists in Group Work* 26, no. 1: 17–30.

Gunther, V. 2010. *Chief Joseph: A Biography*. Santa Barbara, CA: ABC-CLIO LLC.

Hatch, T. 2012. *Osceola and the Great Seminole War: A Struggle for Justice and Freedom*. New York: Macmillan.

Hoch, J. E., and J. H. Dulebohn. 2013. "Shared Leadership in Enterprise Resource Planning and Human Resource Management System Implementation." *Human Resource Management Review* 23, no. 1: 114–25.

Hofstede, G. 1991. *Empirical Models of Cultural Differences*. In *Contemporary Issues in Cross-Cultural Psychology*. Pp. 4–20. Lisse, Netherlands: Swets and Zeitlinger Publishers.

———. 1980. *Culture's Consequences: International Differences in Work-Related Values*. Beverly Hills, CA: Sage Publications.

Hofstede, G., and G. J. Hofstede. 2005. *Cultures and Organizations: Software of the Mind*. New York: McGraw-Hill.

House, R., P. Hanges, M. Javidan, P. Dorfman, and V. Gupta. 2004. *Culture, Leadership, and Organization: The GLOBE Study of 62 Societies*. Thousand Oaks, CA: Sage.

House, R., M. Javidan, P. Hanges, and P. Dorfman. 2002. "Understanding Cultures and Implicit Leadership Theories across the Globe: An Introduction to Project GLOBE." *Journal of World Business* 37, no. 1: 3–10.

Humphreys, J., K. Ingram, and C. Kernek. 2007. "The Nez Perce Leadership Council: A Historical Examination of Post-Industrial Leadership." *Journal of Management History* 13, no. 2: 135–52.

Krumm, B. L., and W. Johnson. 2011. "Tribal Colleges: Cultural Support for Women Campus Presidencies." Emerald Group Publishing Limited. Pp. 263–89.

Lawson, R. M. 2013. *Encyclopedia of American Indian Issues Today*. Santa Barbara, CA: Greenwood.

Likert, R. 1961. *New Patterns of Management*. New York: McGraw-Hill.

Marshall, J. M. 2005. *The Journey of Crazy Horse*. New York: Penguin Group.

Marshall, J. M., III. 2001. *The Lakota Way: Stories and Lessons for Living*. New York: Viking Compass.

Mattern, M. 1999. "The Powwow as a Public Arena for Negotiating Unity and Diversity in American Indian Life." In D. Champagne, ed., *Contemporary Native American Cultural Issues*. Pp. 129–44. Walnut Creek, CA: Altamira Press.

McGregor, D. 1960. *The Human Side of Enterprise*. New York: McGraw-Hill.

McLeod, M. 2002. "Keeping the Circle Strong." *Tribal College Journal* 13, no. 4: 10–3.

McLure, B., and T. Stanco. 1996. "The Peloton: Riding the Winds of Change." *Leadership Abstracts* 9, no. 12: 1–8.

Meyer, J. F., and G. Bogdan. 2001. "Co-Habitation and Co-Optation: Some Intersections Between Native American and Euroamerican Legal Systems in the Nineteenth Century." *American Transcendental Quarterly: 19th Century American Literature and Culture* 15, no. 4: 257.

Miller, D. L. 1978. "Native American Women: Leadership Images." *Integrated Education* 91, no. 15 (January–February): 37–39.

Nagel, J. 1997. *American Indian Ethnic Renewal: Red Power and the Resurgence of Identity and Culture*. New York: Oxford University Press.

Pewewardy, C. 2002. "Learning Styles of American Indian/Alaska Native Students: A Review of the Literature and Implications for Practice." *Journal of American Indian Education* 41, no. 3: 22–56.

Piner, J., and T. Paradis. 2004. "Beyond the Casino: Sustainable Tourism and Cultural Development on Native American Lands." *Tourism Geographies* 6, no. 1: 80–98.

Redpath, L., and M. O. Nielsen. 1997. "A Comparison of Native Culture, Non-Native Culture, and New Management Ideology." *Canadian Journal of Administrative Sciences* 14, no. 3: 327–39.

Resnick, M. 1997. *Turtles, Termites, and Traffic Jams: Explorations in Massively Parallel Microworlds*. Cambridge: MIT Press.

Scott, W. R. 1981. "Developments in Organization Theory, 1960–1980." *American Behavioral Scientist* 24, no. 3: 407–22.

Smith, D. H. 1994. "The Issue of Compatibility between Cultural Integrity and Economic Development among Native American Tribes." *American Indian Culture and Research Journal* 18, no. 2: 177–205.

Spears, L. C. 1994. "Servant Leadership: Quest for Caring." *Innerquest* 2: 1–4.

Stewart, D., J. Gladstone, A. Verbos, and M. Katragadda. 2014. "Native American Cultural Capital and Business Strategy: The Culture-of-Origin Effect." *American Indian Culture and Research Journal* 38, no. 4: 127–38.

Stewart, D., A. K. Verbos, C. Birmingham, S. L. Black, and J. S. Gladstone. Forthcoming. "Being Native American in Business: Culture, Identity, and Authentic Leadership in Modern American Indian Enterprise." *Leadership, Social Entrepreneurship in Indian Country USA: Lessons from Tribal Enterprises*.

Stogdill, R. M., and A. E. Coons. 1957. *Leader Behavior, Its Description and Measurement*. Columbus: College of Administrative Science, Ohio State University.

Stubben, J. D. 2001. "Working with and Conducting Research among American Indian Families." *American Behavioral Scientist* 44, no. 9: 1466–81.

Taylor, F. W. 1913. *The Principles of Scientific Management*. London: Harper & Brothers.

Utley, R. M. 2014. *Sitting Bull: The Life and Times of an American Patriot*. New York: Henry Hold and Company LLC.

Verbos, A. K., J. S. Gladstone, and D. M. Kennedy. 2011. "Native American Values and Management Education: Envisioning an Inclusive Virtuous Circle." *Journal of Management Education* 35, no. 1: 10–26.

Verbos, A. K., and M. T. Humphries. 2014. "A Native American Relational Ethic: An Indigenous Perspective on Teaching Human Responsibility." *Journal of Business Ethics* 123, no. 1: 1–9.

Wakshul, B. 1997. "Training Leaders for the 21st Century: The American Indian Ambassadors Program: Medicine Pathways for the Future." *Winds of Change* 12, no. 2: 24–28.

Warner, L. S., and K. Grint. 2006. "American Indian Ways of Leading and Knowing." *Leadership* 2, no. 2: 225–44.

Weber, M., A. M. Henderson, and T. Parsons. 1947. *The Theory of Social and Economic Organization*. New York: Oxford University Press.

Wheatley, M. J. 1992. *Leadership and the New Science: Learning about Organization from an Orderly Universe*. San Francisco: Berrett-Koehler.

White, R. K., and R. Lippet. 1953. "Leader Behavior and Member Reaction in Three Different Climates." In *Group Dynamics Research and Theory*, 3d ed., edited by D. Cartwright and A. Zander, 318–35. New York: Harper and Row. Online at https://babel.hathitrust.org/cgi/pt?id=mdp.39015071810092;view=1up;seq=332.

Whiteman, G., and W H. Cooper. 2000. "Ecological Embeddedness." *Academy of Management Journal* 43, no. 6: 1265–82.

Woods, P. A., N. Bennett, J. A. Harvey, and C. Wise. 2004. "Variabilities and Dualities in Distributed Leadership Findings from a Systematic Literature Review." *Educational Management Administration and Leadership* 32, no. 4: 439–57.

Young, M. 2005. "Living in the Land of Death: The Choctaw Nation, 1830–1860." *Western Historical Quarterly* 36, no. 4: 508–9.

Yukl, G. 1989. "Managerial Leadership: A Review of Theory and Research." *Journal of Management* 15, no. 2: 251–89.

10 BUSINESS ETHICS AND NATIVE AMERICAN VALUES

Carma M. Claw, *New Mexico State University*
Amy Klemm Verbos, *University of Wisconsin–Whitewater*
Grace Ann Rosile, *New Mexico State University*

ABSTRACT

Native American worldviews can form a foundation for business ethics, particularly in Native American–owned and –operated enterprises. However, there is great diversity in Indian Country, and the basis for ethical behavior can vary from nation to nation. In this chapter we introduce two distinct traditional ways of being: one that is practiced by the Diné (also known as Navajo) and another that is shared by the Anishinabek. Each provides implications for business, leadership, and ways of participating in commerce. The Diné principle purports that ethics begins with each individual and that it is inseparable from everything we do. The Seven Grandfather/Grandmother Teachings are human *responsibilities* to be practiced in all that we do. Thus each ethic applies to American Indians from those respective traditions in the business realm. We recommend that Native peoples seek their own tribes' wisdom for insight on ways of being and doing that provide ethical guidance to apply in their own business settings. For Native peoples this should be a welcomed perspective, because it offers more culturally appropriate and relevant material for business decision-making and practice.
KEYWORDS: Native American ethics, Diné teachings, Seven Grandfather Teachings, tribal business ethics

INTRODUCTION

NOW MORE THAN EVER IT IS IMPORTANT FOR NATIVE AMERICAN business people to set themselves apart by bringing who they are, as Native people, into their business practices. Business ethics has been described as "the application of ethics to the special problems and opportunities experienced by business people" (Kubasek et al. 2015, 16). Currently, there is an urgent need to bolster ethical business behavior across and throughout the business sector.

An amoral practice of business—one that dismisses ethics in favor of pursuit of profits alone—leads to unethical, often illegal, and sometimes horrific behavior in the business context. For example, in 2008, Stewart Parnell, the CEO of Peanut Corporation of America, knowingly directed that salmonella-tainted peanuts be sold, which sickened over seven hundred people, killing nine and triggering the biggest food recall in history (Estes 2014). Parnell was criminally convicted and sentenced to twenty-eight years in prison (Stafford 2015). The United Nations Global Compact is pressing for corporate social responsibility with its more than twelve thousand participants to counter amoral business practices. The related business education initiative, the Principles for Responsible Management Education (PRME), has more than 650 participants.[1]

Many Native American worldviews can make a positive contribution to doing business in a good way, minimizing negative impacts while providing guidance for decision-making that leads to ethical behavior. The chapter, divided into three parts, illustrates this through two examples. In the first part we draw on Diné tribal wisdom to outline one worldview, and in the second part we introduce the Seven Grandfather/Grandmother Teachings.[2] The third part of the chapter contains business examples and implications for business. Although these insights are a mere sliver of tribal wisdom on ways of being and doing, they serve as examples to help guide American Indian businesses toward consistency with and attention to culturally relevant ethical business decision-making.

For Native Americans, Western business education may erode or replace long-established holistic teachings, and this chapter provides a counterperspective. For non-Native business students, it introduces a different way of thinking about one's ethical values and responsibilities and how those might guide a person to better decisions. The chapter's principal objective is to encourage American Indian employees, managers, and business owners to contemplate and connect more deeply with traditional ethical values to manage workplace situations. Ethics are at the core of who we are as Native peoples; it is the very essence of our responsibilities as human beings. Our aim is to elevate moral awareness and improve understanding of how these values may be impacted by, as well as enacted within, organizational contexts and situations (Taft and White 2007).

NII'HOOKAA' DIYIN DINE'É (HOLY PEOPLE OF THE EARTH)

In the Diné world (Diné means "the People" in the Navajo language), ethics is at the core of how the Diné identify themselves: Nii'hookaa' Diyin Dine'é

(Holy People of the Earth). When the Diné were placed within the four sacred mountains of their territory in what is now the southwestern part of the United States, they were imparted with the divine powers and characteristics of the tribe's deities, the Holy People. This cardinal designation initiates not only individual but also societal accountability. One is instilled to be mindful, conscientious, and cautious in all thoughts and actions *within* the greater kinship of all earthly entities and the cosmos. Each child is taught that every element of the human body is precious, powerful, and sacred. The tips of our human tongues are generators of world-changing words and effects, and even unspoken thoughts and actions (even in solitude) are sufficient to impact others. We cannot separate ethics from anything we do because our principal teachings are imbedded in our creation as Diné.

This designation pervades the overarching concept of Sa'ah Naagháí Bik'eh Hózhoon, the fundamental tenet that informs the People of how to live ethically. A loose translation of this concept is "one's lifelong endeavor toward existing in harmony and balance within the cosmos." A vital aspect to all teachings is one's awareness within the context of the greater community, including Earth and the universe. There is recognition that no one is infallible; therefore, one is expected to practice and strive humbly to fulfill these teachings daily. The principal concept of Sa'ah Naagháí Bik'eh Hózhoon is broken down by Diné College into a framework comprised of four elements: *nitsahakees* (thinking); *nahatá* (planning); *iiná* (living); and *siih hasin* (assurance).[3] This chapter focuses on Nitsahakees, the process through which one undertakes a conscious, constructive, contemplative action to become self-identified, self-aware, and self-disciplined. This is lifelong learning that includes knowing where you come from (the clans of your mother, father, maternal grandfather, and paternal grandfather), values and beliefs taught through stories and ceremonies, family, community, and how you are uniquely positioned on this path in relation to your values and beliefs.[4]

Through Nitsahakees, a Diné person comes to understand her place first within the Diné clan system, then that place relative to family, community, nature, and the universe. This practice nurtures and develops deeply rooted values. The person endeavors to achieve balance and harmony in *iiná* (living) through practicing such values as autonomy, wisdom, love, compassion, empathy, strength, endurance, kindness, acceptance, perseverance, equality, uniqueness, kinship, and justice. As such, Diné core values are readily identifiable as an ethical value system. It is through lived experiences, self-discipline, and self-awareness that a Diné person gains understanding of his or her true essence. This evolutionary process unfolds differently in each person's life, and it is unique to that individual. These values are taught by many Diné elders as teachings handed down through generations, often via oral stories that do not conform to a traditional Western view of science, philosophy, or theory. Yet in tribal critical race theory, Brayboy (2005) aptly explains that our stories are our theories. Native "science" is valid and legitimate knowledge, as eloquently explained by Cajete (2000) and others (see, e.g., Atleo 2004; James 2001; Wildcat 2009).

Carma Claw shares one story:

> As a young girl, I joined my grandmother at dawn for the daily corn pollen offering. I translate her wisdom as the following: "All a person might need to know is the first phrase of this offering to survive and thrive on this earthly world: *Kodóó hózhóo naashaa dóó*." My translation of this phrase is "From here forward, may I strive to exist and be in balance and harmony." She taught me, "The mind is extremely powerful; we must respect ourselves and be aware of our actions because we are powerful beyond our understanding." It is difficult to pursue the path of Sa'ah Naagháí Bik'eh Hózhoon, but it is possible with every new day as a fresh opportunity to fulfill its teachings.

In Diné teachings ethics cannot be separate from *anything* we do. It follows that these values inform our actions, behaviors, and decisions within our professional lives. In the Diné worldview, notions of gratitude, humor, accountability, confidence, contemplation, generosity, and more are so valued and honored that they are embedded via ceremony and daily habit to make them an embodiment of a Diné. Diné teachings include important ideas of fairness, equity, and community. Our behaviors are relational (affecting those within our community) and holistic (encompassing the physical, mental, emotional, and spiritual realms). There is structure and order within chaos in the universe (Cajete 2000), including the ethical lives of people—that is, sometimes ethical decisions may be unambiguous and explicit, but sometimes dilemmas are also chaotic. This is acknowledged and accepted, so there is no one-size-fits-all solution. The ontological approach of Diné philosophy is such that it is ingrained in everything, including how to live ethically.

SEVEN GRANDFATHER/GRANDMOTHER TEACHINGS

The Seven Grandfather/Grandmother Teachings come from a sacred story told by Anishinabek elders.[5] This story tells of the first elder, who as a child went on a journey to the spirit world and encountered seven spiritual beings, the Seven Grandfathers or Grandmothers, depending on the telling. Each gives the child one gift that is revealed over the course of the journey to bring the gifts back to the people (see, e.g., Benton-Banai 1988 [2010]; Verbos and Humphries 2014; Verbos, Kennedy, and Claw 2016; Wood-Salomon 2002–2003; Wood-Salomon 2013). The child is on a long journey and arrives home as the first elder. The gifts are translated from the original Native languages as *wisdom, love, respect, bravery, honesty, humility,* and *truth* (see, e.g., Benton-Banai 1988 [2010]; Verbos and Humphries 2014; Verbos, Kennedy, and Claw 2016; Wood-Salomon 2002–2003). These are the human *responsibilities* toward others and all things created. One is to practice the teachings in all contexts, including contemporary business. One key understanding is that if you do not actively practice a teaching, you are doing its opposite. The opposite is as evil as the teaching is good (see, e.g., Benton-Banai 1988 [2010]). It can therefore be helpful to contemplate both how to balance the teachings and how to avoid each teaching's opposite in discerning your human responsibility in a given business situation.

This chapter humbly contemplates the possible meaning of each teaching.[6] *Wisdom* is to be shared to help all the people; it is not to be hoarded or used to exploit others. *Love* is to honor others and care for them. This includes the value of generosity, as it is loving to help others in need. *Respect* is to honor all of creation; it extends to all things animate and not just to people and animals. This honoring is to remember that if, for example, an animal gives its life to become our food and clothing, we must honor its sacrifice. So too must we keep the Earth in a good way, working to find ways that we will not damage it in our dealings. *Bravery* is to persevere in the face of adversity and to have the courage to live in accordance with the teachings. *Honesty* is to tell the truth. This is often forgotten in business, but it builds strong relationships. *Humility* is to remember that we are not greater, nor lesser, than any other. We must be humble toward creation, not wasting the Earth so that there is nothing left for future generations. Humility and respect demand that there be no discrimination against employees, customers, or others. *Truth* is to honor who we are as Native peoples, to have integrity. This means doing what we say we will do and acting in accordance with the teachings. It is acknowledged that this is difficult to do and that balancing these responsibilities requires great effort and perseverance.

In Bodewami cultural tradition, the community shares with its members according to need rather than providing equally to all. Acquisitiveness is not a part of the culture. Rather, giving away one's possessions is common. The teachings are our *responsibilities as human beings* but extend to all of creation, not just to other human beings. Bodewami culture, as in other Native and indigenous cultures, recognizes and honors spirit as animate in rocks, water, trees, plants, and animals. Ethical responsibilities toward creation are a part of other indigenous traditions (see, e.g., Spiller et al. 2011) and are found in emerging perspectives such as radical human ecology (Williams, Roberts, and McIntosh 2012) but are not generally part of business ethics discourse. Native peoples have ceremonies that celebrate these connections and help us to remember our responsibilities and the interconnectedness of everything.

IMPLICATIONS FOR BUSINESS

How do Sa'ah Naagháí Bik'eh Hózhoon, the concept of Nii'hookaa' Diyin Dine'é, and the Seven Grandfather/Grandmother Teachings apply to business? Sa'ah Naagháí Bik'eh Hózhoon is a philosophy based on an enduring (lifelong and beyond) perspective. The four tenets are contemplation, planning, life, and assurance (hope). This model of dynamic, adaptive, diverse, multidimensional, and interdependent systems of all entities is well-known by many indigenous cultures (Cajete 2000). This chapter provides examples of Native American values applied to and enacted in American Indian businesses.

The following functional areas of business are organized in twelve sections because as Native peoples we are governed by many occasions where the number twelve is appropriate. Twelve months, and in Diné, when the language was created there were twelve kernels to represent the origin and growth of vocabulary, and originally there were twelve leaders to manage the People in times of crises. The twelve functional areas of business include a living code of ethics, strategy, sales and marketing, finance and accounting, human resources, technology and equipment, production and operations, supply chain, customer services, research and development, organizational culture, and legal. In each area a concept of the teaching is applied to illustrate how indigenous ethics do and can enable indigenous businesses to be successful on their own terms.

LIVING CODE OF NATIVE ETHICS

We borrow the phrase "living code of ethics" from Verbos et al. 2007, because it describes imbuing an organization with ethical values in action through authentic leaders infused through its policies, practices, culture, actions, and interactions. This relational ethic (see, e.g., Verbos and Humphries 2014) would be "how it is" within the organization and would further provide a deeper meaning within a Native American community context. Since the "living code of ethics" concept was developed for Western businesses, we add "Native" here but realistically it should be specific to the tribe where the business is located. For those who follow Sa'ah Naagháí Bik'eh Hózhoon, for example, it would be a "living code of Diné ethics" and for those who follow the Seven Grandfather/Grandmother Teachings, it would be a "living code of Anishinabek ethics."

A living code of Native ethics would also extend beyond the living human beings within the organization to refer also to the spirit of things viewed from a Western viewpoint as inanimate but that are animate or spirit-filled from a Native American standpoint. These living codes of Native ethics are aspirational, difficult to follow without great attentiveness, and subject to human weakness and assimilation into Western business practices. Yet this is the value added to a Native American business, and it is something to aspire to create. This overarching concept would be infused into each of the other aspects of a business as described below. In contemplating the extent to which you have attained a living code of ethics in your business, ask whether the actions and interactions of people with others—whether human, four-legged, or a part of creation—is done with respect, care, kindness, generosity, and other important values? Have those who sacrifice for the business been honored? Is there waste or sustainability? Do we live our values?

STRATEGY

Long-term planning and perspective is not new to Native cultures. It is the basis for our growth and development, and continued existence as unique indigenous peoples. Our grandparents remind us that in addition to seeking a quality of life for ourselves, we are also responsible for impacting the lives of future generations. We exist as a legacy of our ancestors. Stewart et al. (forthcoming) describes how Native identities and cultural beliefs of the business leaders of six tribes have enhanced their business practices. Using the Seven Grandfather/Grandmother Teachings, a leader would contemplate the impact of a decision on all things animate, including rocks, trees, water, and nonhuman as well as human beings. Traditional Native American conceptions of time differ from Western linear clock time (Verbos, Kennedy, and Gladstone 2011), and indigenous knowledge incorporates sustainability as a part of a commitment to past and future generations (James 2001; LaDuke 1999; Wildcat 2009). Some indigenous philosophers and scholars delineate these farsighted practices as being cognizant of the next "seven generations" and as transplanar wisdom.[7] This would impact a leader's position on sustainability and using nonreplenishing natural resources.

In contemporary business strategy, the central aspect is long-term planning; it begins with a vision and mission, assessing strengths and weaknesses, and using resources toward achieving a competitive advantage (David and David 2015). The conventional practice is a recurring linear process of analyzing the system, implementation, and measurement of the plan. What if a strategist employed a circular system to plan its mission and vision as opposed to a linear approach? A system open to the view of how chaos *and* balance, warrior *and* harmony, and that male *and* female aspects exist the same spaces?

SALES AND MARKETING

Interpersonal skills to build sustainable, respectful, and honest relationships is key in sales and marketing. The ideas of being self-aware, self-disciplined, and accountable are forms of understanding your cultural capital in the context of business. These are to be contemplated within the context of the greater kinship and community, including business partners. Are you aware of who your partners are and what their core values are as business entities? If expert knowledge is available to understand what and how to pursue a market, does the wisdom of *why* and *why not* also enter into consideration? In marketing, businesses rely heavily on brands and symbols as a language to convey products. Language is the basis for cultural strength and symbols are part of language. Examples include the Kokopelli figure, the *Yei-bi-Chei* figures, the Zia sun, feathers, arrows, and circles. How might marketing products be different if the Diné concept that every element of the human body is precious, powerful, and sacred is observed? One illustration is the case about the National Football League's Washington, DC, team refusing to change a racially insulting name while claiming to honor Native people. Native peoples are very much connected to this savage caricature through historical and present-day experiences (Claw and Verbos 2015). Another case is the long-lived practice of industries claiming to "find inspiration" from all cultures and commodifying such "finds." The "products" are often sacred to a group of people, but companies extract and exploit them without regard for those connected to the items.

FINANCE AND ACCOUNTING

Financial sustainability, achieved through finance and accounting, is critical for a business to continue to exist; without cash resources or the account of financial assets and resources, a business will become insolvent or bankrupt. Much like a cornstalk, squash, bean, or tobacco plant needs nurture, care, and attention, so do the finances and accounting of a business. Many nations have cautionary stories about how particular characters paid for their greedy practices, with their skin, eyes, tail, dignity, and so on. Fiscal resources must develop and grow in a manner consistent with the teachings of Native ethics to have integrity and value beyond economics. In financial forecasting, strategic leadership might draw on the tenet that culpability initiates not only at individual levels but also at levels beyond, including company and societal levels. In addition, how can quarterly, annual, and five- and ten-year financial plans be supplemented with seven-generation perspectives?

In 2014, Ho-Chunk, Inc., owned by the Winnebago Tribe of Nebraska, celebrated twenty years of tribal business operations. Its long-term mission is "to provide the Tribe with a large enough income stream from its business operations to enable the Tribe to reach economic self-sufficiency" (Ho-Chunk 2014). Self-sufficiency is a key ethical teaching in many tribes. In Diné teachings, self-sufficiency is a virtue of being a warrior.[8] Ho-Chunk, Inc., offers a glimpse of the warrior ethic when President and CEO Lance Morgan is unequivocal in stating, "I think it is imperative that our top people have some understanding of the tribal mindset and its unique characteristics" and "[n]ever again do I want us to be at the mercy of outside interests who want to take what is ours" (Ho-Chunk 2014). Together, these expressions exemplify needing both *hózhó'jii* (blessing way) and *naayée'jii* (warrior/protection way) teachings of Being in the world as Native peoples. The finances and accounting are supported by the Winnebago tribal philosophy in a culturally relevant manner.

HUMAN RESOURCES

People are the lifeblood of any organization. The Diné and Anishinabek lessons of being respectful, honest, humble, truthful, caring, and contemplative can be applied to the human side of business. These teachings may result in managers who are empathetic and self-aware, thereby creating positive and productive relationships toward the betterment of employees and the company. Hiring employees with such managerial competencies is likely to affect decisions within the company, perhaps with a more positive, enduring, and relational perspective as opposed to adversarial positions. For instance, if leadership employs a relational attitude during an acquisition, as opposed to a hostile takeover, it might reduce the all-too-common corporate culture clash experienced in such transitions. If they serve a company where bravery and courage are needed to confront issues like an acquisition, they are still moderated by obligations toward others and all things created.

The concepts of *balance* and *justice* may also serve in times when certain relatives, like family or community, overly appeal to the relations aspect. Sometimes these appeals to relationships might result in overreaching professional business standards. The concept of *kinship* is not unidirectional. It is important that tribal preferences do not result in entitled attitudes and irresponsible employees.[9] Respect, autonomy, and justice should be afforded to managers and owners from employees as well. Another example of Ho-Chunk's Native philosophy in business is in its executive management. Humility, honesty, respect, love, strength, and endurance are evident in the business philosophy of Ho-Chunk, Inc., as they conduct operations using their tribal wisdom. One example is gender equality, as espoused by many tribes: Ho-Chunk's executive team includes Annette Hamilton, vice president and COO, and Sharon Frenchman, chief administrative officer.

TECHNOLOGY AND EQUIPMENT

Technology is using and applying tools and equipment toward accomplishing a task. For the Diné the ability to incorporate new ideas, including technology, focuses on the "infusion of new people rather than by borrowing or duplication" (Iverson 2002, 19). Trade networks, ceremonial connections, and shared art and cultural elements are examples of how *infusion*—not imitation—occurs through acknowledgment and consideration before the decision is made to accept and integrate new technology. The Diné are selective and deliberate about what and how to infuse new elements. From time immemorial, indigenous peoples have existed as ever-dynamic, ever-evolving people in a complex cosmos—living in concert within changing ecologies, times, circumstances, knowledge, culture, and so on (Claw 2015).

Consider how some Diné transfer the qualities of the horse to automobiles, an example of both extending relationships beyond humans and of accepting and integrating technology with respect, wisdom, and ceremony. They say an automobile has a brain, heart, energy, "wind life," and body, hence they care for cars in unique ways. What difference might there be in managing information systems if they are treated as a respectable entity with life and energy? Diné philosophy advocates having proper credentials and ceremony to work with all entities—human, nonhuman, and the cosmos. Might the occurrence of chronic ailments, (repetitive use, musculoskeletal issues, vision problems, etc.) as well as time away from work be reduced if nonhuman entities such as hardware and software are respected?

Today, Diné lessons of being mindful and contemplative may be applied to the nonhuman side of a business. A manager with empathy, bravery, and self-awareness is likely to also have the wisdom to acknowledge, contemplate, and decide *what* technology to integrate and, perhaps more importantly, *how*.

PRODUCTION AND OPERATIONS

Production is transforming materials into usable goods and services. In conjunction and with the support of technology and labor, the *operations* of a business create the items it sells. As pragmatic societies, the production of items used as utensils, clothing, food, and weapons has been a part of indigenous life from time immemorial. The corn fields and other foods are essential to survival. From organizing the fields to actually working the fields to the bounties of harvest time, there are many reasons corn is a symbol of sustainability, prosperity, and continued existence as Diné. While the farming economy provides sustenance in a form "relative to us," the community of exchanges in goods also strengthens our societies. "Relative to us" means we refer to corn by kinship, and our biological responses to our own indigenous foods seem to better support our health and well-being.

Life lessons, timeless stories, ceremonial rites, and family values are propagated alongside the plant fields. Planning, negotiating terms for exchanges, participating in physical labor, and harvesting are still instrumental in sustaining our communities today. The more modern example of such production is the economy of sheep in Dinétah. While the Diné recognize that life as a Navajo is held in a fragile balance, they also "inherently embraced expansion" (Iverson 2002, 21). Furthermore, they understand the economic benefits of animals like sheep and horses, as they are thoroughly integrated into Diné society, complete with ceremonial prayers and songs. Like other Native cultures, they are a practical society with desire for security and prosperity; and material production is a form of that pursuit of community well-being as well as cultural expression. Today, production and operations management can be exercised in a manner consistent with the same desire for security and prosperity, and in pursuit of continuing to exist as unique Native peoples.

SUPPLY CHAIN

Vendors, distributors, and other business partners are another essential part of moving products to markets. It is not enough in any circumstance to "claim" Native heritage as the basis to be a business partner. Knowing what your business brings to the relationship is key. How and why should your company be chosen as a part of another's supply chain? And how should a Native American business choose its supply chain partners? The corporation owned by the Cayuga Nation of New York uses a seven-generations viewpoint on how the organization endeavors "to find Full Circle Solutions to benefit the collective future of not only the company, its customers and its manufacturers, but for all of Creation" (Ongweoweh Group Full Circle Solutions 2015). This example of Native thought as inclusive and encompassing is further elucidated by "the interconnectedness of all elements of the world" in Ongweoweh Corporation's social responsibility statement: "Ongweoweh Corp is aware of the interconnectedness of all elements of the world, and is committed to sustaining the balance of life forces. This methodology is applied to Ongweoweh's business approach" (Ongweoweh Group Full Circle Solutions 2015). Recognition of the interconnectedness of all elements is a reminder of the need for love (caring, to treat others well), bravery (to make right actions), and truth (integrity, moving practices beyond our company to others we deal with).

CUSTOMER SERVICE

Assisting those who buy products or services is serving the customer. JoDonna Hall Ward talks about her small businesses located in Kayenta, Arizona, on the Navajo Nation (Small Business Revolution 2015). While not explicitly stating that she incorporates Diné values into her business, her statements about the daily process of serving her customers illustrate Diné values of humility, respect, relationships, and love (caring) as emphasized by both the Diné and the Anishinabek. "Always have respect for the community first," she states. "And, if you can do that, you will always stay in business." Consideration and respect for community is a Native value. Another example from her story is, "Am I getting rich? No, I am not. But, it's that satisfaction is more valuable, I think, than anything else." Her honesty speaks to staying true to her mother's teachings and is complete with love for her mother, her community customers, as well as tourists. For many Native peoples, profit is not defined only in economic terms but also as gains and benefits for family, community, and the environment.

RESEARCH AND DEVELOPMENT

Innovation and process, product, and material improvements are ongoing aspects of business. Indigenous societies continually researched, developed, tested, and validated their products (utensils, medicines, foods, and clothing). Early Indians developed and improved weapons (spears and bow and arrows). As farming developed, they created food-storage systems—from baskets to more durable pottery and then larger enclosed areas to preserve staples for winter. Clothing from buckskin developed into woven wool rug dresses (and blankets) and then to velvet products. Medicinal and healing practices continue to be holistic to address a person's condition as a whole (Alvord and Van Pelt 1999). Improved versions of such items are still used today by many Native nations including the Diné and the Anishinabek.

In the creation and development of new products and services, knowledge and wisdom are equally essential. It is important that Native peoples combine knowledge with wisdom to avoid innovations that are destructive to the environment, creation, or people. Bravery, most especially the aspect of perseverance, is a necessity to finding solutions that are good and that respect others and the Earth; love (caring) is also key so that neither creatures nor creation are harmed in developing, testing, or using our products. There must be conscientiousness, cautiousness, and accountability in business decisions. An example of a company that uses Native wisdom in its products is Sister Sky, a Native-owned company founded by sisters Monica Simeon and Marina TurningRobe, enrolled members of the Spokane Tribe. The sisters began the business in 1999. Its mission and vision are:

> Our Mission:
> Create Natural Solutions from Native Roots. Our products are gentle and natural. Free of petro-chemicals and parabens. Never animal tested. Earth friendly packaging and USA Made.

> Our Vision:
> Promoting health, wellness and sustainability for ourselves, our communities and our planet by respectfully sharing authentic Native American herbal wisdom (Sister Sky 2016a).

The company states that it "strives to make a positive impact through job creation and charitable giving." Sister Sky "has a 100% Native American employment rate and donates a portion of profit to the Salish Language School of Spokane and the Native Youth Leadership Alliance" (Sister Sky 2016b).

ORGANIZATIONAL CULTURE

Schein's (2010) classic tome on organizational culture identifies three levels, progressing from unconscious to visible. First are unconscious, taken-for-granted, underlying assumptions that determine behavior, thought, and feeling within an organization. Second are espoused beliefs and values stated in missions, visions, organizational values, strategies, philosophies, and organizational goals. These may or may not be consistent with behaviors—inconsistency causes dissonance, which negatively affects the people within an organization. The third level of organizational culture exists at the surface as myths, stories, and observed behavior, which includes myths and stories about ethics and ethical behavior. An example of espoused beliefs would be a values statement adopting the Seven Grandfather/Grandmother Teachings as organizational values. Practicing and balancing all seven teachings are important to building an ethical organizational culture with a living code of Anishinabek ethics. To bring these to the unconscious level, people need to internalize them as the way to behave within the organization. Similar to how Native culture is shared and conveyed as collectively defined beliefs, values, behaviors, customs, and philosophies, stories within companies can also convey how their teachings are practiced in the organization. Learning and preserving culture is applying and living it through everyday actions. A sustainable culture is infused with the language that carries its teachings. When possible, use of Native language to convey deeper meaning and connection to Native culture can be more effective and useful.

Sister Sky demonstrates the second and third levels of organizational culture, but to determine the first level requires an embedded, ethnographic study within an organization. Sustainability values are evident in the Oneida Nation's corporate philosophy: "Oneida Nation's 'Seven Generations' Philosophy as referenced in our name highlights our belief that what is said and done today will affect the next seven generations. With that in mind, our business philosophy maintains an eye toward the future, focused on sustainable growth for both our tribal economy and that of the surrounding area" (Oneida Seven Generations Corporation 2016). Service to the community is evident in Bay Bank, which became solely owned by the Oneida Nation of Wisconsin in 2000 and provides both "federally funded programs to directly assist tribal members" as well as "some unique mortgage and entrepreneurial programs to assist Oneidas in obtaining housing and starting business ventures" (Bay Bank 2016).

In this context, from a Native philosophical viewpoint, *sustainability* includes environmental accountability, cultural preservation, as well as long-term economic stability toward sustainable growth. This should also be true in the context of business practice. How can understanding your Native culture help you build or create your sustainable corporate culture in a manner that is consistent with your values and ethics? Corporate culture impacts the bottom line. What legacy will your business leave?

LEGAL

Laws bring about order, proscribe and permit, and are intended to be just, but at times human laws are not. In addition to human laws, there are natural laws and traditional laws, which govern actions and behaviors. *Natural laws* for the Diné are those that are observable, like the rising sun and moon, the changing seasons, and the order of the stars. *Traditional laws* are used to direct proper human conduct as prescribed by the Holy People (Yazzie 1994). Ceremonies are used to restore balance and harmony for transgressions against the teachings of the deities. Navajo *customary laws* are human laws based on historical customs of the people. Laws continue as a part of Native nations just as they always have. Although business laws are mostly borrowed from Western law, many tribal courts draw on traditional laws. The perception of lawless, savage, and uncivilized are discredited by these ancient rules that still govern Native communities.

There is an ethical component to human law, which can be formed for good or for ill. Businesses lobby to enact human laws, mostly in the interest and service of profit, and when those laws oppress or bully workers or others, allow for the destruction of the environment, or trample indigenous human, cultural, labor, or sovereign rights, there is a lack of honesty, respect, integrity, humility, and wisdom. It is the brave and true organization that goes above and beyond the expediency of mere legal compliance to practice what is right and just.

CONCLUSION

These teachings help us to meet the standards of our ancestors, our responsibility to all of creation and to future generations. Native businesspeople must actualize the teachings by applying them and living the standards. By imbuing one's tribal wisdom throughout an organization, a living code of Native ethics may bind together tradition with business and promote doing business in a way that honors our ancestors. These teachings provide strength and perseverance in our times of trial and tribulations as Native people, and they continue to help us adapt and survive. They are tested, validated practices that continue to support the survival and well-being of our communities as our citizens live and practice them in their lives, businesses, and professions. There are a myriad of ways in which business behavior in an American Indian context, imbued with American Indian worldviews, could elevate business to new realms. This may be challenging, requiring bravery and perseverance, but holds promise to create a truer path to building a sustainable future.

DISCUSSION

1. Is there a word for *ethics* or a translation for the idea of ethics in your Native language? Does the concept apply to work, trade, and other businesslike aspects of life? To what extent do you find businesspeople in your community following this tradition?

2. Do people who treat ethics as separate from business impact what part of themselves they ask employees to bring into their professional lives? Is it ethical to ask them do so?

3. What is at stake when ethics is left out of business operations?

4. What are the dangers of setting aside our indigenous ethics when conducting business?

EXERCISE

Consider this table, which illustrates the four possible ways that law and ethics intersect. Working in groups of three or four, come up with one to three behaviors or business practices that fall into each category. For example, it is both *legal* and *ethical* to pay employees a living wage with such benefits as health insurance and a retirement plan. It is *illegal* and *unethical* to require employees to "clock out" and continue working. It is *legal* but *unethical* to require an employee to work for minimum wage with no possibility of a

FOUR POSSIBLE WAYS THAT LAW AND ETHICS INTERSECT

Legal and Ethical	Illegal and Ethical
1.	1.
2.	2.
3.	3.
Legal and Unethical	**Illegal and Unethical**
1.	1.
2.	2.
3.	3.

raise, so that they must rely on governmental assistance or charity to make ends meet. It is *illegal* but *ethical* to allow employees to form a labor union and collectively bargain in a country that makes this conduct illegal. If you cannot think of a business application, then come up with something outside of business.

Once you have your list, consider the behavior or practice from the standpoint of the Seven Grandfather/Grandmother Teachings. Ask whether the action is wise, respects others and creation, is honest, is true (has integrity) with who Native people are, requires bravery (including perseverance), is loving (caring), and whether it requires humility. Now consider the opposites of the Seven Grandfather/Grandmother Teachings. Ask whether the action is foolish or ignorant (the opposite of wise), does not respect others or creation (the opposite of respect), is dishonest (the opposite of honesty), is false or incongruent with who we are as Native peoples (the opposite of truth), displays hate or indifference (the opposite of love), and whether the behavior is arrogant or displays hubris (the opposite of humility).

Individually, write a five-minute reflection paper about what you learned from this analysis. You may consider the following questions to guide your reflection: Did it make you think differently about any of the business behaviors or practices? What is a key takeaway from the discussion? Would following the Seven Grandfather/Grandmother Teachings help business managers to make better choices? How?

Notes

1   The participants of the United Nations Global Compact agree to ten principles pertaining to human rights, labor rights, environmental protection, and anticorruption (see www.unglobalcompact.org). The PRME consists of six principles intended to develop managers who will work toward an inclusive and sustainable global economy (see www.unprme.org).

2   The Ojibwe, Bodewami, and Odawa Nations (in English, the Chippewa, Potawatomi, and Ottawa, respectively) share these teachings. The ethical dilemma in writing this is, on the one hand, our contribution to academia is our unique voices and wisdom; but on the other hand, it can also result in (1) divulging too much cultural knowledge, and/or (2) exposing the knowledge to misinterpretation and/or misappropriation (Smith 2012). However, sharing this knowledge is also a form of resistance in creating spaces and places for ourselves as present-day indigenous business students, practitioners, and scholars by imparting our own perspectives. As Verbos, Gladstone, and Kennedy (2011, 12) have described the condition, "America's indigenous people are virtually invisible in U.S. management and education and literature."

3   It should be noted that Sa'ah Naagháí Bik'eh Hózhoon was not always compartmental-
ized, explained, or taught in a framework method. Traditionally, it is instilled by
example, through practice, and through stories told by elders in the Diné language. It
is a continual, circular, and repetitive process.

4   In Diné communities, *family* does not merely denote a nuclear family but encompasses clan and community—an extended notion also found in other Native
traditions.

5   Herein, for convenience, we refer to these three nations as Anishinabek, meaning "the
People," although the Bodewami also use Neshnabek to mean "the People". The
Ojibwe, Bodewami, and Odawa Nations (in English, the Chippewa, Potawatomi, and
Ottawa, respectively) were at one time known as the Three Fires Confederacy and
share many stories in common. The nations were splintered into smaller tribes during
colonization in the United States and Canada. There is no author of the Seven
Grandfather Teachings; rather, it is ancient wisdom that is passed down through
generations. As such, we disclaim any authorship of the story or the teachings. This
does not fit well into Western ideas of authorship and citation.

6   Stated here is one person's interpretation, gleaned from oral tradition and writings by
others, previously cited, as well as unattributed writings. It should not be considered
to be a definitive or complete understanding. It is an example of how the stories and
traditions of each tribe, relative to responsibilities toward others and creation, can be
brought forward in a positive way in American Indian business dealings to bring out
the fullness of who we are as Native peoples.

7   Gladstone 2014 describes *transplanar wisdom* as insight from past, present, and future
emerging from all directions like a sphere and known through stories.

8   The term *warrior* in Diné is distinctly different than the meaning in English. The
virtues of a warrior are those embodied in the stories of the twin heroes who rid the
world of various monsters.

9   Tribal hiring preferences are permitted by federal law as an exception to the antidis-
crimination provisions of Title VII of the Civil Rights Act of 1964. Many tribes adopt
these preferences as a business practice.

References

Alvord, L. A., and E. C. Van Pelt. 1999. *The Scalpel and the Silver Bear: The First Navajo
Woman Surgeon Combines Western Medicine and Traditional Healing.* New York:
Bantam Books.

Atleo, E. R. (Umeek). 2004. *Tsawalk: A Nuu-chah-nulth Worldview.* Vancouver: UBC
Press.

Bay Bank. 2016. "About Us." Online at www.baybankgb.com/About-Us.aspx. Accessed on
July 6, 2016.

Benton-Banai, E. 1988 [2010]. *The Mishomis Book: The Voice of the Ojibway.* Minneapolis:
University of Minnesota Press.

Brayboy, B. M. J. 2005. "Toward a Tribal Critical Race Theory in Education." *Urban Review*
37, no. 5: 425–46.

Cajete, G. 2000. *Native Science: Natural Laws of Interdependence.* Sante Fe, NM: Clear Light Publishers.

Claw, C. 2015. *May We Find Balance.* Knowledge in Indigenous Networks. Online at http://indigenousknowledgenetwork.net/2015/10/28/may-we-find-balance/. Accessed on October 28, 2015.

Claw, C., and A. K. Verbos. 2015. "The Consequences of Sports Teams' 'Indian' Mascots: Implications for Native Americans." Paper presented at the Academy of Management. Vancouver, Canada. August 2015.

David, F. R., and F. R. David. 2015. *Strategic Management: A Competitive Advantage Approach, Concepts and Cases.* Upper Saddle River, NJ: Prentice Hall.

Estes, B. 2014. "Prosecuting over Peanuts: How the PCA Scandal Can Inform More Effective Federal Criminal Enforcement of Food Safety Laws." *Review of Litigation* 33: 145–82. Online at www.lexisnexis.com/hottopics/lnacademic. Accessed on January 4, 2016.

Gladstone, J. S. 2014. "Native American Transplanar Wisdom." In C. Spiller and R. Wolfgramm, eds., *Indigenous Spiritualities at Work: Transforming the Spirit of Business Enterprise.* Pp. 21–32. Charlotte, NC: Information Age Publishing.

Ho-Chunk, Inc. 2014. *2014 Annual Report.* http://hochunkinc.com/downloadable%20 forms/2014%20FINAL%20ANNUAL%20REPORT-final.pdf. Accessed on January 9, 2016.

Iverson, P. 2002. *Diné: A History of the Navajos.* New Mexico: University of New Mexico Press.

James, K., ed. 2001. *Science and Native American Communities: Legacies of Pain, Visions of Promise.* Lincoln: University of Nebraska Press.

Kubasek, N. K., M. N. Browne, L. J. Dhooge, D. J. Herron, L. L. Barkacs, and C. Williamson. 2015. *Dynamic Business Law.* 3d edition. New York: McGraw Hill Education.

LaDuke, W. 1999. *All Our Relations: Native Struggles for Land and Life.* Cambridge, MA: South End Press.

Oneida Seven Generations Corporation. 2016. "Welcome to Oneida Seven Generations Corporation." Online at www.osgc.net/. Accessed on July 6, 2016.

Ongweoweh Group Full Circle Solutions. 2015. "Corporate Social Responsibility." Online at www.ongweoweh.com/core-competences/. Accessed on January 29, 2016.

Schein, E. H. 2010. *Organizational Culture and Leadership.* 4th edition. San Francisco: John Wiley and Sons.

Sister Sky. 2016a. "About Us." Online at www.sistersky.com/Sister_Sky_s/1817.htm. Accessed on July 6, 2016.

———. 2016b. "Giving Back." Online at www.sistersky.com/category_s/1904.htm. Accessed on July 6, 2016.

Small Business Revolution. 2015. *The Blue Coffee Pot: A Small Business Revolution Mini-Documentary.* Online at https://vimeo.com/139172800. Accessed on January 27, 2016.

Smith, L. T. 2012. *Decolonizing Methodologies: Research and Indigenous Peoples.* London: Zed Books Ltd.

Spiller, C., L. Erakovic, M. Henare, and E. Pio. 2011. "Relational Well-being and Wealth: Māori Businesses and an Ethic of Care." *Journal of Business Ethics* 98, no. 1: 153–69.

Stafford, L. 2015. "After Dramatic Day, Ex-CEO Gets Twenty-Eight Years." *Atlantic Journal-Constitution*. September 22.

Stewart, D., A. K. Verbos, C. Birmingham, S. L. Black, and J. S. Gladstone. Forthcoming. "Being Native American in Business: Culture, Identity, and Authentic Leadership in Modern American Indian Enterprises." *Leadership*.

Taft, S. H., and J. White. 2007. "Ethics Education: Using Inductive Reasoning to Develop Individual, Group, Organizational, and Global Perspectives." *Journal of Management Education* 31, no. 5: 614–46.

Verbos, A. K., J. A. Gerard, P. R. Forshey, C. S. Harding, and J. S. Miller. 2007. "The Positive Ethical Organization: Enacting a Living Code of Ethics and Ethical Organizational Identity." *Journal of Business Ethics* 76, no. 1: 17–33.

Verbos, A. K., J. S. Gladstone, and D. M. Kennedy. 2011. "Native American Values and Management Education: Envisioning an Inclusive Virtuous Circle." *Journal of Management Education* 35, no. 1: 10–26.

Verbos, A. K., and M. Humphries. 2014. "A Native American Relational Ethic: An Indigenous Perspective on Teaching Human Responsibility." *Journal of Business Ethics* 123: 1–9.

Verbos, A. K., D. M. Kennedy, and C. Claw. 2016. "Native American Values Applied to Business Ethics." In *Tribal Wisdom for Business Ethics*, edited by G. A. Rosile. Bingley, UK: Emerald Group Publishing Limited.

Verbos, A. K., D. M. Kennedy, and J. S. Gladstone. 2011. "'Coyote Was Walking . . .': Management Education in Indian Time." *Journal of Management Education* 35, no. 1: 51–65.

Wildcat, D. R. 2009. *Red Alert: Saving the Planet with Indigenous Knowledge*. Golden, CO: Fulcrum Publishers.

Williams, L., R. Roberts, and A. McIntosh, eds. 2012. *Radical Human Ecology: Intercultural and Indigenous Approaches*. Ashgate Publishing Company: Burlington, VT.

Wood-Salomon, Z. 2002–2003. 7 Nokomis/Grandmother Teachings.

———. 2013. Personal communication. September.

Yazzie. 1994. "Life Comes from It: Navajo Justice Concepts." *New Mexico Law Review* 24 (Spring), no. 2: 176.

11 COYOTE LEARNS TO MANAGE A HEALTH PROGRAM

Joseph Scott Gladstone, *New Mexico State University*

ABSTRACT

This chapter extends the business principles discussed throughout the book and applies them to managing tribal health programs. This being a book about management practice, this chapter does not discuss the myriad health challenges facing American Indian communities or developing policy that mitigates these problems. Much literature exists discussing tribal health problems (Dixon and Roubideaux 2001), policy (Rhoades 2000), and culturally relevant clinical practices (Dixon and Iron 2006), and readers are directed to those sources to explore the production and application of Indian health policy and clinical practice. Despite the many successful efforts to understand culturally specific approaches to treating, preventing, and advocating for political support to fund tribal health programs, there remains a need for a talented workforce to carry out public health activities in tribal communities. Hahn (1999) points out that public health program managers inadequately translate public health knowledge into effective action. They often have insufficient resources and poor knowledge about how to manage those resources.

This chapter offers practical solutions to public health problems and specifically focuses on organization management: the day-to-day operation of a small health program. We look at program management from a business perspective—that is, thinking about tribal management as an organization manager rather than a policy maker. The chapter briefly explores strategy, funding, worker motivation, and program marketing as each applies to managing a tribal health program. This chapter takes a different approach to teaching management practice within Indian Country. It embraces Verbos, Kennedy, and Gladstone's (2011) lesson to draw on traditional tribal teaching to illustrate Native American perspectives on management practice.

KEYWORDS: tribal health programs, tribal management, traditional tribal teaching methods

INTRODUCTION

COYOTE WAS WALKING ALONG WHEN HE CAME ACROSS AN announcement for a manager position in a tribal health program. The tribe wanted to fight a disease that was harming them. "That sounds interesting," Coyote said. "I like a good fight. I think I'll give that a try." So he applied for the job and got it. Although Coyote had much experience with a good fight, he wasn't very experienced with program management, so he wasn't quite sure how to effectively manage his program. Fortunately for Coyote, Mouse was managing another program next door.

Coyote saw Mouse sitting at her desk, so he yelled over to her: "Mouse! I was just hired to run this program, and I really don't know what to do. Can you help me?"

"What is your plan?" Mouse asked Coyote.

"Plan?" Coyote asked. "I'm supposed to fight a disease. So I will fight it. That is my plan."

"How much money do you have to help you to fight this disease and help these people get better?" Mouse asked Coyote.

"Not much," Coyote said. "Oh, and the people I have working for me don't do a very good job, no matter how much I beat them."

Mouse said to Coyote, "You should think of your program as a business. This means that you need a plan. You need to know how to manage your money and the people who help you as you try to help the community."

"Think about my program as a *business*?" Coyote was confused. "Isn't a business all about making money? My program isn't supposed to make money, it's supposed to spend it."

"Not quite," Mouse replied.

THE FIRST RULE OF BUSINESS AND THE BUSINESS OF PUBLIC HEALTH

Mouse told Coyote that the very first rule in business is to buy low and sell high. She added that any entrepreneur who cannot follow this very important rule should either seek a different career path or learn how to successfully follow the first rule. This rule, she said, applies to health administration. Mouse then connected the first rule of business to the first rule of public health program operation: gain high program performance at low cost. A program administrator's goal is to produce the greatest good for the community, with the least amount of money spent. Since most tribal health programs are grant driven, this means maximizing the amount of community good from the grant funding. When it comes to the idea of profit, for-profit businesses and public-funded health programs have the same goal: receive a large return for an investment.

"But I don't think I'm supposed to make any money," Coyote said to Mouse. "Is that not what it means to be a nonprofit? Not make money?"

Mouse responded by teaching Coyote that when thinking about an investment, there is no rule that says that an investment must be low. There is no known law that places a low cap on operating funds for tribal health programs. The greater the base investment in any business venture, whether for cash profit or for community gain, the greater the return if the investment is well managed. Gaining profit (in this case, increased quality-of-life for the community) is the goal for any tribal health program manager. "Let's talk more about what can slow up your program and how to get around those obstacles," she said to Coyote.

OBSTACLES IN TRIBAL HEALTH BUSINESS SUCCESS

Mouse continued Coyote's lesson by helping him anticipate and react to obstacles that exist in tribal health program management. These obstacles could include weak strategic planning, insufficient funding, an unskilled workforce, and program marketing.

STRATEGIC PLANNING FOR TRIBAL HEALTH PROGRAMS

Mouse said to Coyote: "For your program to succeed, you need a strategy. In your earlier travels you learned that strategy is 'the processes and tactics an organization uses to effectively achieve its goals.'"[1]

"I remember seeing that," Coyote said.

"*Strategic planning* is an act that any new program manager must do when taking charge of a health program," Mouse continued. "The program strategy guides your program's operations. *Strategy* identifies your program's goals and outlines its objectives. Without this first step, Coyote, you will find yourself wandering all over the place because you will have very little idea about where to go."

Coyote was curious about what Mouse had to say. "Okay," he replied. "What do I do first?"

"Well," Mouse said, "you need to understand that most tribal health programs are grounded in public health science. Public health's guiding philosophy focuses on serving community (Katz and Felton 1965). Public health exists for the welfare of the community, and being such, health programs are required to work with community insight and desires. A tribal health program manager must know as much about community *needs* as understanding community *wants*. For example, public health science recognizes the risks of teen pregnancies, both the health risks to the baby in addition to the social and economic impact on the teen mother and the community that she lives in."

Mouse continued: "Although teen pregnancy is an important problem from a public health perspective, you need to ask if it is a problem for a community that places high value on its future, its Seventh Generation. Is teen pregnancy a problem for a community whose members value being a grandparent? A tribal health program manager must weigh out initial plans when public health science conflicts with community values. With community input a program manager can discover what is important to a community and, with that community, set long-term goals for the program. Perhaps not even creating a program that a community does not value."

ENTREPRENEURIAL THINKING IN TRIBAL HEALTH PROGRAM MANAGEMENT

"Wait," Coyote interjected. "Isn't my job supposed to be creating a program? Won't I get in trouble for *not* creating one?"

"Not exactly," Mouse replied. "Of course, you are still supposed to create the program that you're hired to do. What changes is how complicated your program is at its beginning. Choosing not to pursue a heath program is entrepreneurial thinking. It is as important for a successful entrepreneur to choose not to enter into a business venture—be it a new product, production mode, or market—as it is important to choose to take such risk. Spending a great deal of time on grant identification and grant writing for a program tackling an issue that is not seen as a problem for a community saves labor costs and expenses needed to carry out such planning activity."

Coyote listened.

"Now simply abandoning a potential program isn't the only option available," Mouse continued. "To return to the hypothetical example, although a community might not find a teen pregnancy prevention program important, a savvy health promotion professional like you can draw upon public health sciences in community health promotion as a way to initiate the program, although perhaps at a much smaller scale than envisioned."

Mouse waited for Coyote to finish taking his notes, then continued. "A classic health promotion theory is the transtheoretical model, also known as the stages-of-change model (Glanz, Rimer, and Vizwanath 2015). This model assumes that people hold certain attitudes toward health issues that affect them, and if some people aren't ready to tackle a problem, they won't tackle it. The same applies to communities. At the community level, this is called the Community Readiness Model (Edwards et al. 2000). So sometimes health issues that might be important to a health program leader might not be important to a community. But don't worry, an issue might not be important simply because a community is not fully informed about the problem. Knowing about these theories, a program manager can plan an objective that leads to a grand strategy goal to reduce teen pregnancies in the community. This first objective could be as simple as informing a community about the public health problems related to teen pregnancy and offering solutions to those potential problems."

Mouse continued: "Note that the overall program goal (reducing teen pregnancy) has not changed, just the strategy to achieve that goal. It is important for a tribal health program leader to be flexible in thinking and drawing on public health theories to guide planning and strategies. So, Coyote, by pulling back on your initial grand effort to pursue a large grant that might fail, your efforts can be directed to a smaller program that could demonstrate success, and in the long term reflect well on the program's ability to meet goals when it applies for larger and more competitive grants."

Coyote had many questions for Mouse. "How do I learn more about competitive strategic management?" he asked.

"Competitive strategic management is discussed in chapter 4 in this book," Mouse said. "A key reward for a competitive health program is the ability to secure funding that leads to the realizing success in reducing health problems within a community. Let's look at funding strategy."

"Okay," Coyote said, and readjusted his sitting position. Mouse had more to teach him about managing his tribal health program.

EXPANDING FUNDING OPPORTUNITIES FOR TRIBAL HEALTH PROGRAMS

"Consider how many tribal health programs exist," Mouse continued. "You might find a program with a single objective—for example, diabetes prevention—and that program is driven by a single funding source such as the Indian Health Service's Special Diabetes Program for Indians (SDPI). The annual grant program SDPI has existed since 1997 and has granted millions of dollars to assorted tribal and urban Indian diabetes programs and demonstration projects (Indian Health Service 2016). A risk that exists with federally funded programs is that funding could end at any time, depending on the whims of the current government. What could happen to efforts of a diabetes prevention program if it lost its only source for operating?"

Coyote stared at the ground just below Mouse's feet, rubbing his chin as if he were deep in thought over her question, although he really did not know the answer. Mouse recognized his look, so she continued her lesson. "If a program lost its sole funding source, it would have to close up shop. So looking at a diabetes prevention program from a financial perspective, a diabetes program manager will actively consider and pursue as many funding opportunities possible."

Coyote nodded as Mouse continued. "Thinking about diabetes prevention through a public health science perspective, a diabetes program manager knows that eating well and exercising regularly can prevent diabetes. These two activities also reduce some cancers and heart disease. These activities also reduce bone and joint disease and increase individual vitality. Since the same activities that prevent and manage diabetes also contribute to reducing and treating other lifestyle diseases, a program manager can evaluate his or her diabetes program's mission and restructure it to serve a greater mission. By expanding a single disease program into a broader program that addresses other community diseases through the same public health strategies, the program manager has opened up the program to many other funding sources, such as cancer and heart disease prevention, nutrition education, physical activity promotion, and so on. Thus, if a program loses one source of funding, it can continue its broader mission and its employees don't lose their jobs."

"Oh! I get it!" Coyote exclaimed. His eyes were wide with excitement. "I don't have to think that my program only needs to be funded only by one source. If I know that my program can treat other diseases the same way that my program treats the one I am fighting right now, I should look for money that targets those other diseases."

"Correct," confirmed Mouse.

"I have another problem." Coyote asked. "My employees are pretty lazy. And no matter how hard I beat them, I can't get them motivated to do work."

"Uh . . . let's talk about this," Mouse replied.

MANAGING THE PUBLIC HEALTH WORKFORCE

"A common complaint in Indian Country," Mouse said, "is that there appears to be many workers who think that their primary job is simply to get paid.

So, Coyote, are you wondering how you and other tribal health program managers can get your employees to work?"

"Yes!" Coyote exclaimed. He was excited to learn how to get people to do what he wanted them to do. He liked telling others what to do. That was his way.

"Well," Mouse began, "in chapter 9 in this book you learned about leadership, which is about being able to influence people toward reaching goals."

"Yes," Coyote said. "I saw that before I got here."

Mouse continued. "A program leader must guide program staff into thinking about helping the program reach its goals, such as either preventing teen pregnancy or preventing diabetes. Health problems we talked about earlier. Of course this might be more challenging to say than to actually do."

"That's for sure." Coyote nodded.

"Let's explore leader behaviors. Some of these might interfere with program workers' efforts to attain program goals. Let's look at some things that keep workers from performing well in their jobs and then let's talk about some solutions to these problems."

Heath program worker motivation

"*Parles-tu français?*" Mouse asked Coyote.

"*Qu'est-ce que tu as dit?*" Coyote asked.

"Okay," Mouse continued, "the word *motivation* comes from the French word *mouvoir*, which means *to move*. When a leader wants to motivate a worker, that leader is trying to get the worker to move, to do some kind of work that helps in the program's effort to succeed in its mission goals. A program leader should not focus on motivating a worker by using the technique described by this saying: 'The beatings won't stop until morale improves.' This just ends up frustrating both the program leader and employees. It is important to understand some basic leadership theories and know when and how to use them."

Leadership and motivation theories

Mouse continued her lesson for Coyote. "Before talking about leadership theories, you as a program leader must know that motivation is intrinsic." Coyote interrupted Mouse, cocking his head while saying the word *intrinsic*. Mouse saw his confusion. "Motivation comes from within a worker. Nobody can force anybody to do work, not even you, Coyote—"

"I just hit them harder," Coyote interrupted, boasting, "and then they are happy to work for me!"

"Even if you feel that you must beat a worker until that worker's morale improves, it will not improve. Change comes from within. This thinking is almost Taoist."

"I know that guy," Coyote said, "we have tea together."

Mouse explained further: "A tribal health program leader must figure out how to help a worker become self-motivated and self-driven so that worker will want to perform work."

"So use a heavier stick." Coyote was quite confident that his way always worked.

Evaluating the leader

Mouse sighed. "Let me tell you about this leadership researcher, McGregor. He noticed that there are two types of leaders, a Theory X leader and a Theory Y leader (McGregor 1960). Keep in mind that McGregor's idea describes how program leaders see their workers—not how workers actually are!"

"I know how all workers are, Mouse," Coyote said with certainty. "They are lazy and just hang out at the office so that they can get paid."

"And your thinking makes you a Theory X leader, Coyote," Mouse pointed out. "Theory X leaders believe that all workers are lazy, so they need to be beaten daily until worker morale improves."

"Works for me," Coyote said.

"Really, Coyote?" Mouse replied, with a strong sense of doubt. "By what I see from my office, your workers spend more time hiding from you than doing work. Let's consider a different way of looking at your workers, a Theory Y way. A Theory Y leader is aware that every worker is an individual. Each worker has a different want or need for joining the program. A Theory Y leader respects each worker as an individual and adjusts his or her leadership technique to fit each worker."

Worker needs

Mouse noticed that Coyote had somehow managed to find a cup of coffee. Sipping from the cup, Coyote had settled in and was ready to learn more, so Mouse continued her lesson.

"One challenge with leading a health program in Indian Country—"

"I know that place," Coyote said between sips. "I've been there."

"—is the number of trained talent (that is, potential workers) in a community from which a program leader can hire to help accomplish program goals," Mouse continued. "There is a problem in tribal communities with high unemployment rates. Some tribal governments might see federally funded health and social service programs as much as employment agencies as they do as health and social service programs. So a program leader might inherit a staff that was hired despite having limited knowledge about how to do public health activities. People might want a job in your program just because the job provides an income and benefits—"

"And that is why they need to be beaten," Coyote interrupted. "They need to learn how to do the job."

"That's thinking like a Theory X boss again, Coyote. No, when you think about a worker joining your program just for a paycheck, that worker is an example of Maslow's first level in his Hierarchy of Needs."

"Hey! I learned that in my psychology class!" Coyote straightened up, happy knowing that something from school was mentioned to him and that he remembered it.

"Yes," Mouse went on. "And you should remember that according to Maslow (1943), people sort out their life's needs in hierarchal order, from bottom to top. The most basic level need is food and shelter, the next level is security, above security people look for social connections and after that they want self-esteem.[2] Once these four levels of needs are fulfilled, people seek self-actualization. Just by wanting to learn how to be a better manager, Coyote, you are fulfilling your need to satisfy your curiosity. You are pursuing a self-actualization need."

"Oh! Then I must be very self-actualized!" Coyote was happy to be included in Maslow's theory. "Have I got some stories to tell you about my curiosity!"

"So I've heard," Mouse said, and continued with her lesson. "A program leader must understand what motivated a worker to join a program. Was the worker motivated to fulfill the most basic of Maslow's needs, income to afford food and shelter? How about social needs? In small communities the workplace may be the only place where a worker can socialize with other people, and that person's desire to show up to work is to have company. It may appear that one worker's focus on a need for food and shelter and another worker's focus on socializing are two needs that don't fit with a program manager's desire to have them contribute to the program mission."

"So . . . ," Coyote was about to give his usual solution to his worker motivation problem (beating his workers), but Mouse stopped him before Coyote suggested it.

"No, Coyote, you are thinking like a Theory X manager," Mouse explained. "A Theory X manager might be motivated to threaten these two to do work or face being beaten, or even fired. But firing people isn't as easy a solution as it sounds. After a person is fired, other workers must fill in the gaps because the fired worker is no longer there. Tasks must be completed and shifts must be filled. If a reservation lacks a deep pool of talented work, the manager might regret discovering that the best available worker was just fired."[3]

"Hmmm." Coyote never realized that firing workers makes things harder for him and others, and that it might not be easy to replace that person when there are not many qualified workers in a reservation community.

"Also, Coyote, some tribes have strict employment policies that give the benefit of the doubt about worker performance to the worker. So your time that could be spent moving your program toward accomplishing its program goal is wasted as you negotiate an employee performance program for the nonproductive worker."

Coyote rubbed his chin as he looked toward Mouse. She knew that he was learning something. "So, Coyote, when you threaten your worker, you create stress between you and that worker. Instead of motivating the worker to do some work, you might accidently motivate the worker to hide from you as much as possible. So again, your Theory X style motivates the worker to do something other than help accomplish program goals."

Coyote was thinking hard now. "So when I beat my workers until they work, I am instead just motivating them to *not* work? That's not what I meant to do."

"Yes, Coyote. This is known as the folly of rewarding A while hoping for B (Kerr 1995). The folly here is that while a manager wants an employee to perform behavior B (for example, clean the fitness center), the manager instead rewards the worker for hiding from the manager because the manager does not work to find a solution to the worker's performance problem."

Coyote had questions for Mouse. "So what do I do with the worker who only shows up to get paid, and the other who just wants to chat?"

"Those are good questions, Coyote. For the worker who wants to get paid, you need to set goals for that worker (Locke and Latham 1990). This is called goal-setting theory."

Coyote scribbled into his notebook. "Goal-setting theory."

Mouse explained: "Often, workers do not work because they simply are not clear about what they are supposed to do."

"Can't they figure that out on their own?" Coyote asked. "Isn't that why some go to college?"

"College teaches them what the job is *about*, Coyote, but they still need to know what the specific job is for the program."

"Oh." Coyote scribbled more notes.

"In short," Mouse said, "you need to set a goal for a worker. That goal should be related to tasks that help the program reach its overall goals."

"Okay," Coyote replied.

"Then you need to get goal commitment," Mouse said.

"Make them promise to finish their goals. Got it," Coyote responded.

"Almost," said Mouse. Coyote looked confused. Mouse continued: "Goal commitment is a two-way street. The worker needs to agree to reach the assigned goal, and you, the boss, need to promise to provide support for that worker to reach that goal. The third step is for you to work hard to keep your promise by ensuring that the worker gets the support, including equipment and supplies to reach his or her goal."

"Okay," Coyote nodded. "I can see that for the worker who only wants to get paid. But what about the chatterbox?"

Mouse said, "You should assess if that person's personality fits with the job. But goal-setting should also help that person stay focused."

Demotivation

Coyote nodded, then asked, "Is there more that I should know about leading my workers?"

"Yes," Mouse replied. "Maslow is only one way to look at worker motivation. Another thing that a program leader needs to consider is what demotivates workers."

Coyote's ears perked up. "Demotivate?"

"Yes. You can hire the smartest and hardest worker to do a job that helps you reach your program goals and take out their excitement to do that work."

"By beating them." Coyote was starting to figure out that his favorite motivation strategy wasn't very good.

"Yes, and in other ways, too." Mouse replied.

Coyote's face revealed an idea. "I will just pay them more money!"

"Actually," Mouse explained, "people don't work only for money (Deci 1975; Herzberg 1968; Locke and Latham 1990). Sure, money is nice to have, but it is not able to motivate workers in the long term. Think about it, Coyote, are you doing this job just for the money?"

"No. I was hired to fight a disease. And you know how much I like to fight something." Coyote winked.

Mouse smiled. "The same applies for your workers. Especially if they are working in an area where they committed a great deal of their life in preparation to do so. Such as your worker with the physical education degree who is using that degree to manage your gym. The money is nice, but that person really wants to apply their knowledge and education to the work that you hired them to do."

"That makes sense," Coyote said.

"Money is not a driving force to do work," Mouse explained. "Rather, many people want to feel that they accomplished something good. In tribal health programs they are motivated to do good, to help their community improve their health. Many workers in tribal health programs have family members who experienced and suffered the diseases that their programs seek to end, and these workers might have the same diseases."

Mouse continued the lesson. "Workers like this come into programs motivated and ready to do great things. However, over time they might become less motivated to do the work they so eagerly started. What happened? A Theory X boss perhaps would think that the formerly motivated worker was simply attempting to look good so as to earn the job, and now that the worker is getting paid, that worker has become lazy. A beating with a good stout stick is the solution to that problem. But a Theory Y boss realizes that beating a worker is a folly, leading the worker to become less motivated to come to work, hoping to cash out as much sick leave as possible."

Coyote listened as Mouse explained further: "Recall that motivation is *intrinsic*—that is, it comes from within an individual, not from the outside via a stick or a bribe like a carrot. It is also related to Kerr's Folly. An action by a leader or a change forced by a bureaucracy can pull the rug out from under a highly motivated worker. So it is very important to understand *why* your worker is excited to do a job and help that worker remain excited."

Worker confidence

"One way to keep an employee excited in doing a job is by improving the worker's skillset," Mouse said.

"What does that mean?" Coyote asked.

"How confident is that person in completing assigned tasks?" Mouse asked. "Perhaps this person would find greater satisfaction in work, self-actualization, if given the opportunity to learn how to perform the job better and discover how the job fits in fulfilling a greater mission to improve the community's health and well-being (Bandura 1997; Lunenberg 2011). How about a worker who joins the program right out of college? For example, let's say you hired a new graduate with a physical education degree to lead the program's physical activity component. Although the worker might know the science behind improving physical health and have some internship experience in the field, they have never before been responsible for an entire subprogram. They might not feel confident in applying what they learned in school and still feel like a student. The Theory X leader might criticize the new graduate for not having learned anything in school; this will quickly demotivate the formerly eager worker who had invested time and effort in a degree that the boss finds valueless."

Coyote listened as Mouse continued. "But the Theory Y manager recognizes that the worker is new and needs to build confidence in applying the new degree as well as learn a new subtrade: management. The Theory Y boss commits time, effort, and resources to mentor the new worker and to give advanced training."

PROGRAM MARKETING

"I have just one more question," Coyote said to Mouse. "I was told that you are really good at program marketing. Can you tell me how to make a really good poster for my program?"

"That is not quite what *marketing* means," Mouse replied. "*Marketing* is a process where you think about how you will fulfill the community's needs to fight the disease that you were hired to fight."

"Oh," Coyote said, as he thought about what Mouse had just explained. "So, just like everything else you have taught me so far, marketing my program is not as simple as I think it is."

"Correct." Mouse nodded. "In its most simple form, *marketing* is based on the Four Ps: product, price, placement, and promotion (Lee and Kotler 2011). Take note that the last thing in this list is *promotion*. That is the last step in marketing. Think about it this way: How can you promote a program that does not exist? For example, let's consider the gym in your fitness program. You, of course, want people to come to this gym, so you want to advertise its location and the hours that it is open. But is your gym ready to be opened to the public? Your gym is a product. It exists to fulfill the community's need to exercise when it is too hot, too cold, too wet, too windy, too dark outside, or any other time when exercising inside is better than exercising outside. Correct?"

"Yeah, I can see that." Coyote replied. "I should not think about making posters for my gym until my gym is ready to be opened."

"Correct." Mouse nodded. "Let's consider another example: your nutrition counseling program. Think about the product that nutrition counseling delivers. You are 'selling' knowledge to your 'customers.' How much are you charging your customers for this product?"

"Nothing," Coyote replied. "The program is free for them."

"Not exactly," said Mouse. "You are at the very least charging your customers, your clients, their *time*. When your clients come to visit your program, they have decided to spend their time with you instead of somewhere else. Instead of choosing to spend their time at your program, your clients could just as easily decide to spend their time somewhere else."

"Oh, I never thought of that," Coyote uttered. "Wait, what about those folks in the treatment center. They don't get to choose to be there."

"Actually, they do," Mouse said. "They could choose to go to jail instead. Program marketing is a process that begins with providing a product that the community you serve finds valuable and worth spending their time and effort to participate in. It needs to be placed in a location convenient for the clients. This means that your gym, demonstration kitchen, and offices for your counselors need to be placed somewhere that your clients can easily access, even if they do not have a car or another ride. Or you can bring your program to them. You also need to place your program hours within a timeframe that works with your customers' schedules. If there are many people who need nutrition counseling, but who also need to work at their own jobs, then it is not good marketing to close your counseling center at 5 o'clock. Is it?"

"No. I guess not."

"Also, think about how much more motivated your counselors might be if they had an opportunity to reach more customers. Your counselors might be willing to work a little later in the evening if they knew they could help more people."

CONCLUSION

"Wow! That was a lot of information to take in," Coyote said.

"Yes. It is," Mouse said, smiling. "And it's only the tip of the iceberg."

"What's an iceberg?" Coyote asked.

"You will need to ask Polar Bear to describe one," Mouse responded. "For now, you should explore other chapters in this book so you can get more ideas and details about how to manage your tribal program."

"I think I will do that." Coyote stood up and went out the door.

Mouse watched Coyote go through the doorway. After he disappeared down the hall, she said to herself, "I think he got a good start. He does need to learn more, but for now he will be fine."

DISCUSSION

1. This chapter was presented quite differently than other chapters in this book. Do you find that bringing traditional storytelling into learning about modern-day organizational management is useful for learning how to manage a business?

2. Is using traditional storytelling appropriate for teaching modern-day business skills?

3. Would you use traditional storytelling to lead your employees? If so, what story do you think is useful to use?

4. What is the main lesson that you found in this story?

Notes

1   See Daniel Stewart's chapter, "Business Strategy: Building Competitive Advantage in American Indian firms," in this book.

2   It is important to mention in a book about American Indian business management that Maslow's thoughts and theory about social needs was inspired by his experience working with the Blood Tribe in southern Alberta, Canada. He was impressed by the way this tribal community supported each other in a social context. This experience is described in his work *Synanon and Eupsychia* (Maslow 1967).

3   See Stephanie Lee Black and Carolyn Birmingham's chapter, "American Indian Leadership Practices," in this book.

References

Bandura, A. 1997. *Self-Efficacy: The Exercise of Control.* Upper Saddle River, NJ: Prentice Hall.

Deci, E. L. 1975. *Intrinsic Motivation.* New York: Plenum.

Dixon, M., and P. E. Iron. 2006. *Strategies for Cultural Competency in Indian Health Care.* Washington, DC: American Public Health Association.

Dixon, M., and Y. Roubideaux. 2001. *Promises to Keep: Public Health Policy for American Indians and Alaska Natives in the 21st Century.* Washington, DC: American Public Health Association Press.

Edwards, R. W., P. Jumper-Thurman, B. A. Plested, E. R. Oetting, and L. Swanson. 2000. "Community Readiness: Research to Practice." *Journal of Community Psychology* 28, no. 3: 291–307.

Glanz, K., B. K. Rimer, and K. Viswanath. 2015. *Health Behavior: Theory, Research, and Practice.* 5th edition. San Francisco, CA: Jossey-Bass.

Hahn, R. A. 1999. *Anthropology and Public Health.* New York: Oxford University Press

Herzberg, F. 1968. "One More Time: How Do You Motivate Employees?" *Harvard Business Review* 46: 53–62.

Indian Health Service. 2016. "Special Diabetes Program for Indians." Online at www.ihs .gov/MedicalPrograms/Diabetes/index.cfm?module=programsSDPI. Accessed on April 11, 2016.

Katz, A. H., and J. S. Felton. 1965. *Health and the Community: Readings in the Philosophy and Sciences of Public Health*. New York: Free Press.

Kerr, S. 1995. "On the Folly of Rewarding *A* While Hoping for *B*." *Academy of Management Executive* 9, no. 1: 7–14.

Lee, N. R., and P. Kotler. 2011. *Social Marketing: Influencing Behaviors for Good*. 4th edition. Thousand Oaks, CA: Sage.

Locke, E. A., and G. P. Latham. 1990. *A Theory of Goal Setting and Task Performance*. Englewood Cliffs, NJ: Prentice Hall.

Lunenberg, F. C. 2011. "Self-efficacy in the Workplace: Implications for Motivation and Performance." *International Journal of Management, Business, and Administration* 14, no. 1: 1–6.

Maslow, A. 1967. "Synanon and Eupsychia." *Journal of Humanistic Psychology* 7, no. 1: 28–35.

———. 1943. "A Theory of Human Motivation." *Psychological Review* 50, no. 4: 370–96.

McGregor, D. M. 1960. *The Human Side of Enterprise*. New York: McGraw Hill.

Rhoades, E. 2000. *American Indian Health: Innovations in Health Care Promotion and Policy*. Baltimore, MD: Johns Hopkins University Press.

Verbos, A. K., D. M. Kennedy, and J. S. Gladstone. 2011. "'Coyote Was Walking . . .': Management Education in Indian Time." *Journal of Management Education* 35, no. 1: 51–65.

12 A NATIVE AMERICAN VALUES-INFUSED APPROACH TO HUMAN RESOURCES

Matthew S. Rodgers, *Ithaca College*
Shad Morris, *Brigham Young University*

ABSTRACT

This chapter discusses how typical Native American values stand apart from the values that are often used to make human resource decisions in corporate America. Our central argument is that human resource practices in the United States can benefit by considering the values that are commonly held by indigenous communities in North America. Consequently, we discuss generally how Native American perspectives can influence corporate recruiting, selection, assessment, development, retention, and compensation/benefits practices. In doing so, we incorporate a case example of how one company incorporated Native American values into each of these HR practices. The overall goal of this chapter is to stimulate thinking about how both Native and non–Native American businesses may infuse their HR practices with an alternative perspective.

KEYWORDS: human resources, values, human capital, social capital

INTRODUCTION

TO SURVIVE IN TODAY'S MARKETPLACE, ORGANIZATIONS MUST manage their resources in a way that differentiates them from their competitors (Barney 1991). Of the resources available to organizations, people are the most likely source of differentiation. In other words, pretty much anyone can access financial capital, technologies are easy to imitate, and processes can often be replicated. Where companies can *really* make a difference is in how they manage their human and social capital. As a resource, *human capital* represents people's knowledge and skills. *Social capital* represents people's social connections with one another. It turns out, how you manage these human resources has a lot to do with how well you do as an organization in the long run (Morris and Snell 2011).

Although many organizations have only recently come to the revelation of the importance of managing human resources, the notion of valuing resources in general, and human resources specifically, is nothing new to Native American communities. Indigenous peoples have long attached a prominence to values that cherish harmony and respect toward fellow human beings as well as with nature (Verbos, Gladstone, and Kennedy 2011). These values drive Native people's interaction with each other as well as their environment. They may also partially explain why some Native Americans have struggled to adjust to the largely capitalistic value systems that drive and guide much of American business and culture. Yet with American business's "newfound" emphasis on valuing the human element in achieving their goals, perhaps there is an opportunity to analyze how traditional Native American values may contribute to how companies approach their employees.

This chapter discusses a Native American values approach to human resources. Our fundamental goal is to begin a conversation of how the traditional values of Native American tribes can serve as an instrumental guide in the choices that companies make regarding their human and social capital.[1] In doing so, we begin the discussion by reviewing the values and approaches that are commonly held by indigenous communities in North America. We then overlay this value system on the most common and critical HR components and propose how a Native American perspective may shape and even in some cases transform these management practices.

NATIVE VALUES

Much has been written about the role of culture on management practices (e.g., Kogut and Singh 1988; Newman and Nollen 1996). Not surprisingly, culture has a profound impact on employee behaviors as well as deciding on the best approach to manage in different cultural environments (Adler 1983). This proliferation of cross-cultural research has led to the revelation that there is much that can be learned in understanding different cultural approaches to management. Rather than the traditional ethnocentric model where one culture influences another, the present learning paradigm in organizational research is that organizations benefit by incorporating the knowledge, capabilities, and values of different cultural environments (Taylor and Wilson 2012).

An important caveat to recognizing the contributions of diverse cultures is that American management research has largely emphasized understanding cultures outside of the United States. This emphasis ignores the potential cultural contributions of people from groups that are indigenous to the United States who have very different cultural perspectives (i.e., Native Americans). This gap in the literature is unsurprising given that the typical mind-set toward Native peoples has been one of acculturation rather than supporting and appreciating their distinct cultural perspectives. However, by ignoring the potential learning offered by Native communities, organizations risk losing out on an opportunity to differentiate themselves from their competitors and to more effectively manage their human and social capital for long-term success. Cross-cultural research classifies American culture as largely individualistic, assertive, and performance driven (Hofstede 2011). These values translate to American business practices that emphasize performance over people, achievement over relationships, short-term over long-term, and growth over sustainability. While there are exceptions to this generalization, this typical American perspective on business traditionally places less emphasis on embracing people as valuable and appreciated resources. This focus probably explains why HR executives typically have less of a role in the top management team in American organizations.

In contrast, reviews of indigenous communities in North America shows that their values stress respect, harmony, communality, and collectivism (Garrett 1999; Verbos, Gladstone, and Kennedy 2011). The fundamental emphasis stemming from these values is that individuals are a critical resource in any community. In order for the community to be successful, there must be an emphasis on respecting the individual as well as building an environment where individuals care for each other and are concerned for the needs of the whole community. This model suggests a different approach to human resources than the usual American approach to business, and it suggests potential improvements that American organizations may be able to incorporate.

The following emphasizes some of these potential contributions by highlighting how Native American values apply to six aspects of human resource management: recruitment, selection, assessment, development, retention, and compensation/benefits. We use the Pechanga Resort and Casino as a case example of how Native American values can be put into action in a corporate setting.[2] The Pechanga Resort and Casino is owned by the Pechanga tribe and strives to operate a business that is not only successful but, most important, is true to its tribal values.[3] The casino employs over four thousand Native and non-Native people and has achieved notable success. In 2015, *USA Today* rated it as the top casino of approximately fifteen US casinos (USA Today 10best).

RECRUITING

Recruitment is where organizations forecast the supply and demand for talent and reach into the talent pool to attract people into the organization. A key idea behind this attraction process is the employee value proposition (EVP), which emphasizes a balance of "give up" and "get." The "give up" side of an EVP details how employees give up something in order to work (e.g., time, flexibility, commitment, effort). The "get" side of the equation is the value that the company offers. While pay and benefits are often emphasized by American businesses, there is often more than just pay and benefits that factors into the attraction process. Other elements include challenging work, a high degree of autonomy, strong friendship and social bonds, the availability of learning opportunities, a reputation in the community, or an image of social responsibility.

Many Native values suggest that companies should truly respect potential employees by emphasizing a holistic approach to the EVP. If you care about your community, you will want to meet their needs, which span beyond a financial arrangement. By purely emphasizing money, organizations disrespect their employees' needs and also reflect a lack of concern for building a community that cares for their employees. Consequently, Native values suggest that organizations should emphasize a thorough understanding of what employees want to "get" from their employer. The Pechanga Casino embraces this approach in that they emphasize understanding the people who work for the casino as well as those who are likely future employees. They know that their employees want to live self-sufficient lives, they want opportunities for development and growth, and they want to be treated fairly by their organization. This keen insight into their employees allows Pechanga to craft an EVP where people want to work for Pechanga, which enables their recruiting efforts.

SELECTION

In selecting potential candidates for positions, many American firms use performance-based competency frameworks to enable decision-making.

The performance-based approach says that employers should focus on the hard skills and competencies because that is what drives organizational performance. As a result, the competencies and skills of high-performing individuals are studied to distinguish what competencies high performers have that more average performers do not. With these competency characteristics in mind, the candidates with the highest possible performance capability can be selected. Although competency-based frameworks have their advantages, Native values typically suggest the importance of harmony and community in the selection process. In other words, one of the keys to lasting success is to have everyone be a strong fit with the organization. This approach implies a values-based logic in making selection decisions. Selection on the basis of specified values is a powerful way of building and maintaining a strong culture. Furthermore, organizational research suggests that hiring employees who have a strong fit with the organization's values benefits both the organization as well as the individuals themselves (Menguc et al. 2015).

A values-based approach to selection is extremely important at Pechanga. With more than six hundred different types of jobs, Pechanga emphasizes a fit with their values across the board. Their mentality is that fit with their culture is everything. Their interview process clearly emphasizes fit, and they turn away qualified applicants who are not a good fit. This sets a strong tone that they want their organization to consistently reflect very specific values and behaviors, and this happens only when employees have embraced those values (i.e., "a good fit"). Overall, they feel that when customers encounter this consistency resulting from fit, they will have a much more beneficial experience, allowing Pechanga to be successful over the long term. In effect, a values-based approach to selection may also include necessary competencies, but if the fit is not there, then competencies will not lead to success.

ASSESSMENT

Performance management is a process that connects the goals of the organization to individual goals and actions. It involves periodic appraisal that compares desired performance to actual performance (usually quantified in some way). Typically, the outcomes of performance assessments are linked with rewards and development activities to stimulate motivation and improve future assessments. Although the concept of performance management has proliferated throughout the business world, it is largely a US business idea with many cultures (e.g., Germany) not incorporating the concept until the last twenty years or so. Moreover, while performance management practices have spread, there is a fair amount of discontent with it on the part of management and employees, with many complaining about fairness, accuracy, a lack of concern for employees, and a short-term focus (Culbert 2010).

Native values generally offer a different perspective on performance management that may be a benefit to this HR practice. While typical performance management puts the emphasis on the individual to improve, Native values place the emphasis on the group. The group has an obligation to care and invest in the individual—the goal being that the individual then becomes committed to the group and cares about making a contribution to the group. Because of this concern, the individual opens themselves up to feedback from the group, especially from those in authority (e.g., elders). Feedback is given in a way that is reflective and dialogue-based. Motivation happens less from the carrot-and-stick approach and more from the internal desire to contribute to a community that values you. Although Pechanga uses a performance management system, theirs is much different than the typical system. Because the company cares intensely about its values, Pechanga emphasizes values in its evaluations. Overall, there is much less focus on quantitative metrics. Pechanga wants to hold everyone accountable to its values. This starts with the organization's leaders, who are promoted only if they reflect a strong fit with the organization's values. If the values of the company are evident throughout the company, employees will buy into the company and want to make a contribution. Pechanga believes that this is the key to success. Consequently, in their decision-making, they emphasize values more than profit because it is the values that will drive the effectiveness of the organization.

DEVELOPMENT

Building human capital is a fundamental element of human resources, where organizations try to build the capabilities of their employees. This process is typically conducted through job experiences, placing people in new experiences and giving them an opportunity to succeed or fail. In addition to job experiences, other forms of development include formal training, coaching, simulations, mentoring, and so on. Although development is generally valued in US organizations, it is not always effective. Many times development opportunities are limited in nature and only offered for a select few, which creates a competitive environment. In addition, there can be a lack of patience with employees who are slower to develop. Some companies strictly follow

General Electric's vitality curve, where a portion of the lowest performing employees are released each year.

While most Native American perspectives would share the general belief in human capital development, the rationale is slightly different. Rather than using human capital as a way to build competitive advantage, the focus is on building a cooperative environment where individuals help each other become better. Native values suggest that relationships are the primary mechanisms for development. Organizational members share freely of their time and knowledge to help their peers improve. Individual learning comes through observation of others as well as gleaning the knowledge of elders. This shows a much stronger commitment to mentoring models that have been proven to lead to greater individual success (Noe 1988). Individuals show their commitment to the group by taking responsibility for their learning and exercising self-discipline. Finally, there is a fundamental patience with "underperforming" group members; they receive the maximum opportunity and investment from the group.

Pechanga holds a strong belief that they want their workers to succeed not just in the organization but also in life. They offer opportunities for intense leadership development training, but rather than a typical skills approach, the emphasis is on getting employees to embrace company values. Furthermore, Pechanga values those who take responsibility for their learning and exercise self-discipline. The company generously offers tuition remission for those who want to advance their education. The overall goal is to help workers develop by investing in them.

RETENTION

In the United States the most common way to get a promotion is to change companies. For many companies talent management means recruiting and buying talent from the outside. About 40 percent of US employees have been with their current employers for less than two years (Bureau of Labor Statistics 2016). Thus the typical mentality is based on the idea of individualism (i.e., everyone for themselves) and a short time horizon. As a result, companies hire people, use them to benefit performance, let them leave, and then repeat the cycle. This approach can benefit organizational performance in the short run, but it also discounts the costs associated with the constant disruption of people leaving. These costs include hiring costs, disruption costs, training costs, costs stemming from missed opportunities, and costs associated with weakening of the organizational culture. While many senior managers discount the costs associated with turnover, there is a growing consensus that turnover reduction is a major source of competitive advantage (Hatch and Dyer 2004).

Native communities usually emphasize a much more collectivistic approach in comparison to the rest of US society. There is a strong commitment on the part of the community to the individual and from the individual to the community. The emphasis is much more of a family orientation, which is by definition long term. This strong mutual commitment allows the community to benefit from stability, an increased ability to work together, and an improved ability to work through the problems and issues facing individuals and the community. Pechanga emphasizes that people are its source of success. They have a strong belief that they benefit when they are committed to their people and their people are committed to the organization. In an industry with a 40 percent turnover rate, Pechanga boasts a 16 percent rate. They want their people to stick around, and they do their utmost to keep their employees. Pechanga is committed to their workers even during times when they have been forced to reduce the workforce. In 2008, during the economic recession, Pechanga had to lay off 350 employees. They hated to do this, but they were determined to express their commitment to these employees. Pechanga gave everyone severance, they provided for placement services and career counseling, and they put together a job fair to help these employees find another employer. Overall, all the employees sensed the concern that Pechanga had for them. In fact, some of these employees were in tears at the company's expression of caring.

COMPENSATION AND BENEFITS

Building a motivated workforce is of immense concern to businesses, and the typical US mind-set is to offer extrinsic rewards (e.g., pay for performance and promotions) to drive employee motivation. This approach taps into the idea that individuals are self-interested and are primarily focused on money and status. This approach creates a fundamental issue for organizations. They must continue to offer extrinsic motivators to get results, yet these motivators can be costly and hurt overall profits. Thus companies are constantly examining their return on investment for their incentive programs as well as any benefits that they offer. This self-interest model directly conflicts with many Native values. Native values emphasize more of an intrinsic motivation, leveraging individuals' connections with their group. By sharing resources, expressing care, being generous, and emphasizing equality, Native values allow individuals to feel part of a community that values them. This motivates individuals to engage in behaviors and actions that strengthen the community.

One of Pechanga's main approaches to compensation and benefits is to be generous. Although these programs can be expensive, Pechanga wants to care for their workers. They offer a good living wage so their employees can meet their needs; they offer benefits that reflect their concern and passion for their workers (e.g., tuition remission, company picnic). These are offered not as an attempt to motivate through extrinsic motivation but rather attempts to get employees to feel the company's concern for them. Although these programs are costly for Pechanga, they attempt to be generous and absorb a good portion of the costs, especially not passing along cost increases to their employees. This model is consistent with what economists have known for years: by paying higher than average wages, employees are more motivated and productive (Krueger and Summers 1988).

CONCLUSION

As noted throughout this chapter, the traditional values of indigenous groups in North America have a lot to say about how corporate HR departments deal with their people. In a business world that is filled with greed, scandal, and competitive maneuvering, Native values would serve as a breath of fresh air to the current system. Such practices may prove to provide a more sustainable source of competitive advantage for companies in today's marketplace. Some companies, such as Pechanga, have already begun to serve as examples as to what a company might look like with Native American values guiding their HR practices. Other companies may benefit by finding their own approach toward infusing their HR practices with Native values.

DISCUSSION

1. What specific Native American values do you feel are most relevant to human resource practices? Why are they relevant?
2. What types of values have you observed in corporate America? How do you feel an infusion of values typically found in Native American communities may help or hinder human resource practices in these companies?
3. How is Pechanga similar or different from other Native American organizations? Do you feel that Pechanga's approaches could be

incorporated in other Native American organizations? How about in corporate America?

4. In what HR practices (e.g., recruiting, assessment, etc.) do you feel Native American values would make the most difference? The least difference? Why?

Notes

1   We acknowledge that not all tribes have the same values. Throughout this chapter we emphasize values that have been discussed in other scholarly articles and ones that apply generally to our case example (e.g., Garrett 1999; Verbos, Gladstone, and Kennedy 2011). Our approach is general, however, and the values we mention may not apply to some tribes. Regardless of the unique values found among different tribes, we believe that the values found among Native Americans (either specifically or generally) stand in contrast to many of the values used in typical American business practices. We hope this article highlights this contrast as well as the potential contribution of Native Americans to HR practices.

2   There are many tribal businesses and casinos throughout the United States, each operating in unique contexts and with different resources. Our focus on Pechanga Resort and Casino does not mean we consider it to be the prototypical example of how Native American values should be applied. There are definitely other Native American businesses that take a different approach by choice or by necessity. Pechanga is only one example, so its generalizability to other contexts should be evaluated. However, we believe our focus on Pechanga may stimulate thinking on how both Native and non–Native American businesses may incorporate Native American values into the various aspects of human resources.

3   Many thanks to Tony Chartrand, vice president HR/talent management at Pechanga Resort and Casino, for his valuable insights into Pechanga.

References

Adler, N. J. 1983. "Cross-cultural Management Research: The Ostrich and the Trend." *Academy of Management Review* 8, no. 2: 226–32.

Barney, J. 1991. "Firm Resources and Sustained Competitive Advantage." *Journal of management* 17, no. 1: 99–120.

Bureau of Labor Statistics. 2016. "Employee Tenure in 2016." US Department of Labor. Online at www.bls.gov/news.release/tenure.nro.htm. Accessed on January 21, 2017.

Culbert, S. A. 2010. *Get Rid of the Performance Review!: How Companies Can Stop Intimidating, Start Managing—And Focus On What Really Matters*. New York: Business Plus Hachette.

Garrett, M. T. 1999. "Under the 'Medicine' of Native American Traditional Values: An Integrative Review." *Counseling and Values* 43, no. 2: 84–98.

Hatch, N. W., and J. H. Dyer. 2004. "Human Capital and Learning As a Source of Sustainable Competitive Advantage." *Strategic Management Journal* 25, no. 12: 1155–78.

Hofstede, G. 2011. "Dimensionalizing Cultures: The Hofstede Model in Context." *Online Readings in Psychology and Culture* 2, no. 1: 1–26..

Kogut, B., and H. Singh. 1988. "The Effect of National Culture on the Choice of Entry Mode." *Journal of International Business Studies* 19, no. 3: 411–32.

Krueger, A. B., and L. H. Summers. 1988. "Efficiency Wages and the Inter-Industry Wage Structure." *Econometrica: Journal of the Econometric Society* 56, no. 2: 259–93.

Menguc, B., S. Auh, C. S. Katsikeas, and Y. S. Jung. 2016. "When Does (Mis) Fit in Customer Orientation Matter for Frontline Employees' Job Satisfaction and Performance?" *Journal of Marketing* 80, no. 1: 65–83.

Morris, S. S., and S. A. Snell. 2011. "Intellectual Capital Configurations and Organizational Capability: An Empirical Examination of Human Resource Subunits in the Multinational Enterprise." *Journal of International Business Studies* 42, no. 6: 805–27.

Newman, K. L., and S. D. Nollen. 1996. "Culture and Congruence: The Fit between Management Practices and National Culture." *Journal of International Business Studies* 27, no. 4: 753–79.

Noe, R. A. 1988. "An Investigation of the Determinants of Successful Assigned Mentoring Relationships." *Personnel Psychology* 41, no. 3: 457–79.

Taylor, M. Z., and S. Wilson. 2012. "Does Culture Still Matter?: The Effects of Individualism on National Innovation Rates." *Journal of Business Venturing* 27, no. 2: 234–47.

USA Today 10best. 2015. "Pechanga Resort & Casino Wins Best U.S. Casino!" *USA Today.* Online at www.10best.com/awards/travel/best-u-s-casino/. Accessed on November 13, 2015.

Verbos, A. K., J. S. Gladstone, and D. M. Kennedy. 2011. "Native American Values and Management Education: Envisioning an Inclusive Virtuous Circle." *Journal of Management Education* 35, no. 1: 10–26.

13 SERVICE MANAGEMENT FOR NATIVE AMERICAN CUSTOMERS

Deanna M. Kennedy, *University of Washington–Bothell*
Denise Bill, *Muckleshoot Tribal College*
Rachael Meares, *University of Washington–Bothell*
Iisaaksiichaa (Good Ladd) Ross Braine,
University of Washington–Seattle

ABSTRACT
The characteristics of services include being an intangible good that is difficult to inventory and produced at the point of consumption. Managing services requires an understanding of the service profit chain. This chain consists of four elements: *service delivery, operational strategy, service design,* and *market demand.* To offer a successful service, a manager needs to attend to each of these service elements and also consider how the elements connect to provide an appropriate service to customers. This chapter discusses how these elements manifest in the services offered by companies. Yet we believe that two additional elements, *access* and *cultural salience,* are important when creating services with Native American customers in mind. We derive support for these additional elements from service stories provided by the Muckleshoot Tribe of the Pacific Northwest. The chapter concludes with insights for service management.
KEYWORDS: service management, service profit chain, Muckleshoot Tribe, culturally appropriate services

INTRODUCTION

SERVICES INCLUDE THE ECONOMIC ACTIVITIES THAT DO NOT necessarily have a physical product but rather intangible outcomes that are difficult to inventory and inseparable from the point of consumption (Fitzsimmons and Fitzsimmons 2010; Krajewski, Ritzman, and Malhotra 2013). In the United States, service organizations employ a majority of the working class and contribute largely to the gross domestic product (GDP) (Bretthauer 2004). As customers, we realize that services are a major part of our day-to-day lives—from purchasing retail services such as coffee and food, to using social services that help provide job training, health care, and housing access. Across all types of services, managers have the opportunity of designing and delivering services that meet the specific needs of their target market. The way in which managers can create a successful service depends on how well they manage their service profit chain.

The service profit chain (Heskett, Sasser, and Schlesinger 1997) features four strategic elements that separate the decisions involved in offering a service into manageable pieces. Adapted from Fitzsimmons and Fitzsimmons (2010), we term these elements as *service delivery, operational strategy, service design,* and *market demand*. Below we describe and present examples of each service element and how one element supports the other. We then discuss how service considerations may need to be extended when the target market includes Native Americans. Based on recent research about attracting Native Americans into educational programs (Verbos et al. 2015), we believe additional elements of *access* and *cultural salience* need to be incorporated into the framework. This chapter offers insights about how these additional elements may help attract and engage Native American customers.

ELEMENTS OF SERVICE MANAGEMENT
SERVICE DELIVERY

Service delivery includes the decisions regarding the *role of service employees* and the *resources* they need to successfully perform the duties of the service at different levels of demand (Fitzsimmons and Fitzsimmons 2010). First, the manager decides how employees will be involved in delivering the service to the customer. That is, what does the interaction between the service employee and the customer look like? Second, the manager decides what resources will be provided for the service. This decision comes from asking what are the instructions, technologies, equipment, and facilities that will be required? By understanding how the service is offered and the resources used to support the service, the manager can further consider the maintenance and management of service quality.

Service quality is the success with which the performance of the service meets the expectation of the customer (Parasuraman, Zeithaml, and Berry 1985). Whether there are few or many customers at any given time, the manager needs to ensure that the quality of the service is perceived to be the same for every customer. As such, contingency plans may be needed for low- or high-demand periods. These plans may be short term, such as holding inventory or an on-call list for service attendants, or long term, including an expansionist plan for adding personnel, enlarging facilities, and increasing resource contracts (Krajewski, Ritzman, and Malhotra 2013). For example, the United Parcel Service (UPS) provides package delivery that in 2014 accounted for approximately one-fifth of the packages delivered worldwide (Sauter, Frohlich, and Stebbins 2015). Their service involves employees who interface with the sender to prepare the package for shipment; employees who sort, stack, and ship the packages via car, truck, or plane; and employees who interface with the receiver of packages through the UPS store or delivery vehicle. To coordinate the service, employees need to have training, technologies, facilities, and vehicles. Yet maintaining service across demand levels has been difficult; UPS has struggled with peak demand around the holidays. In 2014 management decided to invest in expanding technologies, upgrading facilities, and adding resources to prepare for peak demand levels (Samaha 2015). In addition, UPS has been able to expand the quality of service by offering extra services (e.g., next-day shipping) to more customers such that they now reach 94 percent of US zip codes and 98 percent of businesses (UPS Pressroom 2016). As UPS demonstrates, service delivery can challenge managers to support roles and resources, especially at peak demand, to ensure service quality.

OPERATIONAL STRATEGY

The *operational strategy* requires managers to question how the service will impact functional areas of the organization (Fitzsimmons and Fitzsimmons 2010). This is a specific type of strategizing that is, in part, influenced by the firm's overall business strategy (see chapter 4). The operational strategy is the application of service management into all the functional areas of the company. For example, a low-cost operational strategy may lead to more standardized delivery systems, including more cost-effective and cheaper resources, that are expected to perform at a lower quality than in other strategies. The operational strategy should also include metrics for measuring quality, satisfaction, and overall success. These metrics can drive the interaction between the service delivery person and the customer, so they should be carefully and deliberately considered. Depending on the service, these metrics could include a focus on costs, profits, customer satisfaction, or customer loyalty.

An example of integrating service into the operational strategy is drawn from the online shoe retailer Zappos. Founded in 1999, Zappos handles over six thousand calls and emails a week (Young 2009). At Zappos every employee is enabled to meet customer needs efficiently and that means handling calls and emails effectively. Indeed, rather than focusing on how fast the call center can handle a call, the customer service agents are rewarded for investing time with their customers, with one call lasting ten hours and twenty-nine minutes (McConnell 2012). As the CEO, Tony Hsieh indicates: "If we're serious about building our brand to be about the very best customer service and customer experience; then customer service shouldn't just be a department—it should be the entire company" (Bulygo 2016).

SERVICE DESIGN

The *service design* requires managers to think about customers' perceptions of the benefits from engaging in the service (Fitzsimmons and Fitzsimmons 2010). The questions posed to managers in this service element focus on what the service truly provides to customers, is it valuable, and how is it presented to the market? Although the service design sounds like a simple task in that the manager needs to state what the service is about, it is actually quite difficult. Indeed, Parasuraman, Zeithaml, and Berry (1985) investigated management and consumer perceptions about service offerings and showed that, at times, there was a disconnect. For example, consumers addressed such attributes as privacy and confidentiality of banking services, and the security features of a credit card services, but executives failed to address these attributes when describing their service. Moreover, understanding the value that customers see in the service can also provide feedback into service quality as outlined in the service delivery section, where the performance of the service is weighed against customers' expectations.

A company that continually strives to set and reinforce customer perceptions about its service is the global coffee retailer Starbucks. The company opened its first store in Seattle, Washington, in 1971 and now has more than twenty-four thousand stores in seventy countries (Starbucks 2016a). Starbucks gauges its service around the customer experience, telling customers to "expect more than coffee." Indeed, they describe what the customers will experience as a "full and rewarding coffeehouse experience" as well as why the service is of value from the "commitment to the highest quality coffee in the world, to the way [Starbucks] engage with [its] customers and communities to do business responsibly" (Starbucks 2016a). Furthermore, Starbucks makes sure the message is shared globally. Norbert Tan, executive director of Starbucks Hong Kong and Macau, stated that "our work goes far beyond the coffee counter. We want to share with the public exactly how our coffee is made and our in-depth knowledge from years of experience" (Starbucks

2016b). Thus, as Starbucks demonstrates, service design is a major task that involves clear communication so that expectations are shared internally, between service employees and managers, and externally with customers.

MARKET DEMAND

The service element of *market demand* brings up questions about customer demand levels and expected demand cycles (Fitzsimmons and Fitzsimmons 2010). Specifically, the manager should thoughtfully consider the characteristics of the market and ask: Are there nuances within the market, and how do needs within the market vary over time? By doing so, the manager may set more accurate expectations about the needs that are being served by his or her service delivery. These considerations can help managers position the service to address the entire market, a niche in the market, or better serve a competitor's market space. For example, Netflix is an Internet television and movie rental provider that began in 1997. Today the company services more than 75 million viewers in over 190 countries (Netflix Investor Relations 2016a). When Netflix began, it provided constant access to content by asking members to keep a list of requested movies online from which typically three movies, in the order listed, were provided via mailed DVDs.

Once customers finished with one DVD, they would mail it back to Netflix and receive another one off their list. This helped Netflix to manage demand by knowing what resources (i.e., rentals) would be needed in the future. Netflix also gained information about the speed with which customers returned movies to replenish inventory. As such, the company could carry less on-hand inventory than its brick-and-mortar competitors. To further manage demand, in 2000, Netflix started a movie recommendation system that could help smooth demand cycles between blockbuster releases. The recommendation system became so important that in 2009 the Netflix Prize was awarded to a team that created an algorithm to accurately predict how much someone would enjoy a movie based on his or her preferences (Netflix Prize Home 2016b). Thus, as Netflix demonstrates, understanding demand and demand cycles affects the opportunities of managing services and grabbing market share from competitors.

ELEMENTS OF NATIVE AMERICAN SERVICE DELIVERY

The chapter thus far has discussed the four elements of the service profit chain and provided examples of how these elements are applied in mainstream services. Yet these service elements may need to be augmented to address specific Native American markets and run a successful business. We high-light two particular elements that may enhance the service profit chain in these markets: *access* and *cultural salience*. Recent research by Verbos et al. (2015) argue that these types of issues, when left unaddressed, create barriers between Native Americans and their attainment of aspirations. Access is a poignant reminder that many Native American communities face locational, technological, or economic limitations and typically experience higher poverty, lower employment, and lower income than nonminorities (Aud, Fox, and KewalRamani 2010; Worthington, Flores, and Navarro 2005). As such, access to services may call for more conscientious attention to where and how service delivery occurs.

Cultural salience is the alignment of the service with the cultural values in appropriate and meaningful ways. Indeed, indigenous peoples have generally seen the destruction of their unique identities over the years (e.g., Denham 2008). As such, reestablishing American Indian cultural values and practices has been an ongoing effort for many tribes (Gone 2009). Scholars have shown that economic development activities that align with tribal values have been more successful than others (e.g., Cornell and Kalt 2007). Thus a similar strategy in service delivery may be key to delivering a service that will be successful in Indian Country. To demonstrate the need for access and cultural salience, this section draws on a specific application in an educational environment. In particular, we reflect on the attention to access and cultural salience by the Muckleshoot Tribe. While the examples share specific service delivery activities, they show how much thought and effort should be given to these elements to create an engaging and successful service for Native peoples.

ACCESS

Native American peoples may have different access to resources than your typical, non-Native customer. For example, Native Americans living on reservations or in rural areas are often beyond the boundary of Internet service providers (Smith 2012). Other, smaller businesses have found innovative means to provide service access. We present a story about incorporating the issue of access into educational services by a Muckleshoot tribal member, Denise Bill, EdD. The Muckleshoot Indian Tribe is comprised of the descendants of the Coast Salish peoples who have lived in the region for thousands of years, with a current population of thirty-three hundred. In 1995 the Muckleshoot Tribal Council made a significant commitment to higher education in the Muckleshoot community by creating the Muckleshoot Training Center. Designed to provide business training for tribal members seeking employment in the newly created Muckleshoot Indian Casino, the center offered computer training and college-level courses through agreements with various partner institutions.

The training center was renamed Muckleshoot Tribal College in 1997, and a partnership with Northwest Indian College was formed in 2002. Students now have the option of pursuing two-year degrees on-site in addition to the programming that was already being offered. Denise has worked in Indian Education for over twenty years, including heading up the Indian Education Program for Seattle Public Schools and serving as dean at the Muckleshoot Tribal School. When describing how the Muckleshoot Tribal college has been successful in attracting and serving tribal members, she offered the following insights:

> The Muckleshoot Tribal College focuses on attracting students through Early College Programs. During the program, care is taken to make sure students are working toward their goals, through activities such as Career Days at Muckleshoot Tribal College. In addition, we realized a need within our market to attain college degrees. To make this accessible to our members, we set up partnerships. The Evergreen State College established its presence at Muckleshoot in 1998 with the Reservation Based/Community Determined program, providing community members the opportunity for a four-year bachelor of liberal arts degree. Clover Park, and later Green River College, began offering its Office Assistant Training program through a federal grant in 2000 to 2016 and continues to offer wide-ranging technology opportunities through the Muckleshoot Occupational Skills Training (MOST) program.
>
> Another partnership, with Antioch University, began its First Peoples' Program at Muckleshoot in 2002, offering a master's in education, bachelor's degree in education, and teaching certification to community members. Also in 2002, Northwest Indian College initiated the Class of 2004, to provide two-year associate of arts transfer degrees. In 2009, Antioch was invited to return and offer a First Peoples' B.A. Degree Program. This alliance demonstrated that when Native students are provided access but can still be present in their home communities, participate in traditional practices, and give back to their tribe, they are likely to persist in completing their educational program.

As this story suggests, access can be a hurdle for tribal members wanting to engage in a particular service. As such, when addressing this element of service management, businesses may need to ask themselves: What are the opportunities to *connect with market community* to understand access needs? What is the *value of addressing access* to the customer and the profit chain?

CULTURAL SALIENCE

When the service and activities can be aligned with cultural approaches that are familiar to the recipient of the service, the service may be more likely to draw market demand. For instance, scholars are increasingly calling out the need to better incorporate Native American values, cultural perspective, and teaching methods in management education. For example, pedagogical approaches, like story creation and storytelling, may better engage Native and non-Native students in inductive and reflective learning in the classroom (Verbos, Kennedy, and Gladstone 2011; Verbos, Gladstone, and Kennedy 2011). By doing so, more Native students may become engaged in educational programs and earn a degree. More broadly, to ensure that services are delivered, strategized, and designed that are culturally salient, managers need to understand the culture of their customers. The cultural director of the Muckleshoot Tribe, Willard Bill Jr., shares a story of a cultural event that resonates with tribal members:

> The Tribal Canoe Journey for the Muckleshoot Indian Tribe is an annual demonstration of our traditional lifeways and an expression of a Sovereign Nation. For thousands of years our ancestors traveled in cedar canoes as their primary mode of transportation. Over the past twenty-five years the Muckleshoot Tribe has been revitalizing our canoe society, beginning with the Paddle to Seattle in 1989, where a shovel nose canoe carved and manned by the tribe participated.
>
> Today the annual Canoe Journey is a full-time endeavor, where the tribe prepares year round in language, regalia, traditional foods, and materials production to be appropriately ready for the next Journey. It is a spiritual journey where we actively engage in song, dance, and prayer and physical sacrifice to honor our teachings and ancestors. Pullers go through rigorous training and sacrifice of themselves while on Journey, proudly representing our people and traditional ways of learning and teaching. Journey has brought back traditional protocol, regalia, language, technology, and history to the Muckleshoot Indian Tribe. In recent years our focus has

been on the youth who participate, and we have now developed a strong cohort of young warriors to carry on our traditions.

We share this story to show that cultural salience is a vital part of tribal life. As such, service management needs to recognize this salience and incorporate it appropriately into service element decisions. To understand cultural salience, hearing the cultural stories and knowing the cultural activities that are valued by the Native peoples helps inform service management. Therefore, we suggest that managers ask how the service will be culturally relevant to customers and how can the service be delivered in a culturally relevant manner? In addition to addressing cultural relevance and salience in service delivery and design, managers need to think about cultural salience in relation to such metrics as customer, vendor, and employee satisfaction, and what does success and/or profitability of the service chain look like?

CONCLUSION

Service management can be guided by the elements of the service profit chain: service delivery, operational strategy, service design, and market demand. However, to manage services for Native people and communities, more may be needed. We suggest that additional elements of access and cultural salience be included in the service profit chain. We provided specific examples from the Muckleshoot Indian Tribe as evidence and support for these additional elements. Based on these elements and examples, we suggest the types of questions that can be used to inform service management decisions. Thus we hope this chapter has provided managers a starting point for well-designed, accessible, and culturally salient services for Native Americans.

DISCUSSION

1. You want to offer business consulting to Native entrepreneurs. How would you approach service management for your consulting firm?
2. Organizations have struggled to bring broadband Internet access to reservations. Why? How might service delivery issues be overcome?
3. Describe the challenges and opportunities of integrating access and cultural salience for Native Americans into service management?
4. In what ways do you think leadership and business strategy drive service management decisions?

References

Aud, S., M. Fox, and A. KewalRamani. 2010. *Status and Trends in the Education of Racial and Ethnic Groups*. Washington, DC:.US Department of Education National Center for Education Statistics, US Government printing Office.

Bretthauer, K. M. 2004. "Service Management." *Decision Sciences* 35, no. 3: 325–32.

Bulygo, Z. 2016. "Tony Hsieh, Zappos, and the Art of Great Company Culture." Web Log Post. Online at blog.kissmetrics.com. Accessed on February 10, 2016.

Cornell, S., and J. P. Kalt. 2007. "Two Approaches to the Development of Native Nations: One Works, the Other Doesn't." In M. Jorgenson, ed., *Rebuilding Native Nations: Strategies for Governance and Development*. Pp. 3–33. Tucson: University of Arizona Press.

Denham, A. R. 2008. "Rethinking Historical Trauma: Narratives of Resilience." *Transcultural Psychiatry* 45: 391–414.

Fitzsimmons, J. A., and M. J. Fitzsimmons. 2010. *Service Management: Operations, Strategy, and Information Technology*. 7th edition. New York: Irwin/McGraw-Hill.

Gone, J. P. 2009. "A Community-Based Treatment for Native American Historical Trauma: Prospects for Evidence-Based Practice." *Journal of Consulting and Clinical Psychology* 77: 751–62.

Heskett, J. L., W. E. Sasser, and L. A. Schlesinger. 1997. *The Service Profit Chain*. New York: The Free Press.

Krajewski, L. J., L. P. Ritzman, and M. K. Malhotra. 2013. *Operations Management: Processes and Supply Chains*. 9th edition. London: Pearson/Prentice Hall.

McConnell, A. 2012. "Zappos' Outrageous Record for the Longest Customer Service Phone Call Ever." *Business Insider*. December 20. Online at www.businessinsider.com /zappos-longest-customer-service-call-2012-12. Accessed on February 10, 2016.

Netflix Investor Relations. 2016a. "Company Profile." Online at https://ir.netflix.com /index.cfm. Accessed on January 29, 2016.

Netflix Prize Home. 2016b. "Congratulations." Online at www.netflixprize.com/index .html. Accessed on January 29, 2016.

Parasuraman, A., V. A. Zeithaml, and L. L. Berry. 1985. "A Conceptual Model of Service Quality and Its Implications for Future Research." *Journal of Marketing* 29, no. 4: 41–50.

Samaha, L. 2015. "United Parcel Service Earnings: What Went Wrong in 2014?" *The Motley Fool*. February 3. Online at www.fool.com/investing/general/ 2015/02/03/ united-parcel-service-earnings-what-went-wrong-in.aspx#.VvhKExK9pdk. Accessed on February 11, 2016.

Sauter, M. B., T. C. Frohlich, and S. Stebbins. 2015. "Customer Service Hall of Fame." *24/7 Wall St.* July 23. Online at http://247wallst.com/special-report/2015/07/23/customer -service-hall-of-fame-2/2/. Accessed on February 11, 2016.

Smith, G. 2012,. "On Tribal Lands, Digital Divide Brings New Form of Isolation." *Huffington Post*. April 20. Online at www.huffingtonpost.com/2012/04/20/digital -divide-tribal-lands_n_1403046.html. Accessed on February 11, 2016.

Starbucks. 2016a. "About Us: Company Information." Online at www.starbucks.com/about -us/company-information. Accessed on March 26, 2016.

———. 2016b. "Newsroom: Building Coffee Knowledge at Starbucks Interactive Experience in Hong Kong." March 24. Online at https://news.starbucks.com/news/starbucks
-interactive-experience-in-hong-kong. Accessed on March 26, 2016.

UPS Pressroom. 2016. "UPS Adds More Than 12,000 Zip Codes to Earliest Delivery
Service." March 21. Online at www.pressroom.ups.com/pressroom/. Accessed on
March 26, 2016.

Verbos, A. K., J. Gladstone, and D. M. Kennedy. 2011. "Native American Values and
Management Education: Envisioning an Inclusive Virtuous Circle." *Journal of
Management Education* 35, no. 1: 10–26. DOI: 10.1177/1052562910384364.

Verbos, A. K., D. M. Kennedy, and J. Gladstone. 2011. "Coyote Was Walking . . . Management
Education in 'Indian Time.'" *Journal of Management Education* 35, no. 1: 27–50. DOI:
10.1177/1052562910384368.

Verbos, A. K., D. M. Kennedy, J. Gladstone, and C. Birmingham. 2015. "Native American
Cultural Influences on Career Self-Schemas and MBA Aspirations." *Equality, Diversity,
and Inclusion: An International Journal* 34, no. 3: 201–13. DOI: 10.1108/
EDI-05-2014-0044.

Worthington, R. L., L. Y. Flores, and R. L. Navarro. 2005. "Career Development in
Context: Research with People of Color." In S. D. Brown and R. W. Lent, eds., *Career
Development and Counseling: Putting Theory and Research to Work*. Pp. 225–52.
Hoboken, NJ: Wiley and Sons.

Young, M. 2009. "Zappos Milestone: Focus on Apparel Footwear News." May 4. Online
at http://about.zappos.com/press-center/media-coverage/zappos-milestone-focus
-apparel. Accessed on February 10, 2016.

14 NATIVE AMERICANS AND MARKETING

A Paradoxical Relationship

Stephanie Lawson Brooks, *Winthrop University*
Cara Peters, *Winthrop University*

ABSTRACT

Native American cultural misappropriation in marketing and advertising is pervasive and paradoxical. Cultural misappropriations of Native American culture persist owing to the assumption of homogeneity among Native American tribes. The purpose of this chapter is to explore how Native American culture has been misappropriated through marketing and advertising and discuss inconsistencies in the usage of Native American imagery, symbols, and cultural motifs. Using a case study methodology, the chapter explores misappropriation of Native American culture across three popular cultural contexts where examples of support and opposition exist. The underpinnings of the paradoxical nature of the phenomenon are examined in an effort to provide possible solutions for tribal members and society at large. Understanding how these stereotypes are interpreted and classifying when and how they are appropriate could aid in the preservation and greater cultural understanding of these nations' histories.

KEYWORDS: Native American, stereotyping, misappropriation, social movement, tribes, advertising, culture, Native American marketing, American Indian

INTRODUCTION

NATIVE AMERICAN FOLKLORE AND IMAGERY ARE WOVEN INTO the tapestry of American history. Native American cultural interpretations are intertwined with the origin story of the United States. Depictions of Native American stereotypes exist throughout American culture—from sports, education, and literature to mass media and advertising (Hanson and Rouse 1987). The use of Native American stereotypes in US culture is pervasive and inconsistent, ranging from idealistic representations of Indian princesses and the Noble Savage to "mystical environmentalists or uneducated, alcoholic bingo-players confined to reservations" (Mihesuah 1996, 9; Merskin 2001). These cultural misappropriations have persisted because of assumptions of homogeneity among Native American nations when in reality there are 566 federally recognized Indian nations that are "ethnically, culturally, and linguistically diverse" (NCAI 2015; NCAI 2003).

Exposure to Native American stereotypes in advertising is commonplace, and these images continue to reinforce stereotypical beliefs about Native American culture (Merskin 2001). Product logos, athletic team mascots, commercials, and print advertisements like the Land O Lakes maiden, Jeep Cherokee, Disney's Pocahontas, and the Washington Redskins are some of the most prominent examples. Simultaneously, given the growing number of Native American–owned businesses and the perennial consumer interest in tribal motifs, an opportunity exists for a unified Native voice to influence how their culture, imagery, and symbols are portrayed by marketers and in popular culture. While each Indian Nation has unique customs and history, current advertising and marketing promotions have not presented these distinctions to the broader public. The purpose of this chapter is to bring a greater understanding of how Native American culture has been misappropriated through advertising and marketing. From this understanding, the underpinnings of the paradox is explored in an effort to provide possible solutions to persistent stereotyping and misappropriation of Native American culture. Understanding when the use of Native American cultural assets are appropriate and authentic is important given that use of Native American names, likenesses, history, cultural references, and folklore are interpreted inconsistently between insiders and outsiders (Locklear 2012).

Through multiple cultural contexts, this chapter explores the misappropriation of Native American culture as well as the inconsistencies in advertising of Native American imagery. Current issues related to Native American stereotyping in popular culture and the resulting backlash are examined, including: (1) retailers' use of Native tribal names, symbols, and traditional dress; (2) misappropriation of Native dress by musicians and music festival attendees; (3) and the controversy surrounding the use of Native mascots in both college and professional sports. The use of Native American stereotypes, the negative effects of stereotyping, and the commercialization of Native imagery and symbols have been examined in the advertising literature; however, researchers have yet to examine these misappropriations across cultural contexts (Leak, Woodham, and Stone 2015; Kim-Prieto et al.

2010; Hanson and Rouse 1987; Merskin 2001; Locklear 2012; Edgerton and Jackson 1996).

ONGOING ISSUES
FASHION INDUSTRY

Fashion retailers have exploited Native American likeness, symbols, and traditional dress for financial gain, with examples ranging from large fashion brands such as Ralph Lauren and Urban Outfitters to individual sellers on Etsy. These retailers recognize the perennial desire for Native-inspired motifs given the cultural mythology they possess (Trebay 2012). For example, Ralph Lauren print advertisements have featured vintage photographs of Native Americans dressed in Western clothing. Some argued the images were offensive given the oppressive reminder of assimilation, while the company claimed it has a history of celebrating America's Native American heritage (Clements 2014). In another example, Urban Outfitters was sued by the Navajo Nation for selling clothing and housewares with the Navajo name and iconic aesthetic (*Navajo Nation v. Urban Outfitters, Inc.* 2013; NPR 2012). The retailer claimed that because the word Navajo is of common usage and cannot be copyrighted, the company had the right to use the word and imagery as it saw fit. The Navajo Nation sued on the basis of the Indian Arts and Crafts Act, which states that it is illegal to claim a product is Native American when it is not produced by Native Americans.

While the Navajo Nation took issue with the usage of their name and likeness with Urban Outfitters, they have worked with other companies seeking to use their name. For example, when Mazda introduced the Navajo SUV, they asked for permission to use the name with sensitivity and in exchange the Navajo Nation approved and was given a vehicle for tribal use (NPR 2012). Etsy is a Web-based handmade goods marketplace for small businesses and individual sellers. Numerous sellers make and market Native-inspired clothing, jewelry, toys, and spiritual items, many of which are not produced by Native Americans (Metcalfe 2012). For example, several postings for headdresses are tagged with terms like "boho, festival costume, and feather hat." Although some merchandise is authentic and crafted by Native American artists, other sellers either claim to be inspired by Native American culture or descendants who do not have active tribal affiliation (Metcalfe 2012). These examples highlight the insensitivity surrounding the use of Native American cultural iconography.

MUSICIANS AND MUSIC FESTIVALS

The use of Native American likeness by musicians in both video and print and the adoption of Native American dress for music festival audiences has grown, as a result of the associated mythology of the culture. For example, in 2012 the band No Doubt's music video featured lead singer Gwen Stefani wearing Native American–inspired outfits. After commenters on social media told the group, "You have disrespected and slighted the entire Native American people with your counterfeit portrayal of our heritage" (Romano 2012), the band responded by removing the video and explaining that, given the group's multiracial background (and the fact that they had consulted with Native American studies experts), they did not intend to offend anyone. In 2014, when Grammy Award–winning artist Pharrell appeared on the cover of the magazine *Elle* (UK edition) wearing a headdress, he claimed his actions were based in honor and respect for Native culture; he further defended his choice by stating he was of Native American descent. Many claimed his actions were dishonorable, as the photo perpetuates the stereotype that all Native American tribes wear headdresses or that if you have a shared ancestry you have the right to commercialize aspects of sacred cultural artifacts (Michaels 2014).

Annual music festivals like Coachella and Lollapalooza have become increasingly popular, grossing more than $183 million in tickets sales in 2014 (McIntyre 2015). Some suggest festival goers embrace a bohemian fashion aesthetic that includes wearing Native-inspired headdresses because "some are bound to explore fantasies of escaping modern society and embracing their 'natural' selves via the otherness of older cultures" (Lynskey 2014). As festival popularity grows, concerns have been raised about the misappropriation of this sacred garment; some festivals have banned the wearing of Native headdresses (Marsh 2015).

TEAM MASCOTS

Controversy over the use of Native American names and likenesses for sports mascots continues. Locklear (2012) presents supporting and opposing viewpoints on the Native American mascot controversy. Supporters claim that use of Native American imagery is an honor and provides nostalgic feelings, while the opposition claims that Native American mascots are offensive, degrading, and perpetuate negative stereotypes (Mercado and Grady 2012; Locklear 2012). Research suggests the use of Native American names and mascots perpetuates negative stereotypes of Native Americans (Wolburg

2006). In 2005 the NCAA banned the use of American Indian mascots with only a few exceptions, including the Florida State Seminoles and the Utah Utes, who maintain sanctioned relationships with the tribes whose names they use (Lukas 2012; Wulf 2014).

While many oppose the use of Native American mascots, others (like the Seminole Tribe of Florida) support the use of their cultural heritage by universities. In response to the NCAA ban on Native American mascots, the Seminole Tribe of Florida passed a proclamation stating they have "an established relationship with Florida State University, which includes its permission to use the name, 'Seminole,' as well as various Seminole symbols and images, such as Chief Osceola, for educational purposes and the Seminole Tribe of Florida wishes to go on record that it has not opposed, and, in fact, supports the continued use of the name 'Seminole' " (FSU News 2005). The Seminole Tribe of Florida also authorized Nike to use its symbols for Fire, Arrow, and Man on Horse for FSU's football jersey without compensation as they believe the relationship is mutually beneficial (Lyden 2015).

Although some Native American–themed sports teams are supported by tribes, others (including several professional sports teams) are not. For example, the Washington Redskins continue to use a name considered derogatory and offensive to Native Americans, and team owner Daniel Snyder has stated that he has no plans to change the name (Wulf 2014). A federal judge recently ordered the cancellation of the Washington Redskins' federal trademark registrations as they were deemed offensive to Native Americans and therefore in violation of the Lanham Act. The Lanham Act does not permit or offer protection for trademarks that disparage individuals or people. Opposing arguments to the use of the Washington Redskins name continue as the case goes to appeal (*Pro-Football, Inc. v. Blackhorse* 2015; Shapira 2015).

POTENTIAL REMEDIES

These examples illustrate ongoing issues surrounding the use of Native American imagery, names, and cultural motifs. Each illustrates inappropriate representations of Native culture, but these contexts also highlight the inconsistencies related to authenticity as well as accepted and appropriate use of Native American cultural symbols. When is the use of Native American cultural symbols appropriate? Why do some tribes approve the use of their likeness for some nontribal marketing purposes? Perhaps these issues arise because of the sheer number of tribes that exist within the United States, with each possessing its own tribal government, cultural heritage, and relationship with the outside community. According to US Census data, tribal businesses accounted for approximately $34.4 billion in receipts in 2007, an increase of over 25 percent since 2002. Native American businesses grew more than 15 percent from 2002 to 2007 (US Census 2012).

The growing sector of Native American–owned businesses faces unique challenges in the marketplace because these businesses operate in both tribal and nontribal settings. Many Native American–owned businesses lack infrastructure and financial resources necessary to compete with non-Native businesses (Bregendahl and Flora 2002). Furthermore, while not always the case, Native American business philosophy often differs from the nontribal marketplace. Native American businesses are often more focused on the natural world and preserving resources; as such, they can be less motivated by profits (Bregendahl and Flora 2002; Verbos, Gladstone, and Kennedy 2011; Caulfield 2011). Native American stereotypes persist in advertising and marketing; however, there are instances when the use of certain imagery, names, and motifs are deemed appropriate. The question remains how, with 566 federally recognized tribes and more than 200 state recognized tribes, will Native Americans present a unified voice that may be necessary to protect their cultural heritage (NCAI 2015)?

Several Native American–owned businesses showcase successful examples of the opportunity that exists to share, protect, and preserve cultural traditions that include an understanding of Native American issues. For example, Famous Dave's Barbecue (founded by David Anderson, an Ojibwe Native of Minnesota) provides leadership training to at-risk Native youth; Anderson also served as the assistant secretary of the Interior of Indian Affairs (Native Youth Magazine 2015). Beyond Buckskin, founded by Jessica Metcalfe, is a website dedicated to reducing Native American stereotyping through education and support of Native American artists. Metcalfe regularly posts editorials and features related to current issues of Native American cultural misappropriation, building awareness and educating the mainstream (Beyond Buckskin.com). The Seminole Tribe of Florida successfully operates several agribusinesses as well as the Hard Rock Hotel and Casino while promoting their cultural heritage through a relationship with Florida State University and heritage tourism ventures including museums, cattle rodeos, and "Real Florida" swamp safaris (Culpepper 2014; Weidman 2010).

Tocabe, a Native American–owned restaurant based in Denver, "gives voice to American Indian cuisine and culture" to their over 80 percent non-Native customer base. The owners, Ben Jacobs and Matt Chandra, travel to

Native American reservations for menu inspiration and attempt to source their goods from Native-owned suppliers (Armitage 2015). Finally, G&G Advertising, a full-service, Native-owned advertising agency, is focused on representing and marketing to Native Americans to "get rid of the myth" (Rothenberg 1999). Founded by Michael Gray, who was raised on a reservation in Montana and is of Blackfeet and Chippewa-Cree ancestry, G&G has created campaigns focused on Native American target markets for the US Census Bureau, the American Indian College Fund, and Wells Fargo (Carstarphen and Sanchez 2012; Wentz 2001). Recognizing that tribes differ from each other, G&G Advertising seeks to find the commonalities among tribes but recognizes the need to segment based on unique tribal demographic differences such as geographic location and socioeconomic conditions (Rothenberg 1999). These businesses set an example of how to market to and support Native American culture, but they only represent individual and incremental contributions and are not representative of all Native American–owned businesses.

Inconsistencies in how Native American culture is marketed are not limited to nontribal businesses and organizations. Some Native business owners struggle with the tensions between producing their wares by traditional means or using modern conveniences to increase the ease of production (Bregendahl and Flora 2002). Conflict also exists among tribes marketing tourism and maintaining authenticity. For example, tourists seek goods and services while visiting reservations; however, there are some tribal members who are concerned about the commercialization of their culture (Bregendahl and Flora 2002). In contrast, tribes like the Miccosukee have sought to "aggressively promote" (Weidman 2010, 4) heritage tourism as a way to maintain their independence and control their way of life (Weidman 2010). For Native American business owners, cultural and business practices are often in conflict, leaving the owner to struggle to determine how to integrate these two practices. Individual businesses can help the cause but collective action may be necessary to educate those who are practicing cultural misappropriation and to bring about social change within the wider culture.

MARKETING STRATEGIES FOR NATIVE BUSINESSES

Positioning is a well-accepted marketing theory which advocates that companies should work toward having their brand occupy a distinct position, relative to competing brands, in the consumer's mind (Ries and Trout 1981). Companies apply positioning strategy by emphasizing the distinguishing attributes and features of their brand or by constructing a unique brand image through various forms of marketing communication. A company's position should be distinctive, differentiating it from competitors, and convey the potential value that the consumer gains from purchasing that particular product.

One way Native American business owners can position their company is by emphasizing the integration of Native American culture and heritage into their business practices and conveying information about those Native American business practices via their marketing communication activities. Compared to most businesses in the marketplace, positioning based off of a Native American culture and heritage would be distinctive and differentiating. However, this strategy may be somewhat paradoxical as Native American business owners may feel like they are exploiting their own heritage and tribal culture for personal financial gain. Given the examples of cultural misappropriation just articulated in this chapter, it appears that non–Native Americans in the United States will most likely want to embrace such a positioning strategy. Thus emphasizing culture and heritage as positioning strategy may improve the business endeavors of Native American business owners. That being said, marketing theory suggests that using a tribe's culture and heritage as a positioning strategy needs to be done appropriately.

Marketing theorists have begun to propose marketing strategies for what they call "postmodern consumer tribes," although they are not examining tribalism in the true sense of the word (i.e., from the perspective of Native Americans in which tribes are based more on kinship and ancestral ties [see Almeida 2014]). Postmodern consumer tribes are small-scale, affectual groups held together through shared passions, life styles, emotions, and consumption practices (Maffesoli 1996). Members of these postmodern consumer tribes seek products and services less for their use value and more for their value in linking consumers to others (Cova and Cova 2001, 2002; Godin 2008; Sharkey 2012; Veloutsou and Moutinho 2009). Examples of these postmodern consumer tribes include French in-line roller skaters (Cova and Cova 2001, 2002), members of online role-playing games (Cova and White 2010), and even brand fans of Apple and Nike (Sharkey 2012).

Research on postmodern consumer tribes provides suggestions for how Native American business owners should approach using their culture and heritage as a positioning strategy in an appropriate way. There are three basic factors that mark postmodern consumer tribalism: (1) a collective sense of belonging, (2) lived experiences with the brand, and (3) authenticity and legitimacy (Veloutsou and Moutinho 2009). With respect to a collective sense of belonging, research suggests that postmodern consumer tribes need to stress their linking value (how the company's products or services support the tribe's being, rather than how to deliver the product or service to consumers) (see Cova and Cova 2001, 2002; Maffesoli 1996). For Native American business owners this requires that they identify a set of visible markers (i.e., relevant Native American symbols and images) and specific business practices (i.e., buying from Native American suppliers) that exemplify their culture and heritage, which they can leverage in their business strategies. These business activities should illustrate to consumers support for the tribe and the linking value between consumers and the tribe (even if limited to purchase, such as a certain amount of purchase being donated to the efforts of tribal organizations to improve living conditions for the tribe).

The second factor that researchers suggest is important for postmodern consumer tribal marketing is lived experiences with the brand. Cova and Cova (2001, 2002) state the members of postmodern consumer tribes exhibit four behavioral roles: (1) adherent, (2) participant, (3) practitioner, and (4) sympathizer. The *adherent* is a devotee to the tribe, in the same way that someone is devoted to a religion through faith. The *participant* attends tribal events and gatherings. The *practitioner* practices the tribal experience in his or her day-to-day life. And the *sympathizer* follows vogues and trends related to the tribe (which is an imagined experience and based on symbolic interaction). Thus research on postmodern tribal marketing suggests that consumers need to either symbolically or experientially participate in tribal practices, activities, and beliefs. Native American business owners who want to use their culture and heritage as a positioning strategy therefore need to provide lived experiences that help consumers identify with the Native American aspects of the business. Incorporating Native American images and symbolism throughout the retail environment and in company advertising is one way to begin to create such lived experiences.

Finally, Cova, Kozinets, and Shankar (2007) also found that postmodern consumer tribes are the protectors of brand authenticity. Postmodern consumer tribe members identify and define what is legitimate and authentic with respect to the brand and related consumer behaviors. There may even be opposition or an adversary that helps define legitimacy for the tribe (Cova and White 2010; Kozinets and Handelman 2004; Badrinarayanan, Sierra, and Taute 2014). Business owners who want to leverage Native American culture and heritage as a positioning strategy must therefore be careful to incorporate images, symbols, and lived experiences that are truly authentic to the tribe's history and culture. The authenticity of business practices becomes the foundation for consumers judging the legitimacy of the business practices, symbols and imagery, and the lived experiences provided by the brand.

PERSISTENT PARADOX

A paradox exists related to the persistence of Native American stereotypes in advertising and marketing; however, there are instances when the use of certain cultural symbols and motifs is accepted by Native Americans. With over seven hundred federally and state-recognized tribes, a challenge exists in finding a unified voice to protect Native American cultural heritage. Founded in 1944, the National Congress of American Indians (NCAI) serves as the unified voice of Indian Country. The NCAI's mission is to: "(1) protect and advance tribal governance and treaty rights; (2) promote the economic development and health and welfare in Indian and Alaska Native communities; and (3) educate the public toward a better understanding of Indian and Alaska Native tribes" (NCAI 2015). Tribal governments operate as sovereign nations within the United States and exercise the right to self-govern (NCAI 2015). While the NCAI and several other organizations seek to educate the greater public about Native American culture, not all tribes cooperate in all dealings.

Paradox exists because of the enduring nature of tribal governments, which historically are responsible for all aspects of economic development and social welfare for tribal members within tribal territory. Many of these tribal governments are in competition for economic resources and capital, making it challenging to partner in broader cultural preservation and education initiatives. For example, the Eastern Band of Cherokee Indians recently voiced opposition to the Catawbas opening a competing gaming business in North Carolina (Toensing 2013). In another example a multi-tribe coalition faced internal conflict over the proper designation for sacred lands, which lead to some tribal members leaving in opposition (Maffly 2015). However, the more than seven hundred Native American tribes will need to coordinate efforts and speak with a unified voice against the misappropriation of their culture. For a social movement to take shape, organizations like NCAI need to mobilize resources, including material (financial and physical capital); moral (unified support for goals); social-organizational (organizing goals and social networks); human (volunteers, leaders); and cultural (prior activist experience, understanding of the issues, collective action) (McCarthy and Zald 1977; Edwards and McCarthy 2004).

Native American tribes have historically lacked the resources to create a sustained social movement, owing to marginalization and exploitation and ongoing scarcity of infrastructure resources, ranging from telecommunications and wireless access to financial capital and the rural nature of many tribal reservations (NCAI 2003). While organizations like the National Congress of American Indians and other groups like Women of All Red Nations and NATIVE exist and provide education and advocacy for Native American culture, there is a void because of the inability to mobilize across all tribes and the lack of many resources necessary to create a sustained social movement. Given the controversy over the use of Native American imagery, the question of when, if ever, is it appropriate and how to accurately use these themes is an important topic to explore. This chapter seeks to explicate the overarching themes and instances where support and opposition exist. Owing to the historical oppression, assimilation, and general disregard for their history, Native Americans carry the burden of these experiences through to their consumption behaviors today (Shim and Gehrt 1996). Understanding how these stereotypes are interpreted and classifying when and how they are appropriate could aid in the preservation and greater cultural understanding of these nations' histories.

DISCUSSION

1. When is the use of Native American cultural symbols appropriate in marketing, advertising, and retail settings?
2. Summarize the most recent developments in the *Navajo v. Urban Outfitters* lawsuit. What lessons can marketers take away from this ongoing dispute?
3. Define *positioning*. Based on the definition provided, how has Tocabe positioned themselves as a Native-owned business?
4. Define *postmodern consumer tribes*. How could Native American businesses use the three factors that mark postmodern consumer tribalism to develop a marketing strategy?

References

Almeida, B. 2014. "Tribal Marketing: Is There a Tribe within a Tribe?" Dissertation, Universidade Catolica Portuguesa.

Armitage, L. 2015. "Tocabe x2: Native American Eatery in Denver Doubles-Down on Success." Online at http://indiancountrytodaymedianetwork.com/2015/03/28/tocabe -x2-native-american-eatery-denver-doubles-down-success-159788. Accessed on December 6, 2015.

Badrinarayanan, V., J. Sierra, and H. Taute. 2014. "Determinants and Outcomes of Online Brand Tribalism: Exploring Communities of Massively Multiplayer Online Role Playing Games (MMORPGs)." *Psychology and Marketing* 31, no. 10: 853–70.

Bregendahl, C., and C. Flora. 2002. "Native American Business Participation in E-commerce: An Assessment of Technical Assistance and Training Needs." US Department of Agriculture, Cooperative State Research, Education, and Extension Service.

Carstarphen, M. G., and J. P. Sanchez. 2012. *American Indians and the Mass Media.* Norman: University of Oklahoma Press.

Caulfield, J. 2011. "Selling the Native Americans." *ProSales.* Online at www .prosalesmagazine.com/business/selling-to-native-americans_0. Accessed on December 3, 2015.

Clements, C. 2014. "Ralph Lauren Apologizes for Native American Ads." Online at http://wgno.com/2014/12/19/ralph-lauren-apologizes-for-native-american-ads/. Accessed on March 29, 2015.

Cova, B., and V. Cova. 2002. "Tribal Marketing: The Tribalisation of Society and Its Impact on the Conduct of Marketing." *European Journal of Marketing* 36, nos. 5–6: 595–620.

———. 2001. "Tribal Aspects of Postmodern Consumption Research: The Case of French In-Line Roller Skaters." *Journal of Consumer Behaviour* 1, no. 1: 67–76.

Cova, B., R. Kozinets, and A. Shankar. 2007. *Consumer Tribes.* New York: Routledge.

Cova, B., and T. White. 2010. "Computer-brand and Alter-brand Communities: The Impact of Web 2.0 on Tribal Marketing Approaches." *Journal of Marketing Management* 26, nos. 3–4: 256–70.

Culpepper, C. 2014. "Florida State's Unusual Bond with Seminole Tribe Puts Mascot Debate in a Different Light." *Washington Post.* December 29. Online at www .washingtonpost.com/sports/colleges/florida-states-unusual-bond-with-seminole-tribe -puts-mascot-debate-in-a-different-light/2014/12/29/5386841a-8eea-11e4-ba53 -a477d66580ed_story.html. Accessed on March 20, 2016.

Edgerton, G., and K. Jackson. 1996. "Redesigning Pocahontas: Disney, the 'White Man's Indian,' and the Marketing of Dreams." *Journal of Popular Film and Television* 24, no. 1: 90–98.

Edwards, B., and J. D. McCarthy. 2004. "Resources and Social Movement Mobilization." In D. A. Snow, S. A. Soule, and H. Kriesi, eds., *The Blackwell Companion to Social Movements.* Pp. 116–52. Oxford: Blackwell.

FSU News. 2005. "Florida State University Thanks the Seminoles for Historic Vote of Support." Online at www.fsu.edu/news/2005/06/17/seminole.support/. Accessed on December 6, 2015.

Godin, S. 2008. *Tribes: We Need You to Lead Us.* New York: Penguin Group.

Hanson, J. R., and L. P. Rouse. 1987. "Dimensions of Native American Stereotyping." *American Indian Culture and Research Journal* 11, no. 4: 33–58.

Kim-Prieto, C., L. A. Goldstein, S. Okazaki, and B. Kirschner. 2010. "Effect of Exposure to An American Indian Mascot on the Tendency to Stereotype a Different Minority Group." *Journal of Applied Social Psychology* 40, no. 3: 534–53.

Kozinets, R., and J. Handelman. 2004. "Adversaries of Consumption: Consumer Movements, Activism, and Ideology." *Journal of Consumer Research* 31: 691–704.

Leak, R. L., O. P. Woodham, and G. W. Stone. 2015. "Felt Discrimination Increases Offensiveness of Stereotyped Out-Group Depictions." *Journal of Consumer Marketing* 32, no. 1: 26.

Locklear, E. 2012. "Native American Mascot Controversy and Mass Media Involvement: Do the Media Promote Racism through Native American Athletic Imagery or Support Those Who Are Offended." *Explorations: The Journal of Undergraduate Research and Creative Activities for the State of North Carolina* 7: 152–59.

Lukas, P. 2012. "Time to Rethink Native American Imagery." ESPN.com. September 26. Online at http://espn.go.com/blog/playbook/fandom/post/_/id/12057/time-to-rethink -native-american-imagery. Accessed on February 24, 2015.

Lyden, J. 2015. "Osceola at the 50-Yard Line." NPR Code Switch. November 28. Online at www.npr.org/sections/codeswitch/2015/11/28/456786680/osceola-at-the-50-yard-line. Accessed on December 3, 2015.

Lynskey, D. 2014. "This Means War: Why the Fashion Headdress Must Be Stopped." *Guardian.* July 30. Online at www.theguardian.com/fashion/2014/jul/30/why-the -fashion-headdress-must-be-stopped. Accessed on December 6, 2015.

Maffesoli, M. 1996. *The Time of Tribes.* London: Sage.

Maffly, B. 2015. "Bears Ears Monument Debate Is Splitting Utah Navajos." *Salt Lake Tribune.* August 6. Online at www.sltrib.com/news/2812195-155/bears-ears -monument-debate-is-splitting. Accessed on December 10, 2015.

Marsh, C. 2015. "Osheaga's Headdress Ban Shows Festival's Zero Tolerance for Cultural Appropriation." *Guardian.* July 17. Online at www.theguardian.com/culture/2015/jul /17/osheaga-music-festival-headdress-cultural-appropriation. Accessed on March 20, 2016.

McCarthy, J. D., and M. N. Zald. 1977. "Resource Mobilization and Social Movements: A Partial Theory." *American Journal of Sociology* 82, no. 6 (May): 1212–41.

McIntyre, H. 2015. "America's Top Five Music Festivals Sold $183 Million in Tickets in 2014." *Forbes.* March 21. Online at www.forbes.com/sites/hughmcintyre/2015/03/21 /americas-top-five-music-festivals-sold-183-million-in-tickets-in-2014/. Accessed on December 6, 2015.

Mercado, H. U., and J. Grady. 2012. "The Ongoing Fight for the Fighting Sioux." *Sport Marketing Quarterly* 21, no. 2: 115–18.

Merskin, D. 2001. "Winnebagos, Cherokees, Apaches, and Dakotas: The Persistence of Stereotyping of American Indians in American Advertising Brands." *Howard Journal of Communications* 12: 159–69.

Metcalfe, J. R. 2012. "Etsy Is a Breeding Ground for . . ." BeyondBuckskin.com. February 2. Online at www.beyondbuckskin.com/2012/02/etsy-is-breeding-ground-for.html. Accessed on December 3, 2015.

Michaels, S. 2014. "Pharrell Apologizes for Wearing Native American War Bonnet." Guardian. June 5. Online at www.theguardian.com/music/2014/jun/05/pharrell -apologises-wearing-native-american-war-bonnet-elle. Accessed on December 6, 2015.

Mihesuah, D. A. 1996. *American Indians: Stereotypes and Realities.* Atlanta, GA: Clarity Press.

National Congress of American Indians (NCAI). 2015. "Tribal Nations of the United States: An Introduction." Online at www.ncai.org/attachments/PolicyPaper_VmQazPE qbvZDMeaDvbupWTSZLmzyzBKOknQRXnUyoVMoyFkEWGH_Tribal%20 Nations%20and%20the%20United%20States_An%20Introduction.pdf. Accessed on December 10, 2015.

———. 2003. "An Introduction to Indian Nations in the United States." Online at www .ncai.org/about-tribes/Indians_101.pdf. Accessed on December 6, 2013.

National Public Radio (NPR). 2012. "Navajo Nation Sure Urban Outfitters over Trademark." NPR. April 5. Online at www.npr.org/2012/04/05/150062611/navajo-nation -sues-urban-outfitters-over-trademark. Accessed on December 3, 2015.

Native Youth Magazine. 2015. "Native Americans in Business." Online at http:// nativeyouthmagazine.com/business.html. Accessed on December 10, 2015.

Navajo Nation v. Urban Outfitters, Inc. 2013. 935 F. Supp. 2d 1147 (D.N.M. 2013).

Pro-Football, Inc. v. Blackhorse. 2015. No. 1-14-CV-01043-GBL, 2015 WL 4096277 (E.D. Va. July 8, 2015).

Ries, A., and J. Trout. 1981. Positioning: The Battle for Your Mind. New York: McGraw-Hill.

Romano, T. 2012. "The Uproar Over No Doubt's Native American Video Gaffe." Daily Beast. November 6. Online at www.thedailybeast.com/articles/2012/11/06/the-uproar -over-no-doubt-s-native-american-video-gaffe.html. Accessed on March 29, 2015.

Rothenberg, R. 1999. "A Native American Ad Agency Bids to Change Tired Images." Advertising Age. August 2. Online at http://adage.com/article/special-report-magazines -the-alist/a-native-american-ad-agency-bids-change-tired-images/61571/. Accessed on February 24, 2015.

Shapira, I. 2015. "Federal Judge Orders Cancellation of Redskins' Trademark Registrations." Washington Post. July 8. Online at www.washingtonpost.com/local/judge -upholds-cancellation-of-redskins-trademarks-in-a-legal-and-symbolic-setback-for -team/2015/07/08/5a65424e-1e6e-11e5-aeb9-a411a84c9d55_story.html. Accessed on March 20, 2016.

Sharkey, T. 2012. "What's Your Tribe? Tap into Your Core Consumers' Aspirations Like Nike, Gatorade, BabyCenter, and REI Do." Forbes. January 25. Online at www.forbes .com/sites/tinasharkey/2012/01/25/whats-your-tribe-tap-into-your-core-consumers -aspirations-like-nike-gatorade-babycenter-and-rei-do/#77e3b5697d6c. Accessed on January 27, 2016.

Shim, S., and K. C. Gehrt. 1996. "Hispanic and Native American Adolescents: An Exploratory Study of Their Approach to Shopping." Journal of Retailing 72, no. 3: 307–24.

Toensing, G. C. 2013. "Eastern Cherokee Opposition to Catawba Casino Fuels US Senate Race." Indian Country Today. September 25. Online at http:// indiancountrytodaymedianetwork.com/2013/09/25/eastern-cherokee-opposition -catawba-casino-fuels-us-senate-race-151437. Accessed on December 10, 2015.

Trebay, G. 2012. "An Uneasy Cultural Exchange." New York Times. March 15, 2012. Online at www.nytimes.com/2012/03/15/fashion/an-uneasy-exchange-between-fashion-and -navajo-culture.html?_r=0. Accessed on December 6, 2015.

US Census. 2012. "Features for Facts: American Indian and Alaska Native Heritage Month: November 2012." Online at www.census.gov/newsroom/releases/pdf/cb12ff-22 _aian.pdf. Accessed on January 20, 2017.

Veloutsou, C., and L. Moutinho. 2009. "Brand Relationships through Brand Reputation and Brand Tribalism." *Journal of Business Research* 62: 314–22.

Verbos, A. K., J. S. Gladstone, and D. M. Kennedy. 2011. "Native American Values and Management Education: Envisioning an Inclusive Virtuous Circle." *Journal of Management Education* 35, no. 1: 10–26.

Weidman, D. 2010. "Global Marketing of Indigenous Culture: Discovering Native American with Lee Tiger and the Florida Miccosukee." *American Indian Culture and Research Journal* 34, no. 3: 1–26.

Wentz, L. 2001. "Gray's Day to Shine." *Advertising Age*. November 19. Online at http:// adage.com/article/news/gray-s-day-shine/53301/. Accessed on March 20, 2016.

Wolburg, J. 2006. "The Demise of Native American Mascots: It's Time to Do the Right Thing." *Journal of Consumer Marketing* 23, no. 1: 4–5.

Wulf, S. 2014. "Why the Use of Native American Nicknames Is an Obvious Affront." ESPN .com. Online at http://espn.go.com/espn/otl/story/_/id/11426021/why-native -american-nicknames-stir-controversy-sports. Accessed on February 24, 2015.

CONTRIBUTORS

DENISE BILL, EdD, University of Washington, has been a teacher, staff development trainer, and administrator in the public education system for twenty years. She was the superintendent of the Muckleshoot Tribal School for two years and currently serves as adjunct faculty for Northwest Indian College, Evergreen State College, and Antioch University.

CAROLYN BIRMINGHAM, a member of the Ojibwa Tribe, teaches MBA students at Florida Institute of Technology. Her interests are in organizational behavior, entrepreneurship, groups, and conflict resolution.

STEPHANIE LEE BLACK is on the faculty at the University at Albany, where she teaches entrepreneurship and conducts research on ethnic entrepreneurship. She also works with the College of Business and the Life Science Department to commercialize new technology. She has experience working in various industries and starting new businesses. Black is a member of the Oglala Lakota Indians from the Pine Ridge Reservation.

IISAAKSIICHAA (GOOD LADD) ROSS BRAINE is a citizen of the Apsaalooke (Crow) Nation and a descendant of the Tsitsistas (Northern Cheyenne) of the Big Sky state of Montana. He is also a member of the Biglodge Clan and Nighthawk Warrior Society. Braine currently serves as the tribal liaison and director of wəɫəbʔaltxʷ—Intellectual House at the University of Washington.

GAVIN CLARKSON is an associate professor in the Finance Department of the College of Business at New Mexico State University and the chief economist for the Fort Sill Apache Tribe. An enrolled member of the Choctaw Nation of Oklahoma, he has consulted, written, and published extensively on tribal sovereignty, finance, economic development, and asset management. He was a contributing author for the current edition of Felix Cohen's

Handbook of Federal Indian Law, providing material on tribal finance, corporations, economic development, and intellectual property. Clarkson earned a doctorate from the Harvard Business School in technology and operations management and is a cum laude graduate of the Harvard Law School, where he was the managing editor of the *Harvard Journal of Law and Technology* and president of the Native American Law Students Association.

CARMA M. CLAW is a fourth-year doctoral student at New Mexico State University. Her research interests include indigenous business management, ethics, and strategy. She offers over seventeen years of industry experience and has a commitment to Native American communities. Claw is Bit'ahnii and a citizen of the Diné Nation.

JOSEPH SCOTT GLADSTONE is enrolled in the Blackfeet Tribe and is a Nez Perce tribal descendent. An assistant professor of management at the University of New Haven College of Business, he holds a PhD in business administration and master's in public health concentrating on program management. Before his academic career, Gladstone worked with the Puyallup Tribal Health Authority in Tacoma, Washington; the Seattle Indian Health Board; the Tucson Indian Center; and the Tohono O'odham Department of Health and Social Services in Arizona.

CHARLES F. HARRINGTON, PhD, is a professor of management and interdisciplinary studies at the Center for Interdisciplinary Studies at the University of South Carolina–Upstate. His principle research interests have focused on American Indian business and entrepreneurship. Harrington has published extensively in these areas as well as on issues facing American Indians in mainstream higher education.

DEANNA M. KENNEDY, PhD, is a member of the Cherokee Nation of Oklahoma and an assistant professor of business at the University of Washington–Bothell. Her work with Native American colleagues aims to increase access to educational materials for business-interested Native American students and practitioners.

STEPHANIE LAWSON BROOKS, PhD, is currently an assistant professor of marketing at Winthrop University. Her research interests focus on collaborative consumption and services marketing. She has published in several peer-reviewed journals, including the *Journal of the Academy of Marketing Science*, *Marketing Letters*, and the *Journal of Consumer Marketing*.

RACHAEL MEARES graduated from the University of Washington–Bothell campus in 2013 with her bachelor's degree. She works in enrollment management, where she developed partnerships across UW campuses with tribal leaders and educators to develop outreach and retention programs for Native American students at the UW–Bothell campus.

SHAD MORRIS is the Georgia White Fellow and an associate professor of organizational leadership and strategy at the Marriott School of Brigham Young University. He has coauthored three books and regularly publishes research on global human resources. Before academia, Morris worked for the World Bank, for Management Systems International, and for Alcoa.

CARA PETERS, PhD, is currently a professor of marketing at Winthrop University. Her interests lie in digital marketing and consumer behavior. She has published in numerous peer-reviewed journals, including the *Journal of Consumer Psychology*; *Consumption, Markets, and Culture*; and the *Journal of the Academy of Marketing Science*.

MATTHEW RODGERS is an assistant professor of management at Ithaca College. He received his PhD in management from Cornell University. His research interests include ethical leadership, abusive supervision, and impression management/political behavior. He has published in numerous journals, including the *Strategic Management Journal*, *Leadership Quarterly*, and *Human Resource Management*.

GRACE ANN ROSILE, professor of management at New Mexico State University, has been a Daniels Ethics Fellow for five years. She headed a team that created a series of seven educational films called "Tribal Wisdom for Business Ethics" (available for free). Rosile also edited the forthcoming book based on these films.

JAMES K. SEBENIUS is the Gordon Donaldson Professor of Business Administration at Harvard Business School. He specializes in analyzing and advising on complex negotiations.

DANIEL STEWART, a member of the Spokane Tribe of Indians, is a professor of entrepreneurship and director of the Hogan Entrepreneurial Leadership Program at Gonzaga University. He holds a PhD (in organizational behavior) and a master's degree (in sociology) from Stanford University. He is the president of Dardan Enterprises, a commercial construction firm.

AMY KLEMM VERBOS, JD and PhD, is an assistant professor of business law at the University of Wisconsin–Whitewater. Her research interests include relational ethics, Native American ethics, indigenous inclusion, gender equity, and the Principles for Responsible Management Education. She is an enrolled citizen of the Pokagon Band of Potawatomi.

INDEX

THE PHD PROJECT

"When we launched The PhD Project you could count the number of Native American college business professors holding a PhD on two hands. With the help of this book, *American Indian Business: Principles and Practices*, and programs like The PhD Project, there are now forty-nine business professors with nine students in business PhD programs."
–Bernard J. Milano, president, KPMG US Foundation, Inc. and The PhD Project

All royalty sales from the purchase of *American Indian Business: Principles and Practices* benefit The PhD Project, which encourages African Americans, Hispanic Americans, and Native Americans to pursue PhDs in business to serve as role models and mentors for minority business students.

The PhD project hosts an invitation-only annual conference in Chicago each November for minority professionals considering doctoral studies, along with discipline-specific conferences for current minority doctoral students throughout their programs to provide encouragement and support. The PhD Project covers all travel, hotel and conference expenses for those who are invited to attend. The application deadline is September 30. Visit www.phdproject.org for more information and an application.

Lightning Source UK Ltd.
Milton Keynes UK
UKHW011028161222
414000UK00003B/150